THE FATHERS
OF THE CHURCH

A NEW TRANSLATION

VOLUME 3

EDITORIAL BOARD

LUDWIG SCHOPP
Editorial Director

RUDOLPH ARBESMANN, O.S.A.
Fordham University

STEPHAN KUTTNER
The Catholic University of America

WILFRID PARSONS, S.J.
The Catholic University of America

ROBERT P. RUSSELL, O.S.A.
Villanova College

ROY JOSEPH DEFERRARI
The Catholic University of America

MARTIN R. P. MCGUIRE
The Catholic University of America

BERNARD M. PEEBLES
St. John's College, Annapolis, Md.

ANSELM STRITTMATTER, O.S.B.
St. Anselm's Priory, Washington, D. C.

GERALD G. WALSH, S.J.
Fordham University

THE WRITINGS OF SALVIAN, THE PRESBYTER

Translated

by

JEREMIAH F. O'SULLIVAN, Ph.D.
Fordham University

The Catholic University of America Press
Washington, D. C.

NIHIL OBSTAT:

        JOHN M. FEARNS, S.T.D.
        CENSOR LIBRORUM

IMPRIMATUR:

        ✠ FRANCIS CARDINAL SPELLMAN
        ARCHBISHOP OF NEW YORK

September 27th 1947

ISBN-13: 978-0-8132-1550-1 (pbk)

Copyright © 1947 by

THE CATHOLIC UNIVERSITY OF AMERICA PRESS, INC.

All rights reserved

Reprinted 1962
Reprinted 1985
First paperback reprint 2008

INTRODUCTION

SALVIAN, the presbyter, was born in Gaul either in the last years of the fourth or the early years of the fifth century. It is very probable that the city of Trier was his birthplace.¹ The two localities in Gaul with which he was most familiar were Arles in Aquitaine and Trier. He has left an artistic description of the natural beauty of Aquitaine² and a doleful account of Trier³ in its hour of desolation. The first destruction of the city, probably witnessed by Salvian's parents, occured in 360, while Emperor Julian was absent on the fatal Persian War. The city was overrun four times during Salvian's lifetime, and he was an eyewitness to its destruction in 406. This and his statement that Trier was the first city in Gaul form the basis for many commentators' conclusions that Trier was his birthplace

Actually, there is no statement in his extant works as to his place of birth. Historically, Trier was the first city of Gaul because it was the home of the Praetorian Prefect of Gaul, a district which included territorial Gaul and Britain as well. Trier was the Rome of Gaul just as Carthage was the Rome of Africa. By imperial decree, Trier's professors and teachers received salaries comparable to their counterparts in Rome, and higher than in any other city in Gaul.⁴ In all historical

---

1 He designates Trier as *"urbs excellentissima"* (*De Gubernatione Dei* 175 n.39), a term he does not apply to any other city in Gaul.
2 *De Gubernatione Dei* 187.
3 The city was destroyed four times up to the time of Salvian's writing *De Gubernatione Dei*. He speaks of witnessing the scenes coincidental with the attack on the city in 406. *Ibid.* 164, 174-176,
4 *Codex Theodosianus* (ed. P. Kruger, Berlin 1923) 13.3.11.

truth, Salvian could consider Trier the foremost city in Gaul, but it does not necessarily follow that he was born there.

In a letter to his dear friends, the monks of Lerins, Salvian interceded for a young kinsman who 'is noble by birth and about whom I hesitate to speak, lest in speaking about him I seem to speak about myself.'[5] The young man's widowed mother still lived in Cologne where she was destitute of the means of self-support or of fleeing the city. As Salvian picturesquely puts it, she lived 'by hiring out her hands to the wives of the barbarians.'[6] This letter offers proof of Salvian's status in Gallo-Roman aristocratic society, yet he repeatedly castigated the aristocracy. The only class more castigated was that of the petty officials whose exactions made the daily existence of the poor intolerable. These exactions continued despite the barbarian conquests.[7]

With the barbarian conquest of northern and eastern Gaul, the offices and machinery of government were transferred from Trier to Arles, in Aquitaine. Doubtless, many who were in no way connected with the government sought a more secure asylum in the south. This possibly accounts for the presence of Salvian and his immediate family in Aquitaine.

Early in life he married Palladia, whose parents were pagan at the time of the marriage.[8] A daughter, Auspiciola, was born of this marriage.[9] Evidently, Palladia's parents remained in northern Gaul, because Salvian speaks of the great distance that separated them.[10] After a long discussion, Salvian and Palladia decided to go their separate ways to monastery and convent. They announced their decision to his parents-in-law,

---

5 *Epistola* 1.238.
6 *Ibid.*
7 *De Gubernatione Dei* 85, 134.
8 *Epistola* 4.242, 243.
9 *Ibid.* 245.
10 *Ibid.* 244.

INTRODUCTION   5

who showed their disagreement by seven years of silence. This attitude occasioned a letter[11] from Salvian, filled with pathos and gilded with rhetoric. It contains both the pleading of a man trained in law and the sincerity of a distraught parent. There is no further mention of Palladia and Auspiciola in Salvian's extant writings.

Salvian entered the monastery of Lerins, and it is here, in all probability, that he was ordained to the priesthood. His monastic companions were notable and honorable. His friend, Eucher, later a bishop, was a biblical scholar.[12] Eucher's wife, Galla, entered a convent, and his two sons, Salonius and Veranus, later became bishops. Salvian taught rhetoric at Lerins and among his fellow teachers could be found Hilary, Caesarius and Honoratus—all notables in the annals of that monastery. It is quite possible that he knew St. Patrick who was a student at Lerins at the same time. Undoubtedly, Salvian had access to the works of Saint Augustine at Lerins and his attitude towards the dogmatic errors of the Arians closely parallels Saint Augustine's plea for tolerance and understanding.

Salvian became famous as a teacher and preacher. Gennadius calls him the master of bishops[13] and Hilarius of Arles names him as a dear friend of the equally famous preacher, Honoratus of Lerins.[14] He lived to a ripe old age, for Gennadius in his *Catologue of Illustrious Men* mentions Salvian as being alive toward the close of the fifth century. At that time he must have been almost one hundred years old.

Compared to St. Augustine, Salvian was not a prolific writer. Gennadius credits him as the author of a volume *On the Value*

---

11 *Epistola* 4.241-250.
12 Eucherius was the author of *Instructiones de quaestionibus difficilioribus veteris ac novi testamenti* (CSEL 31).
13 Gennadius, *Catalogus virorum illustrium*, Migne, PL 58. 1059-1120 (No. 68).
14 *Sermo de Vita Sancti Honoratii Arlatensis*, Migne, PL 50.1260.

of *Virginity*; four books *To the Church;* a treatise *On the Satisfaction for Sins;* five books *On the Present Judgment;* one book in exposition of the last part of *Ecclesiastes;* one book of letters; one book of verse; many homilies written for bishops; and many books concerning the sacraments.[15] His extant works are those *On the Present Judgment,* a book of *Letters* and four books *To the Church.* Of these, *On the Present Judgment,* is the most important as an historical document.

Though Gennadius mentions that the work is composed of five books, our present edition has eight. We know the treatise not as *On the Present Judgment,* the name given by Gennadius, but as *The Governance of God.* Judging by the context, the treatise, as we have it, is incomplete, because it stops abruptly shortly after Salvian has begun to develop his theme.

Salvian's style is rhetorical and repetitious. The fact that he taught rhetoric may partly account for this. Apparently, he wrote in the manner in which he preached, and, in all probability, his extant writings, at least in substance, originated as sermons. It is quite evident that Salvian wrote with an eye to his audience. He wrote about his own times and, like every commentator on things contemporary, he assumed his audience was informed as to his subjects. His treatise *The Governance of God* might well be entitled *A Report on the State of the Nation.* The state of the nation, according to Salvian's observations and appraisal, was bad because of the sins of men. Consequently, the calamities which had befallen and were falling on the Roman Empire were God's punishment on man, who was not about to go to perdition, but who had already arrived there. He argued that the ruin of his time was the result of sin and greed.

---

15 Gennadius, *Catalogus virorum illustrium,* No. 68.

INTRODUCTION

Salvian wrote his famous and oft-quoted treatise in the ten years[16] prior to 450, when the political and social disintegration of the Empire had reached its nadir. The Emperor was no longer the First Magistrate of Rome, but an Eastern despot. His prowess no longer consisted in leading his armies, but in playing palace politics in Milan or Ravenna, cities chosen less for their tactical military importance than as gateways to escape the ever threatening hordes of barbarians. Within the imperial circle, intrigue and espionage consumed a large portion of the energies of the occupants. Stilicho, of German descent, saved the Empire for Theodosius, but was assassinated with the Emperor's tacit consent in 408. Two years later, Alaric the Visigoth plundered Rome and, on his death in the same year, the Visigoths turned north and took possession of Aquitaine. The Visigoths later became one of Rome's trusted allies and Theodoric lost thousands of his men in turning back Attila in the battle of the Catalaunian Plains (452).

The Alani, Burgundians, Vandals and Franks had definitely crashed the Rhine barrier early in the fifth century. Salvian witnessed the destruction of Trier in 406, the year of the breakthrough. The Franks were supreme in Belgium, the Burgundians in the territory north of Aquitaine, while the Vandals pushed through into Spain. These onrushing tribes lived off the land as they went, isolating and defeating the small contingents of the Roman army encountered on their way. The Visigoths compelled the Vandals to flee to North Africa, the imperial granary of Rome. Salvian lived in years when his native Gaul was without government or political stability and, like the prophet Jeremias, whom he quotes so frequently, he wept for the lamentable state of his homeland.

---

16 He mentions the capture of Toulouse (439) by the Visigoths, but makes no mention of the threat of Attila and the Huns (450-452). In all probability the work was completed between these two dates, 439 and 450.

Salvian boldly laid the sins of the century at the feet of the officials and landed aristocracy. The government, represented by the curial official, was the tax-gatherer and, as such, merited special claim to odium. Actually, the curial was a tyrant,[17] but Salvian failed to mention that circumstances compelled this official to be tyrannical. By imperial decree,[18] the curial could not enter the religious calling and he could not choose his calling in life.[19] He was born a curial and died a curial; worse still, the imperial government declared the amount of the tax and the unfortunate agent who could not collect the required amount was compelled to donate the deficit from his own possessions.[20] Naturally, the curials were harsh in their levies and in their mode of collection. It is this harshness which Salvian assails. His attack is general rather than specific.

Taxes in the later Empire were extremely heavy. There were direct taxes on the individual, land, houses, animals, inheritances, senators, tradesmen and merchants. Indirect taxes were levied on exports, imports and goods sold at auction or in the public market. Despite an imperially imposed price control, the equivalent of the modern "black market" dictated prices. Taxes were levied on land and as a poll-tax on the individual.[21]

For the proper imposition of this land tax, the Empire was surveyed and measured into parcels, on each of which was

---

17 *De Gubernatione Dei*: '*quot curiales fuerint, tot tyranni sunt*' 134.
18 *Codex Theodosianus* 12.1.59.
19 No other class or group in Roman society was surrounded with a mass of legislation as was the curial class. Section 12.1, '*De decurionibus*,' of the Theodosian Code has 192 distinct laws governing the duties and privileges of the curial class.
20 *Codex Theodosianus* 2.23.2.
21 The best short treatment of this highly controversial subject is Ferdinand Lot's *L'Impot foncier et la capitation personelle sous le bas-Empire* (Paris 1928) 1-82. Useful also is R. Thouvenot's study 'Salvien et la ruine de l'Empire romain,' *Mélanges d'archéologie et d'histoire de l'École francaise de Rome*, 38 (Paris 1920) 145-168.

INTRODUCTION 9

imposed the same sum of money as a tax.²² This parcel of land was called a *caput* or a *jugum*, hence the terms *capitatio* or *jugatio*.²³ The size of the parcels of land varied inversely in proportion to the fertility of the soil.²⁴ Each section had a real value of approximately four thousand dollars and its real value probably was greater than its assessed value. Taxes were payable on the first day of the financial year, 1 September, and on 1 January and 1 May.²⁵ In addition to the regular yearly tax, some emperors levied extraordinary taxes on each *jugum*. The regular *capitatio* on land returned to the imperial treasury over two billion dollars each year from the lands of the Empire.

The poll-tax, whose amount varied, is also called *capitatio*. Every individual in the Empire was liable to this poll-tax, with the following exemptions. (1) All who paid the *capitatio* on land. This means that the poll-tax was a tax supplementary to the land tax and was a direct tax on those who did not possess landed property. (2) All persons above the social status of plebeian were exempt. The plebeians, however, if they possessed landed property, did not pay poll-tax. Thus, those subject to the poll-tax were: the dwellers in towns, who were plebeians and did not possess land; the *coloni*, who worked on the land but did not possess it; the slaves. After an imperial edict of Diocletian, the tax was levied exclusively on *coloni* and slaves. Since the *coloni* were propertyless, their masters had to pay the tax;²⁶ consequently, the masters demanded more and more services from their *coloni*.²⁷

---

22 Lactantius, *De Mortibus Persecutorum*, Migne, PL 7. 189-276, (No. 23), has an excellent description of the high-handed methods employed by government officials while making the survey.
23 Ulpian, *Digest* 50.15.14, has a detailed account of the land census.
24 F. C. von Savigny. 'Über die römische Steuerverfassung.' *Vermischte Schriften* (Berlin 1850) 67-148.
25 The financial year from 312 onwards was called *indictio*. The same word was applied to the amount to be levied during the financial year.
26 *Codex Theodosianus* 11.1.12; 11.48.3.
27 F. C. von Savigny, *op. cit.*, pp. 67-148. A law of 370 dispensed women

The *coloni* class was ever on the increase numerically, for, when small property owners were unable to pay the curial demands, they sought a nearby landed proprietor and begged his patronage.[28] Patronage theoretically meant physical protection by the lord and service by the tenant in return for that protection. The tenant lost the ownership of his property to the patron, but he did not lose the liability for taxes, which pursued him even into his semi-servile status.[29] The lord paid the tenant's capitation tax and assumed proprietorship over the land and person of the indebted one.[30] This is the background against which Salvian's strictures upon the harshness of the *curiales* must be read and understood. It was this official attitude which caused the revolt of the Bagaudae, or Peasants, in Southern Gaul.[31]

This official policy of the Roman fisc created a class which was one of the primary causes of the social and political disorder in Gaul. Salvian condemned the large landed proprietors as brigands and robbers.[32] They benefited directly from the unrelenting policy of the *curiales,* because, with each bankrupt peasant who sought their protection, they increased not only their land but their potential armies. Their estates, or *latifundi,* extended over many acres; even in the France of today the towns of Savigny and Vitry recall the patrician names of Sabinus and Victor.

---

who had made a vow of chastity, widows too old to re-marry, male adolescents (younger than twenty years), and women until married, from paying this tax. (*Codex Theodosianus* 13.10.4).

28 *De Gubernatione Dei* 141.
29 *Ibid.*: 'cum possessio ab his recesserit, capitatio non recedit; proprietatibus carent et vectigalibus obruuntur.'
30 *Codex Theodosianus* 13.10.1,4.
31 The word *Bagauda* is apparently of Celtic origin, signifying a peasant or rustic; also a robber. Aegidius Forcellinius, *Totius Latinitatis Lexicon* (Padua 1805) 1, p. 297, states that it is not a Latin word. See also Du Cange, *Glossarium,* 'Bagauda.'
32 *De Gubernatione Dei* 95.

From the middle of the third century, an imperial decree debarred the wealthy landed class from army commands.[33] However, they were the civil administrators and directors of the balance of economic power.[34] The large landed proprietor was a law unto himself, defying the State and its agents by refusing to pay the *capitatio* and by also refusing to pay licenses for commercial transactions. He exercised jurisdiction over and, according to Salvian, tried the cases of those on his estates.[35] He maintained a retinue of retainers and, on occasion, could convert his dependents into a small army. The *patronus* was the law. With his extensive estates sometime widely separated, with his ever-readiness to accept more and more dependents until their dependency became absolute, the days of feudalism and the feudal lord were not too beyond Salvian's last years.

Salvian understood the evil influence on society of this large and powerful class and bitterly bemoaned the fate of the unfortunates whom circumstances and the *curiales* compelled to relinquish their little holdings and with them, their freedom. Because of their wealth in land, the landed proprietors were the real wielders of the little power remaining in Gallo-Roman society. Their wealth was in the land; their interests were their own.

This attitude of the landed aristocracy was only one of the many symptoms of social decay. From fourth and fifth century sources, even from pagan authors, the general impression is one of an extremely corrupt society. The aristocracy was selfish, the officials were venal and the populace was corrupt.

---

[33] Ferdinand Lot, *La Fin du monde antique, et le début du moyen âge* (Paris 1938) 147-153.
[34] *Ibid.*, p. 147.
[35] *De Gubernatione Dei* 144.

According to Salvian,[36] the games and spectacles epitomized the worst aspects of society.

In Salvian's estimation, the circus, amphitheatre and theatre had a most corrupting influence on the people. He must have been familiar with the huge amphitheatre at Trier where Constantine had ordered some captive Frankish chiefs thrown to the wild beasts. The populace was shouting itself hoarse at the games while that city was being taken in 406. Yet, the games went on, and Salvian furnished a vivid picture of the lustful delirium of the populace while their city was being ruined.[37] Shortly thereafter, the city fathers requested the Emperor for the means of holding the games as the best aid to relieve the people's distress.[38] When the Vandals were taking Carthage, Salvian says, it was difficult to distinguish between the shouts of those at the games and the cries of those who fell defending the walls of the city.[39]

Salvian's accounts of this mania for games and amusement are well authenticated by other authors. The number of holidays in a year reached 175, and each holiday was celebrated with supplied amusement. The expenditure for one set of games often reached $250,000, and this was either State or individually financed. Horse racing was the most popular sport, some horses winning over 300 prizes. Gladiatorial combats between professionally trained fighters frequently ended in their deaths. Animal baiting was made exciting by throwing condemned criminals to the wild beasts.[40] There were also

---
36 *Ibid.* 154.
37 *Ibid.* 174-176.
38 *Ibid.* 178.
39 *Ibid.* 172.
40 The best general accounts of Roman society are by L. Friedländer, *Roman Life and Manners under the Early Empire*, 4 vols. (trans. by L. A. Magnus, J. H. Freese and A. B. Gough, London 1908-13), and by Sir Samuel Dill, *Roman Society in the Last Century of the Western Empire* (2nd ed. London 1933).

the mimes, stage performances whose portrayal of the lustful was vivid and corrupting.

Salvian regarded games and spectacles as the most perverting influence on Christians. A frequenter of those scenes and enactments had practically abandoned his baptismal vows 'to renounce the devil, his works and pomps,' because the games were the work of the devil. Men preferred the circus and amphitheatre to God's temple, and those who happened to be attending Mass departed from the church when the noise of those attending the games reached their ears.[41] In 393, Theodosius decreed that games were not to be held on Sunday,[42] but, apparently, this law was unheeded in Salvian's day. The new society was without purpose or morality, a people who had lost all sense of obligation.

Any appreciation of Salvian, more moralist than historian, must take into account not only the man but his times. He lived in the age of Sts. Ambrose, Augustine and Jerome. Organized monasticism was gaining a foothold in the West, with its hub at Lerins. The spirit of St. Martin of Tours permeated the minds of men akin, in religious zeal, to Salvian. On the other hand, paganism was making its last stand. Its devotees were mostly intellectuals and aristocrats who believed in the *Roma Dea* and whose pagan sincerity was as ardent as that of the most devoted Christian.

In between the earnest Christians and pagans was the huge mass of the lukewarm, so thoroughly castigated by Salvian. To them he applied the Scriptural text: 'because you are lukewarm, I will begin to vomit you out of My mouth.' These men gave outward obeisance to Christianity, but were not above practicing the heathen ritual.[43] They were Christians extern-

---
41 *De Gubernatione Dei* 163-164.
42 *Codex Theodosianus* 2.8.20.
43 Witness his castigation of the inhabitants of Carthage, *De Gubernatione Dei* 207-219.

ally, but inwardly they wondered why Rome achieved its greatest power under pagan auspices and was enduring the calamities of their own day under Christian rulers. They belonged to the fringe of intellectual paganism and practical Christianity.

It was for and against such men that Saint Augustine wrote *The City of God;* Orosius, *The Seven Books Against the Pagans;* Salvian, *The Governance of God.* These three works comprise a trilogy against the learned pagan and the lukewarm Christian. All three authors were learned in pagan lore and, when occasion demanded, Salvian spoke the thought common to pagan and Christian alike. His knowledge of Roman history and Roman law was extensive. These subjects were the common heritage and education of the cultivated Roman. According to him, their use was not in proving the past greatness of the State, but in recognizing the providence of God, who rewards and punishes the acts of man.[44] There is a God who watches over man; there is a City of God in heaven, and a City of God on earth. Man can attain his ultimate objective in heaven only by creating and living in a state of holiness on earth. The most secure way of doing this is to put into practice the Sermon on the Mount. Salvian's thesis is an implementation of Saint Augustine's *City of God*[45] and his two principal

---

44 This forms the theme for his *De Gubernatione Dei,* and special attention is given to its historical aspects in the first three books.

45 Salvian's thesis on the cause of Rome's downfall goes much further than St. Augustine's. The latter is sympathetic to Rome in its hour of misery and reminds the city of its eternity. Salvian has an underlying antagonism to the Roman Empire. Its past glories belong to the past. It was rewarded with world power for its virtues, but, now that it has become corrupt, its power is passing into the hands of the barbarians who are being rewarded for their virtues. He intimates very clearly that the future belongs, not to Rome, but to the barbarian tribes, because they are chaste. They have become the salvation of the Roman Empire because of their strict morality. Salvian looks to the future and realizes that the destiny of Europe belongs to the Teutonic tribes.

works, *The Governance of God* and the *Appeal Against Avarice in the Church*, each serves to present it.

The second treatise, sometimes called *Ad Ecclesiam*, is known more generally under the title *Contra Avaritiam*. In all probability Salvian divested himself of all property when he entered the monastery of Lerins. He was unable, as we have seen, to succor a young kinsman of his who appealed for aid. The thesis of *Ad Ecclesiam* is a strong exhortation for almsgiving to the Church as a means of acquiring merit in the future life. Man owes a debt to God and he must repay this debt. The donation of property to the Church is an excellent way of repaying this debt, in part, provided it is given with the proper intention. Only in this way will it be acceptable to God. In developing his theme, he repeatedly uses the words, *solvere debitum*, thus foreshadowing the advent of the *Penitentials*.

Nine letters of Salvian are extant. Their content ranges from a request for aid (*Epistola I*) to an explanation to his bishop, Salonius, for writing anonymously the treatise *Ad Ecclesiam* (*Epistola* IX). Actually, he used the name Timothy, a name which was causing some Christians to think this was an apocryphal work of St. Paul's companion, Timothy. When pressed for an answer on authorship, Salvian went to great lengths explaining why and how the treatise was written, but in no place does he definitely admit its authorship. The Latinity of his *Letters*, particularly of Letter VII, is more than usually rhetorical and gramatically puzzling.

There have been many editions of *Opera Salviani* since the sixteenth century. German scholars have devoted much attention to his thought and Latinity. For this reason, I have used the critical editions by Francis Pauly, *Salviani Presbyteri Massiliensis Opera quae superunt*, CSEL 8 (Vienna 1883) and by C. Halm, *Salviani Presbyteri Massiliensis Opera quae supersunt, MGH, Auctores Antiquissimi* 1. 1 (Berlin 1877), and, in general, followed the former text. A translation of the first work appearing in this volume has been rendered by Eva M. Sanford, *On the Government of God* (Columbia Records of Civilization; New York 1930) to which I am greatly indebted.

I wish to acknowledge my debt for library facilities to Dr. Kenneth S. Gapp, Librarian, Princeton Theological Seminary, to Mr. Howard L. Hughes, Librarian, Trenton Public Library, and to Rev. Carl R. Nagele.

SELECT BIBLIOGRAPHY

Texts:

F. Pauly, Salviani Presbyteri Massiliensis, *Opera quae supersunt*, CSEL 8 (Vienna 1883).

C. Halm, Salviani Presbyteri *Massiliensis, Opera quae supersunt*, MGH, *Auctores Antiquissimi 1.1* (Berlin 1877).

Secondary Sources:

P. Boissonade, *Life and Work in Mediaeval Europe* (New York 1927).

A. C. Cooper-Marsdin, *History of the Islands of the Lerins* (Cambridge 1913).

Joseph Declareuil, *Rome the Law-Giver,* (New York 1926).

Samuel Dill, *Roman Society in the Last Century of the Western Empire* (London 1933).

Samuel Dill, *Roman Society in Gaul in the Merovingian Age* (London 1936).

Alois Haemmerle, *Studia Salviana* (Landshut and Neuberg 1891-1899).

Ferdinand Lot, *La fin du monde antique et le début du moyen âge* (Paris 1938).

Ferdinand Lot, *L'impôt foncier et la capitation personelle sous le bas-Empire et a l'épogue franque* (Paris 1928).

L. Mery, *Etude sur Salvien, prêtre de Marseille* (Marseille 1849).

A. F. Ozanam, *La civilization au cinquième siècle* (Paris 1855).

Jean-Remy Palanque, *Saint Ambroise et l'empire romain* (Paris 1933).

M. Rostovtzeff, *Social and Economic History of the Roman Empire* (Oxford 1926).

Eva M. Sanford, trans., *On the Government of God* (New York 1930).

E.G. Sihler, *From Augustus to Augustine* (Cambridge 1923).

R. Thouvernot, 'Salvien et la ruine de l'empire romain' in *Melanges de l'école francaise de Rome*, (1918-1919) 145-146.

W. Zschimmer, *Salvianus der Presbyter von Massilia und seine Schriften* (Halle 1875).

CONTENTS

	Page
INTRODUCTION	3
THE GOVERNANCE OF GOD	
Text	21
LETTERS	
Text	233
THE FOUR BOOKS OF TIMOTHY TO THE CHURCH	
Text	265
INDEX	373

THE GOVERNANCE OF GOD

(De gubernatione Dei)

CONTENTS

Page

Dedicatory Preface: To Salonius 25

Book One 27

Theories of the ancient philosophies on the governance of God. The unholy are unworthy of temporal prosperity. The just should not bemoan their afflictions. The just subdue the strength of the body to increase the strength of the soul. Adversities are not arguments against God's governance. God's governance is proved by human governance. Proofs of God's governance taken from Scripture. God's gifts are as great in our day as then. Why does God not kill all sinners? God's mercy. God's severity.

Book Two 55

Scriptural examples established God's governance. Scriptures attest God's universal presence. God is favorable to the just and unfavorable to the unjust. God judges and protects the just. God's judgment is universal. David protected and punished as just and unjust. David's repentance. God protected the just and punished their persecutors. The existence of a present and future judgment.

Book Three 67

Objections of unbelievers. The sufficiency of God's word on the mysteries of God. Definition of faith. Great numbers of Christians unobservant of evangelical precepts. The examples set by the Apostles. Saint Paul. God's commandments are obligatory. Chastity among men. The disorders in the world. Disrespect for God in the churches. Prevalence of vices.

Page

Book Four 90
> Duties of Christians. Examples of Jews applicable to Christians. Relation between God's goodness and our tribulations. Unworthy Christians are more culpable than slaves. Denunciation of the nobility. Their oppression of the poor. God's chastisement and our sins. God's governance and God's existence are one. The Incarnation and man's ingratitude. Christians more wicked than pagans. Scandals given by Christians.

Book Five 127
> The law. Heretics less culpable than the orthodox. Scriptures in use by the heretics. Virtues of the heretics. Exactions of civil officials. The *Bagaudae*. The lot of the poor. The greed of officials.

Book Six 151
> Christians and the games and spectacles. The sins occasioned by spectacles, games and theatres. Attending spectacles is to renounce baptismal vows. The spectacles and the misfortunes of the Roman Empire. Barbarian invasions. The ingratitude of Christians.

Book Seven 185
> Romans uncorrected by calamities. Comparison of Romans and barbarians. Barbarian conquest of Aquitaine, Gaul, Spain and Africa. Crime and punishment. The crimes of Carthage. The virtues of the Vandals. The theories of Socrates.

Book Eight 224
> The sin of flattery. Our adversities and God's governance. Pagan practices among African Christians. God and His priests. Attitude of the Africans to men in religion. God's punishment of the Africans.

THE GOVERNANCE OF GOD

PREFACE

SALVIAN greets the holy Bishop Salonius in the Lord.
Almost all men who have believed that it is man's cultural obligation to produce a literary work by intensive mental application have taken special care, whether they deal with matters beneficial and right or unprofitable and base, to embellish their narrative with a splendor of words and, by the style they use, to focus attention on the very topic they wish to discuss. It is therefore to this style that the majority of profane writers, whether they use the medium of prose or of poetry, have given special attention. They do not give sufficient consideration to the suitability of the subjects they choose, as long as whatever is said is either recited in elegant and polished verse or narrated in lucid prose.

All these writers have pursued in their works their own objectives only, and, more mindful of their own glorification than of profit to others, they have striven, not to be considered wholesome and helpful, but to be eloquent and subtle. Therefore, their writings are either vainly bombastic, or notoriously false, or corruptingly obscene or filthy in expression. Indeed, the result of this is that, while pursuing praise of their own ability, they expend so much effort on unworthy subjects that they seem to me not so much to enhance as to condemn their talents.

On the other hand, I am a lover more of deeds than of words and seek after what is useful rather than public acclaim. I strive that wholesome lessons derived from facts be praised in me, not vainly wordly ornaments. Therefore, in my little treatise, I do not want meretricious ornaments. I want medicines which are not so much pleasing to the ears of the idle as they are profitable to the minds of the sick. I hope that from both palliation and profit I shall receive a great reward in heavenly gifts.

If my medicine does cure certain men of the unfavorable opinion they harbor of God, my reward shall not be little because I have benefited many. If, however, this benefit is not realized in full, the very attempt to be beneficial will, perhaps, not be without reward. A mind, zealous for good and consecrated to love, has the compensation that accompanies goodwill, even though full accomplishment of what is begun is not attained.

Here, therefore, I shall begin.

BOOK ONE

SOME MEN say that God is indifferent and, as it were, unconcerned with human acts, inasmuch as He neither protects the good nor curbs the wicked. They say that in this world, therefore, the good are generally unhappy; the evildoers, happy. Because I am addressing Christians, the Holy Scriptures alone should suffice as a refutation of this charge. But, because many have some pagan disbelief in them, perhaps they can also be enticed by proofs taken from chosen and learned pagans. I am about to prove that these pagans did not even think in such a matter about God's carelessness and indifference. They were ignorant of the true religion and could never have known God, because they did not know the Law through which God is known.

The philosopher Pythagoras, whom Philosophy herself looked upon as her master, spoke thus when discussing the nature and benefactions of God:[1] 'The soul, passing at will and diffused throughout the world, is the source from which all things born have their life.' How, therefore, is God said to neglect the world which He loves so fully that He spreads Himself over the entirety of the world?

Plato and all the Platonic Schools acknowledge God as the governor of all creation. The Stoics bear witness that He remains, taking the place of the helmsman, within that which He directs. What could they have felt more proper and more reverent regarding the concern and watchfulness of God than to

---

[1] Cicero, *De Natura Deorum* 1.11,27; Lactantius, *Institutiones Divinae* 1.5,17.

have likened Him to a helmsman? By this they understood that as the helmsman in charge of a ship never lifts his hand from the tiller, so never does God remove His inmost attention from the world. Just as the helmsman steers, completely dedicated in mind and body to his task, taking advantage of the wind, avoiding the rocks and watching the stars, in like manner our God never puts aside the function of His most loving watch over the universe. Neither does He take away the guidance of His providence, nor does He remove the tenderness of his benign love.

In this way there arose that saying of mystic origin by which Maro wished to prove himself not less a philosopher than a poet when he said: 'God truly traverses all lands, the expanse of the sea and the depths of the heavens.' Cicero also said: 'Neither can God, who is understood by us, be understood in any other manner than as a mind disengaged, free and isolated from all mortal materiality, having full cognition of all things and directing them.'[2] Elsewhere he said: 'Nothing is more outstanding than God,' and, therefore, of necessity the world is ruled by Him. God, therefore, is neither obedient nor subject to anything in nature: He Himself rules all nature. Perchance, we who are most manifestly wise believe that He whom we credit with ruling all things, rules and neglects at the same time.

Therefore, when all men, even those not of our faith, under the compulsion of sheer necessity, have proclaimed that the universe is known and moved and ruled by God, how can He at the present day be thought indifferent and unconcerned? Is it not God who is fully cognizant of all things by perception, who moves all by His strength, who rules by authority and protects in His bounty? I have said what men foremost in both

---

2 Both quotations are taken from Lactantius, *op. cit.* 1.5, 12; 1.5,25.

philosophy and eloquence have thought of the majesty and management of the Most High. I have brought forward the greatest masters of both philosophy and eloquence so that I could prove more easily that all agreed; or, if they disagreed, then they did so without carrying conviction. Indeed, I am unable to find any who differ in judgment from them, beyond the absurdities of the Epicureans and some of the would-be Epicureans. As these men have linked pleasure with virtue, so have they linked God with carelessness and disinterestedness. It is clear that those who think in this manner follow the frame of mind and opinion of the Epicureans, just as they practice their vices.

(2) I do not think we need utilize Scriptural testimony at this time to prove such an obvious fact, especially since Holy Writings refute so clearly and fully all the claims of those ungodly men. By meeting their subsequent false representations, we can refute even more fully those already made. They say that God, since He neither protects the good nor punishes the wicked, is disinterested in all things; that in this world, therefore, the status of the good is decidedly worse than that of the evil. They say that the good, of a certainty, live in poverty, the wicked in plenty; the good in sickness, the wicked in health; the good in sorrow, the wicked in joy; the good in misery and low estate, the wicked in prosperity and high estate.

In the first place, I ask those who either grieve or charge that these conditions are as they are: whether they are sorry for the holy ones, that is, those who are true and genuine Christians, or for the false and imposters? If for the latter, unnecessary is the sorrow which mourns for the unhappiness of the wicked, since all evil men become worse-living as they become successful. They rejoice that their devotion to wickedness has so much success; on this account alone, therefore, they should feel most miserable in order that they may cease from their wickedness. This wickedness consists in claiming the name of religion for their evil gains and in bestowing the title of sanctity on paltry business transactions. If the misfortune of these men are compared with their own misdeeds, they are less wretched than they deserve, because, no matter what their misfortunes, they are not as pitiable as they are wicked.

In no way, therefore, should one grieve for them because they are not rich and happy. How much less should we grieve for the holy ones, because, no matter how wretched they may seem to those who misunderstand, they cannot be other than happy. It is unnecessary that anybody should think them unhappy because of sickness, or poverty, or for other circumstances of this kind, in the midst of which they are sure they are happy. No one is unhappy because another thinks he is, but only because he himself thinks so. They who are truly happy in mind cannot be wretched because of the erroneous judgment of some other person. I think no persons are happier than those whose actions are governed by their own convictions and vows. Holy men are humble because such is their wish. They are poor because they delight in the practice of poverty. They are without desire for display before others because they scorn it. They are without honors because they flee from honors. They mourn and exult in mourning. They are weak and rejoice because they are infirm. The Apostle has said:[3] 'When I am weak, then I am strong.' Rightly did the man, to whom God Himself spoke, think when He said:[4] 'My grace is sufficient for you, for power is made perfect in infirmity.'

Therefore, we must never grieve over the affliction of bodily

---
3 2 Cor. 12.10.
4 2 Cor. 12.9.

sickness which, we understand, is the mother of strength. Whatever that may be, whosoever are truly holy must be called happy because, in the midst of hardships and bitterness, there are no happier persons than they who are happy because they wish to be. Indeed, there are wont to be some whose objectives are foul and indecent and who, in their own opinion, are happy because their wishes are fulfilled. Despite that, they are not happy, because they should not desire the things they do. In this respect, holy men are happier than all others because they have what they wish for and they cannot, in any way, have better things than what is already in their possession. Toil, fasting, poverty, humility and sickness are not burdensome to all those who are willing to bear them, but only to those who are unwilling. The mental attitude of him who sustains these burdens determines whether they are light or heavy. No matter how light the task, it is heavy to him who performs it unwillingly. No matter how heavy, it seems light to him who executes it willingly.

Perhaps we are to think that the Fabii, Fabricii and the Cincinnati, those past masters of the virtues of olden times, bore a heavy burden in being poor, when they did not wish to be rich. All these men devoted their full energies and efforts to the advantage of all, and by their personal poverty enriched the increasing wealth of the State. Did these men, eating their cheap and simple fare before the very fire over which it was cooked and who delayed partaking of it until evening, groan and sorrow over their frugal and rural mode of life? Did they feel badly that they, in a greedy desire for wealth, did not hunt for talents of gold? They even placed legal limits on the use of silver. Did they, who judged a patrician unworthy of the Senate because he wished to be enriched by ten pounds of silver, think that their illicit greed was being punished because they did not have purses bulging with gold coins?

Poverty was not an object of contempt. Wearing one short and rough garment, men were fetched in those days from the plough to the *fasces;* perhaps, as they were being garbed in the consular robes, they wiped their dusty sweat with the imperial robes in which they were about to be garbed. Then, magistrates, though poor, had a rich State. Now, the power of the rich makes the State poor. I ask: What blindness and insanity make men believe that large private wealth can remain, while the State is impoverished and needy? Such, then, were the Romans of old, and as they, not knowing God, condemned wealth, so do those who follow the Lord today spurn it.

Why, then, do I speak of those men who, for the sake of spreading Roman imperial power, scorned their private wealth and transferred it to the public treasury and who, although individually poor, were nevertheless in plenty, because the State was rich? What of certain Greek philosophers who, through no motive of public service, but with greed for glory, despoiled themselves of the use of almost all personal property? And not only this, they elevated their convictions to the lofty summit of contempt for death and sorrow on the grounds that the wise man is happy even though shackled with chains and subject to punishment. They deemed the power of virtue to be so great that a good man could never be an unhappy man. If, therefore, these men who sought no compensation for their effort beyond momentary praise are adjudged not unhappy by some wise men, how much more are the religious and holy of our day to be thought not unhappy? In this life they possess the joys of their faith and will obtain the rewards of blessedness in the next.

(3) One of these men, about whom I am lamenting, speaking to a certain holy man who knew the true faith, that is, that God rules all things and tempers His rule with moderation and guidance in accordance with His knowledge of the necessities of human beings, asked: 'Why are you sick?' He was speaking according to his reasoning and judgment, and meant: 'If, as you think, God rules all things here and now, if He is the controller of all things, how is it that a man whom I know to be a sinner is healthy and strong, while you of whose holiness I have no doubt are sickly?' Who does not wonder at the man who in the depths of his heart thinks that the merits and virtues of holy men are worthy of so great recompense that bodily strength in this life must be their reward?

I answer, not in the name of one holy man, but of all holy men. Are you asking, whoever you are, why holy men are weak? I answer briefly—the holy make themselves more weak because, if they were strong, they could hardly be holy. I am of the opinion that all men receive strength through food and drink and become weak through abstinence, thirst and fasting. There is nothing strange in the fact that they are weak who cast aside the use of those means by which others become strong. And the reason why they cast them aside is, as the Apostle said of himself:[5] 'I chastise my body and bring it into subjection: lest perhaps, when I have preached to others, I myself should become a castaway.' If the Apostle thought he should seek to weaken his own body, who can wisely avoid doing so? If the Apostle feared the strength of the body, who can reasonably expect to be strong? This is why men dedicated to Christ are weak of their own volition. Be it far from me to think holy men are neglected by God, as my opponents

---

5 1 Cor. 9.27.

argue. Instead, I am confident that they are loved more by Him. We read that the Apostle Timothy's body was very weak. Was he who wished to be weak for the purpose of pleasing Him neglected by the Lord, or was he displeasing to Christ because of his infirmity? The Apostle Paul himself, although Timothy was suffering from severe infirmities, allowed Timothy to take and taste only a little wine.[6] This means that Paul, while wishing Timothy to take his own bodily weakness into account, did not desire Timothy to develop full bodily vigor. And why did he do this? Surely, for no other reason than, that, as he himself says,[7] 'the flesh lusts against the spirit: and the spirit against the flesh,' for, he says, 'these are contrary one to the other, so that you do not the things that you would.'

Someone has wisely said about this point that, if we cannot do what we hope to do because of the resisting strength of the body, then the flesh must be made weak so that our hopes can be realized. He said:[8] 'Bodily weakness sharpens the vigor of the mind and, when muscular strength is impaired, bodily strength is transferred to mental strength. Our hearts do not burn with vile passions, and latent desires no longer seethe in an unbalanced mind. Our senses do not wander wantonly over various delights. The soul alone rejoices, exulting over the weakness of the body as over a conquered enemy.' This, therefore, as I have said, is the reason for bodily weakness in holy men. You, I think, do not deny that such is the case.

(4) But, you say, perhaps there are other and greater sufferings, that is, the holy suffer many hard and bitter trials

---
6 1 Tim. 5.23.
7 Gal. 5.17.
8 Salvian is actually quoting himself: Epistle 5.221-222, which is almost identical.

in this life: they are captured, tortured and cut in pieces. That is true. But what can we say, since the prophets were led away into captivity and the Apostles also suffered torture? Certainly, we cannot doubt that God was especially concerned for them at that time, since they underwent those sufferings for Him. Perhaps you say this is additional proof for you that God neglects everything in this world and reserves all for judgment in the next, since at all times the good have suffered all the evils while the wicked have done them all. This does not seem to be the statement of an unbeliever, especially since it acknowledges a future judgment by God.

But we say the human race is to be judged by Christ in such a way that we also now believe that God rules and dispenses all things in accordance with His reason. As we now affirm belief in God's future judgment, so do we now teach that God is always our judge in this life. While God governs us, He judges us, because His governance is His judgment.

In how many ways do you wish me to prove this: by reason, example or authority? If by reason, who is so devoid of human intelligence and so foreign to that very truth of which I speak that he does not acknowledge and see that the beauteous structure of the world, the inestimable magnificence of the heavens above and of the regions below, are ruled by Him who created them, and that whosoever made these elements will also govern them? He surely regulates all things with reason and forethought as He fashioned them in power and majesty, since even in the performance of human acts nothing is done without reason. In like manner all things derive their totality from Providence, just as the body draws its life from the soul. Therefore, in this world not only empires and provinces, affairs civil and military, but even the lesser offices and private homes, the cattle themselves and the smallest kinds of domestic animals are kept in check only by human arrangements and planning as if by hand and helm.

Without doubt, all these things are performed in accordance with the will and judgment of the Most High God, so that the whole human race, in regulating its lesser parts and members, has for a model God's governance of the entire universe. You say that in the beginning God legislated and arranged for His creatures. Then, acting contrariwise, after the universe was created and perfected, He removed and put from Himself all concern with things earthly. You say that He was shunning toil perhaps, and so removed Himself from His creation. You also say that, avoiding the annoyance of weariness or being engrossed with other problems, He forsook a portion of His affairs because He could not cope with the whole.

(5) You say that God removes from Himself all care of human beings. What, then, is our rational basis for divine worship? What is our reason for worshiping Christ, or what hope have we of appeasing Him? If God neglects the human race in this world, why do we daily stretch forth our hands to heaven? Why do we seek the mercy of God with unceasing prayers? Why do we hasten to the houses of the Lord? Why do we humbly pray before the altars? There is no basis for prayer if the hope of being answered is taken away. You see, therefore, how foolish and useless it is to make public assertion of your belief. Indeed, if your assertion is accepted, there is absolutely nothing left of our worship.

Perhaps you take refuge in the following argument, and say that we worship God out of fear of a future judgment and that we take special pains with elaborate worship in this life with the purpose of winning absolution on the day of judgment that is to come. What else did the Apostle Paul mean when he preached daily in the church and ordered us to offer constantly our prayers, entreaties, requests and thanks to our God? And what was the purpose of thus beseeching God? What else but, as he himself said,[9] 'that we may lead a quiet and peaceful life in all chastity.' As we see, he orders us to pray to and beseech the Lord for our daily needs, and he would not so order unless he were confident that our prayers could be heeded.

How, therefore, does anybody think that the ears of God are open for granting future favors, but closed and deaf to our present needs? Why do we, when praying in church, ask God for daily well-being if we do not firmly believe that He hears us? We should not offer votive offerings for our safety and prosperity. Rather, in order that the propriety of the request may win favor for him who asks, we should speak thus: 'Lord, we do not request prosperity in this life, nor do we beg humbly for immediate favors, because we know that your ears are deaf to such petitions and you do not give ear to prayers of this kind. We ask only for those things which are for the future, after death.'

Grant that a petition of such a nature is not without its use, but on what rational basis does it rest? If God removes His care and ceases to be concerned with this world and closes His ears to the entreaties of His supliants, then, doubtless, He who does not hear our prayers for present needs does not hear our prayers for future needs. It may be we are to believe that Christ does or does not pay attention according to the variety of our prayers. This means that He closes His ears when we ask for immediate good and opens them when we request future good.

There is nothing more to be said about this. This way of thinking is so stupid and silly that I must beware lest what is said for the honor of God might seem instead to do Him

---
[9] 1 Tim. 2.1-4.

wrong. So great and awe-inspiring is the reverence due to His Sacred Majesty that not only should we shudder at mention of those things said against His worship, but even what we say in defense of His worship must be said with great fear and submissiveness.

If it is foolish and irreverent to believe that divine Love disdains the care of human affairs, then He does not disdain them. If He does not disdain them, He rules them. If He rules, He judges by the very act of ruling, because there cannot be rule without constant judgment by the ruler.

(6) Perhaps some may think that which is made evident by reason is insufficiently proved unless supported by examples. Let us see how God ruled the world from the beginning. I will show that He always governed all things, and so I teach that He also judged at the same time as He ruled. What does Scripture say? 'God formed man from the slime of the earth and breathed into him the breath of life.'[10] And what then? 'He placed him in a paradise of pleasure.'[11] What next? He handed him the Law. He gave him instructions and trained him in the principles of conduct. What followed then? Man transgressed the sacred mandate, was subjected to judgment, lost paradise and took on the penalty of damnation.

Who is it who does not see that God is both judge and ruler in all this? God placed Adam in paradise in innocence; He expelled him as a criminal. Adam was established in paradise by decree; he was expelled by judgment. When God established him in a place of delight, He decreed so as a ruler; when He expelled him as a criminal from that kingdom, He was acting as judge. This is the established fact about the first man, that is, of the father. What about the second, that

---
10 Gen. 2.7.
11 Gen. 2.8.

is, the son? 'It came to pass,' says Holy Scripture, 'after many days that Cain offered of the fruits of the earth, gifts to the Lord. Abel also offered of the firstlings of his flock, and of their fat; and the Lord had respect to Abel and to his offerings. But to Cain and his offerings, He had no respect.'[12]

Before I speak of the more manifest judgment of God, in those instances of which I have already spoken there is I think, a certain severity of judgment. I mean that God, by accepting the sacrifices of one brother, rejected that of the other, and judged very openly of the righteousness of one and the wickedness of the other. But this is not all. Cain paved the way for his future crimes by leading his brother into the wilderness, where, with secrecy as his patron, he committed his crime. He was at once the most wicked and foolish of men in believing that, for committing the greatest of crimes, it would be sufficient if he avoided the witness of men, when in fact God was to witness his fratricide. Because of this, I think he then shared the opinion held by many today: that God pays no attention to earthly affairs; neither does He see those done by wicked men. There is no doubt that Cain, when summoned by the word of God after his misdeed, answered that he knew nothing of his brother's murder. He believed God was so ignorant of what had been done that he thought this most deadly crime could be covered by a lie. But it turned out otherwise than he thought. When God condemned him, he realized that God, whom he thought had not seen his crime of murder, had seen him.

Here and now I wish to put a question to those who deny that God rules, looks after and judges human affairs. Do the accounts of all those things of which I have spoken differ widely? I think that He who is interested in the sacrifice is

---

[12] Gen. 4.2-16.

present. He who chastises Cain after the sacrifice rules. He who makes inquiries about the murdered man from the very man who killed him is concerned. He who condemns the wicked murderer by a just verdict judges. In this incident there is also something suitable to the question at issue. Indeed, let us not wonder today that holy men suffer certain hardships, when we realize that God, at the time of Cain and Abel, allowed the first of His holy men to be killed by the worst sort of crime. For what reason God allows such things it is not within the scope of human weakness to know fully, nor is it now the time to discuss this. For the time being, it is sufficient to prove that all things of this sort happen, not because of the negligence or indifference of God, but because they are permitted by His wisdom and dispensation. We can never call Him unjust, in whom we cannot deny that divine judgment exists, because the will of God is the highest Justice. Neither is what God does unjust, because man cannot grasp the force of divine justice. But let me return to my purpose.

(7) We see from what I have said that nothing is done without God's concern, because His divine will regulated some, His forbearance endured others, and His sentence punished others. There are some, perhaps, who think that I have not proved sufficiently, by citing only a few examples, the points on which I have been speaking. Let us see if I cannot make this clear through universal application. God, according to the Holy Scriptures, seeing that the human race had multiplied alike in numbers and wickedness, said[13] 'that the wickedness of men was great on the earth and that all the thought of their hearts was bent upon evil at all times. He repented that He had made man on the earth. And being touched in-

---
13 Gen. 6.5-7.

wardly with sorrow of heart, He said, "I will destroy man, whom I have created, from the face of the earth." '

Let us consider how both the solicitude and severity of the Lord are shown equally in all these words. First He said, 'And God seeing'; secondly, 'He was touched inwardly with sorrow of heart'; thirdly, 'I will destroy man whom I have created.' In the first statement, wherein it is said that God sees all things, His care is shown. In the statement that He has sorrow is shown the dread of His wrath. The statement about His punishment shows His severity as a judge. Holy Scripture says, 'God repented that He had made man on earth,' not that God is affected by emotion or is subject to any passion. Rather, the Divine Word, to impart more fully to us a true understanding of the Scriptures, speaks as if in terms of human emotions and, by using the term 'repentant God,' shows the force of God's anger. Besides, God's anger is the punishment of the sinner.

What followed next? 'When God saw the earth was corrupted, He said to Noah, "the end of all flesh is come before Me; the earth is filled with iniquity through them, and I will destroy them with the earth." '[14] And then what? 'All the fountains of the great deep were broken up and the flood gates of Heaven were opened. And the rain fell upon the earth forty days and forty nights.'[15] And a little while later: 'And all flesh was destroyed that moved upon the earth.'[16] And again, 'And Noah only remained alive and they that were with him in the ark.'[17] Here and now I wish to ask them who call God indifferent to human affairs whether they believe that at that time He either cared for earthly affairs or judged them. I think that He not only judged, but did so in

---
14 Gen. 6.12-13.
15 Gen. 7.11-12.
16 Gen. 7.21.
17 Gen. 7.23.

a twofold manner, for, by preserving the good, He showed that He was a bountiful giver of awards, and, by condemning the wicked, a severe judge.

But these arguments may seem to have little authority with the foolish, since these events took place before the flood, as if it were in another age. This is like saying that either at that time there was a different God, or He was unwilling to care for the world afterwards. Through God's gift, I can prove what I say by examples from each generation since the flood, but their great number forbids detailed enumeration. Certain of the more important examples are sufficient because, since God doubtless is the same for the greater and lesser instances, that which is acknowledged of the greater must also be understood of the lesser.

(8) When, after the flood, God blessed the generation of men, His blessing begot a huge multitude of men and God spoke to Abraham from Heaven.[18] He ordered him to depart from his own country and seek a foreign land. Abraham was called and he followed; he was led and established. From poverty he came to riches; from obscurity, to power. Downcast by his wanderings, he became most exalted in honor. Yet, lest what was given to him by God should be considered only an undeserved gift, he who rejoiced in prosperity was proved by adversity. Toil, danger and fear followed. He was upset by traveling, fatigued by exile, heaped with reproach and deprived of his wife. God ordered the sacrifice of his son to Himself; the father offered the son and, in so far as the intention in his heart was concerned, sacrificed him. Again came exile, again fear, the hatred of the Philistines, the plundering by Abimelech. He suffered many evils, but re-

---
18 Gen. 12.1.

ceived equal compensations because, though he was brought low by many, he was delivered from all.

Further, in all these instances which I have recounted, is it not God who examines Abraham, invites him, guides him, takes care of him, sponsors him, protects him, bestows gifts on him, tests him, exalts him, avenges him and judges him? He examines him because He chose him as the one best from all others; invites him because He called him; guides him because He led him to the unknown; takes care of him because He visited him by the oak tree; sponsors him because He promised things to come; protects him because He guarded him among strange peoples; bestows gifts on him because He made him opulent; tests him because He wished him tested by bitterness; exalts him because He made him more powerful than all others; avenges him because He avenged him on his opponents; judges him because, in avenging him, He judged.

God added to this narrative of events when He said:[19] 'the cry of Sodom and Gomorrha is multiplied and their sin is become exceedingly grievous.' The cry of Sodom and Gommorrha is multiplied, He said. Well did He say that sins can cry out. Great surely is the cry of sinners as it mounts from earth to heaven. But why does He say that the sins of men cry out? It is because God says His ears are assaulted by the cries of our sins that the punishment of sinners be not delayed. Truly it is a cry and the cry is great when the love of God is overpowered by the cries of sins to the extent that He is forced to punish the sinners. The Lord shows how unwilling He is to punish even the gravest sinners, when He said that the cry of Sodom ascended to Him. This means: My mercy urges Me to spare them, but the cry of their sins

---
19 Gen. 18.20.

compels Me to punish them. When He had said this, what followed? Angels were sent with messages to Sodom.[20] They set out and entered the city, where they were treated well by the good and abused by the wicked. The wicked were blinded; the good were saved. Lot, with tender care, was led out of the city, which was burned with its evil inhabitants. At this point I ask whether He burned the evil with or without passing judgment? He who says God punished the Sodomites without passing judgment asserts that God is unjust; if, on the other hand, He destroyed the wicked after passing judgment, He judged them. Certainly He judged, and His judgment is, as it were, a likeness of the Judgment that is to come, for it is well known that hell will be a flaming mass for the future punishment of the wicked, just as flames from heaven destroyed Sodom and its neighboring cities.

In the present instance, God wished to proclaim the Judgment that is to come when He sent fiery death from heaven upon a wicked people, just as the Apostle also says that God by overthrowing the cities of Sodom and Gomorrha condemned them, thereby setting an example for those who will live wicked lives.[21] However, His act in that instance possessed more mercy than severity. That He so long delayed their punishment was due to His mercy; that He at last punished them, to His justice. When God sent His angels to Sodom, He wished to prove to us that He is even unwilling to punish the wicked. This was certainly for the purpose that, when we read what the angels endured from the Sodomites and we see how excessive were their crimes, how infamous their vices and how obscene their lusts, God could thereby prove to us that He was unwilling to destroy them. They themselves compelled their own destruction.

---

20 Gen. 19.1.
21 2 Peter 2.6.

(9) I could mention innumerable examples, but I am afraid that, in striving to prove my point sufficiently, I seem to be composing a history. Moses was pasturing his flock in the desert, saw a bush burning, heard God speaking from the bush, received His commands, was exalted in power and sent to Pharaoh, to whom he came, spoke, and whom he vanquished after being scorned.[22] Egypt was smitten. The disobedience of Pharaoh was chastised, and not in one way only; guilty of manifold sacrilege, he was tormented by a variety of punishments. What was the result? Ten times he rebelled, ten times he was chastised. What do we say to that? I think you must recognize in all these happenings that God equally cares for and judges human affairs. In Egypt, God's judgment was not one but many, for, as often as He struck down the rebellious Egyptians, so often did He judge them.

But, after the events I have mentioned, what happened next? The Israelites were released and, having celebrated the Passover, despoiled the Egyptians and departed in riches. Pharaoh repented, gathered an army, overtook the fugitives, pitched camp beside them, but was separated from them by darkness. The sea was dried up. Israel crossed over and was freed by the obliging overflowing of the waves. Pharaoh followed, the sea flowed over him and he was destroyed by the covering flood. I think the judgment of God is manifest in those events which took place; indeed, not only His judgment, but also His moderation and patience. It was through His patience that the rebellious Egyptians were often struck down. It was because of His judgment that they were condemned to death for persisting in their arrogant obstinacy.

Thus, after these things were accomplished, the Hebrew people, victorious without a battle, entered into the desert. Travelers without a route, wanderers without a path, but with

---

[22] Exod. 3.

God as a guide, honored by divine comradeship, powerful in their heavenly leadership, they followed a moving column of cloud by day and of fire by night. This cloud took on suitable degrees of color according to the changing hours of the day. Its muddy blackness was distinct in the light of day and its flaming splendor lit up the gloom of night.

Consider also the springs which suddenly gushed forth. Consider the wholesome waters either pure as found or altered to purity, retaining their former appearance, but changed in their properties. Consider the peaks of mountains opened by gushing brooks, the dusty fields flooded by new torrents, the flocks of birds sent into the camps of the wanderers, since God in His most indulgent mercy supplied them not only with their human needs but also with alluring delicacies. Consider again the food given for forty years through the daily ministration of the stars. The heavens, shedding sweet foods, offered an abundance not only for nourishment but for delight. Consider that the men felt in no parts of their bodies the increases and decreases natural to human beings; their nails did not grow, their teeth did not decay, their hair remained at one length, their feet were not inflamed, their clothing was not torn, their shoes were not worn, and thus the dignity of the men was so conspicuous that it enhanced their mean garments. Consider, moreover, God's descent to earth for the purpose of instructing His people. He accommodates Himself, God the Son, to earthly eyes. The huge mass of ordinary people, admitted to the association of divine familiarity, became strong in the power of this sacred friendship. Consider the thunders, lightnings, the terrifying blasts of heavenly trumpets, the fearful noises throughout the sky, the heavens rumbling with holy sounds, the fires and fogs and clouds filled with God. Consider the Lord speaking face to face with man, the Law ringing from His divine mouth, the pages of the book of stone inscribed by God's finger with letters and accents, the people learning and God teaching, as if it were one school of heaven and earth, with men and angels all but intermixed.

For thus it is written that, when Moses had taken the words of the people to the Lord, the Lord said to him:[23] 'now will I come to you in the darkness of a cloud that the people may hear Me speaking to you.' And a little later:[24] 'Behold thunders began to be heard and lightning to flash and a very thick cloud to cover the mount.' Again:[25] 'The Lord came down upon Mount Sinai, in the very top of the mount.' And then:[26] 'He spoke with Moses. And all saw that the pillar of cloud stood at the door of the tabernacle. And they stood and worshiped at the doors of their tents. And the Lord spoke to Moses, face to face, as a man is wont to speak to his friend.' Such being the case, does God seem to have care for mankind, giving them so much, helping them so much? He shared His speech with a vile mortal, as though admitting him into the association of divine fellowship. He opened to him His hands filled with undying riches. He nourished the people with a cup of nectar, and fed them with heavenly food. I ask, what greater evidence of His governance could He show, what greater proof of His affecttion than that man, going through this life, possess a glimpse of the happiness in the next?

(10) Perhaps you will now answer that God formerly exercised this care over mankind, but does not now do so. Why are we to believe this? Is it, perhaps, because, though reaping fields full of grain at harvest time, we do not now eat

---
23 Exod. 19.9.
24 Exod. 19.16.
25 Exod. 19.20.
26 Exod. 33.9-11.

manna daily as the Israelites then did? Is it because we do not catch quail that fly into our hands, though we devour all manner of birds, cattle and beasts? Is it because we are not granted waters gushing from apertures in the rocks, though we pour the products of our vineyards into our wine cellars?

I have more to add to this. We ourselves, who say that the Israelites were then cared for by God who now neglects us, would absolutely not accept the choice of their circumstances if we could receive their past favors in exchange for our present good. We would not want to lose what we now possess so that we could have what they then utilized. It is not that their condition then was better than ours now, but that they who were then fed through the ministration of heaven and God preferred their formerly full bellies to the favors they then received. They were saddened by the base remembrance of flesh meats, growing sick in their abominable desire for onions and garlic; not because their former diet was more nourishing, but rather, experiencing then what we do now, they scorned what they had and longed for what they had not. We praise more the things that are gone than those of the present; not that, if we had the opportunity to choose, we would prefer to possess them forever, but because it is a well known imperfection of the human mind to want what it has not. As the proverb says:[27] 'Another's goods please us, and ours please others more.'

To this can be added something that is approximately general to mankind: man is always ungrateful to God and feels himself bound through an innate and native vice to belittle the blessings of God, lest he acknowledge being indebted to God. But, enough on this topic. Let me return to my proposi-

---

27 Syrus v. 28 (ed. Ribbeck).

tion begun a little while ago, although I think I have amply proved what I proposed. Let me add something more, if you please, since, in the prosecution of a case, it is better to prove a point beyond all requirements than to fall short in presenting evidence.

(11) On being freed from the yoke of Pharaoh, the Hebrews transgressed when they were near Mount Sinai and were immediately smitten by God for their transgression. Thus is it written:[28] 'the Lord therefore struck the people for their guilt on occasion of the calf which Aaron had made.' What greater and more manifest judgment could God have made regarding sinners than that punishment immediately follow their sins. Yet, since all were guilty, why was not condemnation visited on all? Because the good Lord struck some with the swords of His sentence in order to correct others by example, and to prove to all at the same time, His judgment by correcting, His love by pardoning. When he punished, He judged; when He pardoned, He loved. His judgment and love were unequal: His love was more evident than was His severity. Surely, therefore, since our most indulgent Lord shows Himself more prone to pardon than to do vengeance, His love claimed the great proportion of the people, although by His divine censure in punishing a part of the Jewish host He exhibited His judgment and severity. That the punishment did not destroy all who were implicated in the crime was a special and singular act of mercy to innumerable men.

But, as we read, He was inexorable in punishing certain persons and families, such as he who was killed for unlawfully gathering wood when the people rested on the Sabbath day.[29] Though his act seemed harmless, the observance of the day

---
28 Exod. 32.35.
29 Num. 15.33-36.

rendered it sinful. There is also the instance of two men in dispute, one of whom blasphemed and was punished with death. Thus it is written:[30] 'And behold, there went out the son of a woman of Israel, whom she had by an Egyptian, among the children of Israel: and fell at words in the camp with a man of Israel. And when he had blasphemed the Name, and had cursed it, he was brought to Moses.' And a little later:[31] 'And they put him into prison till they might know what the Lord would command. And the Lord spoke to Moses, saying: "Bring forth the blasphemer without the camp and let those who heard him put their hands upon his head: and let all the people stone him."'

Was not the judgment of God immediate and manifest? Was not His sentence pronounced by heavenly decision as if it followed our earthly legal procedure? First, the sinner was arrested; secondly, he was led, so to speak, before the judgment seat; thirdly, he was accused; then he was imprisoned; lastly, he was punished by the authority of the divine judgment. Furthermore, he was not only punished, but punished on the basis of evidence so that God's justice and not His authority seemed to condemn the accused. This, indeed, is an example contributing to the correction of all men so that none should allow thereafter what the whole people had punished in the person of one guilty man. For this reason and by this judgment does God act now, and always has acted, so that the penalties inflicted on one may serve for the correction of all.

Thus it was when Abiu and Nadab, men of priestly blood, were consumed by fire from heaven. In their case, God wished to show, not judgment alone, but judgment immediate and impending. For thus is it written: that when the fire sent by God had consumed the holocaust, 'Nadab and Abiu, the sons

---
30 Lev. 24.10.
31 Lev. 24.12-14.

of Aaron, taking their censers, put fire therein, and incense on it, offering before the Lord strange fire, which was not commanded them. And fire coming out from the Lord destroyed them: and they died before the Lord'.[32] What else did He wish to show but His right hand stretched over us and His constantly threatening sword? He punished the sin of the aforesaid in their very act, and their crime was scarcely committed before their sin was punished. And not only this was accomplished in their case, but much more.

Since in them not a wicked intention, but a misdirected carelessness, was punished, the Lord indeed made it clear of what punishment they who sin through contempt of divine authority would be deemed guilty when even they who sinned through thoughtlessness were smitten by God. The Lord also made it clear how guilty they would be who acted against the express orders of their Lord, when those who simply acted without mandate were punished as they were. God also wished us to be mindful of our correction by the severity of a salutary example so that all laymen would understand how much they should fear the wrath of God. Neither could the merits of the parent priest snatch his sons from punishment nor did the privileges attached to the sacred ministry save them.

But what do I say of those whose thoughtlessness, in a way, affected God and overflowed to His heavenly injury? Mary spoke against Moses and was punished. She was punished only after a trial. First she was called to be judged, then accused, and then scourged. In the accusation she received the full force of the sentence, and in leprosy she atoned for her crime. A punishment of this nature humbled not Mary alone but also Aaron. Though it was unbecoming for the high priest to be deformed by leprosy, the punishment of the Lord flayed him

---

[32] Lev. 10.1-2.

also. Nor was this all. Aaron, as a partner in guilt, also was involved in Mary's punishment. Mary was punished by leprosy that Aaron might be punished by shame.

Moreover, in order that we may recognize the inexorability of the form of divine judgment, God was not moved by the intercession of him who was injured. For we read that the Lord spoke thus to Aaron and Mary.[33] 'Why then were you not afraid to speak ill of my servant Moses? And being angry with them, He went away. And behold, Mary appeared white as snow with a leprosy. And Moses cried to the Lord, saying: "O God, I beseech Thee, heal her." And the Lord answered him, "If her father had spitten upon her face, ought she not to have been ashamed for ten days at least? Let her be separated seven days without the camp, and afterwards she shall be called again."' Let what I have said be sufficient for this portion of the discussion and this part of the book. It is an unending task to discuss all the instances. It is indeed exceedingly long to enumerate them even without discussion. But, however, let me add another.

(12) The Hebrew people repented their departure from Egypt and were struck down. They grieved at the fatigue and the toil of the journey and were afflicted. They craved flesh meat and were scourged. Eating manna daily, they desired to satiate their gluttony with forbidden foods. Their intense greed was sated, but they were tortured in that satiety. For, as Scripture says:[34] 'As yet their meat was in their mouth, the wrath of God came upon them and He slew very many among them and laid low the chosen men of Israel.'

Og rebelled against Moses and was destroyed. Core made rebuke and was overwhelmed. Dathan and Abiron murmured

---
33 Num. 12.8-15.
34 Ps. 77.30-31.

against him and were swallowed up. Scripture says:[35] 'And the earth opened and swallowed up Dathan: and covered the congregation of Abiron.' Two hundred fifty leaders, as Scripture testifies, who were called upon by name to speak at the time of the council, rebelled against Moses:[36] 'And when they had stood up against Moses and Aaron, they said, "Let it be enough for you that all the multitude consists of holy ones and the Lord is among them. Why lift you up yourselves above the people of the Lord?"' And what happened after this? Scripture says:[37] 'And a fire coming out from the Lord killed the two hundred fifty men who had offered the incense.'

When their crimes were so great, heavenly solicitude was of no avail. As often as they were corrected, so often amendment did not follow. As we are not corrected, even though soundly scourged, so they, though constantly struck down, did not mend their ways. What is written? 'The following day all the multitude of the children of Israel murmured against Moses and Aaron, saying, "You have killed the people of the Lord."'[38] What followed? Fourteen thousand and seven hundred men were struck down and consumed by divine fire.

Since the multitude all had sinned, why were not all punished, especially since, as I have said, none escaped from Core's mutiny? Why did God wish the whole assembly of sinners to be killed on the former occasion, but only a portion at the latter time? It is because the Lord is filled with both justice and mercy and in His indulgence He gives way to His love, and in His will to teach a lesson He gives way to His severity. On the former occasion He gave way to His sev-

---
35 Ps. 105.17.
36 Num. 16.3.
37 Num. 16.35.
38 Num. 16.41.

erity so that the punishment of all the guilty would profit to the betterment of all. On the latter occasion, He gave way to mercy so that all would not perish.

Although He acted mercifully, the punishment, of a portion of the people so often repeated, did not profit them, and thus He finally condemned all to death. This should be of profit, at the same time, to our fear and amendment, lest, perhaps we, not corrected by their example, be punished like them by extinction. What became of them is not in doubt. Although the whole Hebrew people departed from Egypt to enter the promised land, none entered except two holy men. For thus it is written: 'The Lord spoke to Moses and Aaron saying, "How long does this wicked multitude murmur against Me? As I live," said the Lord, "according as you have spoken in My hearing, so will I do to you. In the wilderness shall your carcasses lie." '[39] What next? 'But your children, of whom you said, that they should be a prey to the enemies, will I bring in, that they know the land which you have despised. Your carcasses shall lie in the wilderness.'[40] And what then? 'All died and were struck down in the sight of the Lord.'[41]

What is it that is lacking in this account of events? Do you wish to see a ruler? Behold Him correcting present evils and regulating the future. Do you wish to see a strict judge? Behold Him punishing the wicked. Do you wish to see a just and clement judge? Behold Him sparing the innocent. Do you wish to see the judge of the universe? Behold Him judging everywhere. As a judge He accuses; as a judge He rules; as a judge He pronounces sentence; as a judge He destroys the guilty—as a judge He rewards the innocent.

---
39 Num. 14.26-29.
40 Num. 14.31-32.
41 Num. 14.37.

BOOK TWO

THE FOREGOING examples which I have cited are sufficient proof that our God is a most concerned observer, a most lenient ruler and a most just judge. But perhaps one of my more ignorant readers is thinking: 'If all things are done now by God as they were done formerly, why is it that the wicked prevail while the good suffer? Why is it that in former times the wicked were made to feel the anger of God; the good, His mercy? Today, it seems, the good for some reason feel the anger of God; the wicked, His favor.' I shall answer in a little while. Because I have promised to prove three points, that is, the presence, governance and judgment of God, I shall do so by three methods, that is, by reason, examples and authority. And because I have already given sufficient proof of them by reason and examples, there remains proof by authority. The examples I have already given should be considered proof by authority, because that is rightly said to be authority by which the truth of things is proved.

Which of the three forementioned points should be first proved by sacred authority: God's presence, His governance or His judgment? I am of the opinion that His presence should be first proved, because He who will rule or judge must doubtless be present in order to rule or judge. The divine Word, speaking through Holy Scripture, says:[1] 'The eyes of the Lord, in every place, behold good and evil.' Behold here God present, looking upon us, watching us through His vision wherever we are. For that reason God said He watch-

---
1 Prov. 15.3.

ed closely the wicked and the good, to the end that He would prove that nothing is overlooked by Him who pries into all things.

So that you may understand more fully, hear what the Holy Spirit testifies in another part of the Scriptures, when it says:[2] 'Behold, the eyes of the Lord are on them that fear Him, to deliver their souls from death and feed them in famine.' This is why God is said to watch over the just, that He may maintain and protect them. Watchfulness by His gracious divinity is the function of His relationship with men. The Holy Spirit says likewise elsewhere:[3] 'The eyes of the Lord are upon the just, and His ears unto their prayers.' See with what kindness Scripture says the Lord acts towards His people. When it says the eyes of the Lord are on the just, His watchful love is shown. When it says that His ears are always open to their prayers, the bounty of the hearer is indicated. That His divine ears are always open to the just portrays not merely God's attention, but almost a kind of obedience in Him.

How are the Lord's ears open to the prayers of the just? How, unless that they always hear and always heed, always grant readily the requests that are heard, and instantly answer what they heed? Therefore, the ears of the Lord are always open to, and always intent on, the prayers of His holy men. How happy would we be, if we ourselves were ready to hear God as promptly as we read of Him promptly heeding us. Perhaps you say that God's watchfulness over the just is of little value to the argument, because the watchfulness of His divinity is not general, but only granted as a special favor to the just.

In answer, Scripture has already testified above that the

---
[2] Ps. 32.18-19.
[3] Ps. 33.16.

eyes of the Lord observe the good and the bad. If you now wish additional proof, look at what follows, for the text continues,[4] 'The countenance of the Lord is against them that do evil things: to cut off the remembrance of them from the earth.' Without doubt, you see, you cannot complain that God does not watch over even the unjust, because you know He watches over all, but this is done with different effect because of the merit involved. The good are watched over for the sake of preserving them; the evil, that they may be destroyed. You yourself, having a place among the last mentioned category, deny that men are watched over by God. Understand that you are not only clearly seen by God, but realize that you are undoubtedly about to be lost. Since the face of the Lord is over against those who do evil, so that He will cut off their remembrance from the earth, it is necessary that you, who wickedly deny that the face of God beholds you, should learn by your perdition the anger of the Beholder. These arguments are sufficient proof of the presence and watchfulness of God.

(2) Let us now see whether He who watches rules us, although the very reason for His watchfulness has within itself the cause of His governance. He does not watch us with this end in view: that, having beheld, He may neglect us. The very fact that He deigns to watch is to be understood as nonneglect, especially since, as Scripture has already testified, the wicked are observed for their destruction, the good for their salvation. By this very fact the stewardship of a divine ruler is shown, for it is the function of just government to govern and deal with men individually, according to their respective merits. But hear fuller testimony on this point.

---

[4] Ps. 33.17.

In the Psalm, the Holy Spirit said to God the Father:[5] 'Give ear, O you who rule Israel.' Israel is interpreted as 'seeing God,' whom, indeed, Christians who believe by faith see by faith and in their hearts. Though God is the governor of all things, it is said that His governance is particularly granted to them who especially deserve to be ruled by divine guidance. Therefore you, whoever you are, if you are a Christian, must believe that you are governed by God. If you completely deny that you and other Christians are ruled by God, then you must realize that you are outside the fold of Christ.

If, as we have already said, you are more interested in what pertains to men in general than to Christians in particular, notice how clearly the Holy Book says that all things are daily ruled by a divine nod and all things are governed by God when it says:[6] 'He loves counsel and knowledge.' For there is no other God but Him whose care is for all. 'For so much then as you are just, you order all things justly, and with great favor you dispose of us.'[7] Here you have God constantly arranging, constantly governing. Yet this passage of Holy Scripture is not only a declaration of divine governance, but of human dignity. The words 'you dispose of us' shows the force of divine governance; the words 'with great favor,' the apex of human dignity.

Elsewhere we read the words of the Prophet:[8] 'Do I not fill Heaven and earth?' He, Himself, tells why He fills all things:[9] 'because I am with you,' as He says, 'to save you.' Behold, the Lord shows us not only His rule and its all pervading fullness, but also the power and benefits accruing from

---

5 Ps. 79.2.
6 Eccli. 39.10.
7 Wisd. 12.15-18.
8 Jer. 23.24.
9 Jer. 42.11.

this very fullness. For the fullness of divinity carries as its reward the salvation of what it fills. Saint Paul, in the Acts of the Apostles said:[10] 'For in Him we live and move and are.' Without doubt He is more than the governor of life, in whom is the very motion of all that lives. Saint Paul did not say that we are moved by Him, but in Him. In this way He taught, to be sure, that our substance is deep-rooted within God's holy strength, because we, indeed, live in Him from whom we draw our very existence.

The Saviour Himself said in the Gospel:[11] 'Behold I am with you all days, even to the consummation of the world.' Christ said that He was not only with us, but even with us all our days. Do you, most ungrateful of men, say that He, who is with us unceasingly, has no care or regard for us? What does He do when with us? Is He with us to scorn and neglect us? And how can it happen that He is with us in our piety and neglects us in our impiety? He says, 'Behold I am with you all days, even to the consummation of the world.'

Indeed, we give a fine interpretation of God's love if we falsely say that He constantly neglects us, while He Himself says He never does neglect us! By this Christ wished to show that He would never take His love and protection away from us, because His presence would not leave us. We turn His divine love into contempt for us and we change His proofs of love into arguments of hatred against us. His statement 'of being with us' we wish to turn into proof of His hatred, rather than of His love. If the Lord had said that He would be apart from us, perhaps we would have less gossip about the indifference of the absent one. It is a proof of greater and more scornful contempt if we are ever neglected by Him who never leaves us. And there is all the more odium in it

---
10 Acts 17.28.
11 Matt. 28.20.

if He always remains with us so that, while never depriving us of His presence, He ever deprives us of His love.

Far be it from us to believe this about a most loving and merciful God, that He would wish to be ever near us, His presence seeming to neglect us in greater aversion. Far be it from us to have uttered this wickedness. I think there is none so evil in the whole human race who would wish to be in another's company because he disliked him. There is none so evil that he would seek to use the other's presence for the sole reason of obtaining greater satisfaction by despising him face to face. Let human nature itself teach and convince us that we wish to be with somebody whose company we seek because we like him. And because we love, we wish our presence to be profitable to him we love. What we cannot deny to a bad man, we take away from God. We make God worse than the worst of men, if we assume that He said He would always be with us for the purpose of more scornfully neglecting us by His very presence. But so much for this argument.

(3) Having proved by Holy Scripture that all things are both watched and ruled by God, it remains now for me to show that most things in this world are judged by His divine power. When the holy David had borne the affronts and insults of Nabal from Carmel, because David delayed vengeance, he was avenged at once by the very hand of God. Shortly thereafter, when his enemy had been defeated and killed by the hand of God, David said:[12] 'Blessed be the Lord Who has judged the cause of my reproach at the hand of Nabal.'

When his rebellious son chased him from his kingdom, the Lord soon delivered him. Not only did the Lord deliver him,

---
[12] 1 Kings 25.39.

but delivered him more fully than the one delivered wished. This was that God might show that the injustice is more grievous to Himself than to those who suffer it. He who avenges beyond the wish of him who is being avenged, what else does he want understood than that he himself is being avenged in him for whom he is doing the avenging? Thus, when, for his attempted patricide, David's son being hanged on a cross not made by human hands, the Scripture says that the punishment, divinely brought on him, was thus announced:[13] 'I bring good tidings, my lord, the king: for the Lord has judged on your behalf this day from the hand of all that have risen up against you.'

(4) You see how the Scriptures prove by divine witnesses that God judges not only by deeds and by examples, as I have already said, but does so today by the very name and terms of judgment. Pehaps you think that God performed special favors for a holy man by directly judging his enemies. The day will fail me if I were to speak about His immediate sentences and judgments in this world. But that you may clearly know that His censure and sacred considerations deal more with actions than with persons themselves, hear how God, the judge, who many times gave sentences favorable to his servant David, often gave decisions unfavorable to him. This happened in a transaction which did not involve many men, or perhaps, what would have aroused God more, in a transaction involving holy men. It happened in the instance of one man, a foreigner, where the action rather than the person demanded punishment.

When Urias, the Hethite, a member of a wicked race and of an unfriendly nation, had been killed, the Divine

---

13 2 Kings 18.31.

Word was immediately passed to David:[14] 'You have killed Urias, the Hethite, with the sword and have taken his wife to be your wife, and have slain him with the sword of the children of Ammon. Therefore the sword shall never depart from your house. Thus said the Lord, "Behold I will raise up evil against you out of your own house; and I will take your wives before your eyes and give them to your neighbor. For you did it secretly: but I will do this thing in the sight of all Israel and in the sight of the sun." '

What do you say to this, you who believe that God does not judge our actions and who believe that He has no concern whatsoever for us? Do you not see that the eyes of God were never absent even from that secret sin through which David fell once? Learn from this that you are always seen by Christ, understand and know that you will be punished, and perhaps very soon, you, who, perhaps in consolation for your sins, think that our acts are not seen by God. You see that the holy David was unable to hide his sin in the secrecy of his inmost rooms; neither was he able to claim exemption from immediate punishment through the privilege of great deeds. What did the Lord say to him? 'I will take your wives before your eyes and the sword shall never depart from your house.'

You see what instant judgment so great a man suffered for one sin. Immediate condemnation followed the fault, a condemnation immediately punishing and without reservation, stopping the guilty one then and there and not deferring the case to a later date. Thus He did not say, 'because you have done this, know that the judgment of God will come and you will be tormented in the fire of hell.' Rather, He said, 'You shall suffer immediate torture and shall have the sword of divine severity at your throat.'

---

14 2 Kings 12.9-12.

And what followed? The guilty man acknowledged his sin, was humbled, filled with remorse, confessed and wept. He repented and asked for pardon, gave up his royal jewels, laid aside his robes of cloth of gold, put aside the purple, resigned his crown. He was changed in body and appearance. He cast aside all his kingship with its ornaments. He put on the externals of a fugitive penitent, so that his squalor was his defense. He was wasted by fasting, dried up by thirst, worn from weeping and imprisoned in his own loneliness. Yet this king, bearing such a great name, greater in his holiness than in temporal power, surpassing all by the prerogative of his antecedent merits, did not escape punishment though he sought pardon so earnestly.

The reward of this great penitence was such that he was not condemned to eternal punishment. Yet, he did not merit full pardon in this world. What did the prophet say to the penitent?[15] 'Because you have given occasion to the enemies of the Lord to blaspheme, the son that is born to you shall die.' Besides the pain of the bitter loss of his son, God wished that there be added to the very loving father an understanding of this greatest punishment, namely, that the father who mourned should himself bring death to his beloved son, when the son, born of his father's crime, was killed for the very crime that had begotten him.

(5) This is the first introduction of divine punishment; the first, but not the only one. A long series of great tribulations followed, and an almost unending succession of misfortunes scarcely left his house. Thamar was corrupted by the madness of Ammon, and Ammon was slain by Absolom.[16] A grave crime was committed by one brother, but it was

---

15 2 Kings 12.14.
16 2 Kings 13.

avenged more grievously by the other. In this way David, the father, was punished for the crimes of both. Two sons sinned, but three suffered for the crime of two; Thamar lost her virginity and the loss of Absolom was mourned in Ammon. Indeed, you cannot tell for which of these two sons the loving father mourned more grievously: for him who was slain in this world by his brother's hand or for him who perished in the next because of death by his own hand.

According to the word of God, misfortunes were piled up from this time on. The father suffered long from the treachery of his son. He was expelled from his kingdom and fled as an exile to escape murder. You do not know of a son more wicked and bloodthirsty. Because he could not kill his father in his attempt to murder him, he defiled him with incest. By heaping crime on crime he achieved an incest beyond all incest. He committed in public a thing most shameful to his father, a crime which is abominable in secret. Not only his absent father was made to look hideous by his son's deadly crime, but the eyes of all were polluted by his public incest.

Is the spectacle of David's flight to be added to this account? Of such a nature was the flight that such a great king, of so great a reputation, greater and more honored than all other kings in the world, fled from his people with but a few servants. In comparison with his recent state, he was indeed poor; in comparison with his customary entourage,[17] he was indeed alone. He fled in fear, disgrace and sorrow, 'walking,' says Scripture, 'with head covered and barefoot.'[18] He was a witness of his former estate, an exile from his former self, almost one who lives after his own death. He was cast down so low that he received the scorn of his own servants, which is grave, or their pity, which is graver still.

---

17 Following Pauly's emendation.
18 2 Kings 15.30.

Siba fed him and Simei did not fear to curse him in public.[19] He was so changed from his former self by God's judgment that he, whom the entire world had once feared, was insulted to his face by a single enemy.

(6) Who are they who deny that God watches over human affairs? Behold how often the Sacred Scriptures have shown in the person of one man that God not only watched but judged. And why all this? Why indeed, unless we may understand that the Lord's censure and coercion on the world will always be the same as they once were.

Thus we read that holy men were heretofore punished by God's judgment so that we would know that we are being judged in the present life with God as our judge. For, as God is eternal, so is His justice. As His omnipotence never fails, so is His verdict immutable. As God is perpetual in His law, so is His justice constant. Therefore, all the holy men in Holy Scripture, amid fear of imminent dangers and the swords of persecutors, demanded the establishment of the immediate judgment of God.

Thus said the just man in the psalm:[20] 'Judge me, O God, and distinguish my cause from the nation that is not holy.' That this might not refer to a future judgment of God, he immediately added, 'deliver me from the unjust and deceitful man.' He indeed demands the immediate judgment of God who begs to be freed from the hand of his persecutor. In his knowledge of a just cause he did well to ask for the Lord's justice rather than His favor, because the best favor is always given to the good cause, provided the cause is judged with justice.

Elsewhere the Psalmist spoke most clearly:[21] 'Judge, O

---

19 2 Kings 16.
20 Ps. 42.1.
21 Ps. 34.1.

Lord, them that wrong me: overthrow them that fight against me. Take hold of arms and shield and rise up to help me.' You see in this instance that he does not demand the severity of a future trial, but only the verdict of an immediate judgment. Here is what he says, 'Take up the shield and grip the sword,' meaning thereby, the shield for protection, the sword for vengeance. God, as a judge, does not need such weapons, but in this world the names of dreaded things are the instruments of dreaded judgments. Speaking to human beings in terms of human affairs, because he was praying for judgment and vengeance on his enemies, he expressed the power of divine chastisement through the instruments used for earthly vengeance.

Lastly, the same prophet showed elsewhere the difference between the present and future judgment of God. What did he say to the Lord about the verdict of the immediate trial? You have sat on the throne, you who judge justice.[22] And what of God's future and everlasting judgment? 'He shall judge the world in equity,' and again, 'He shall judge the people in justice.'[23] By these words, He distinguished the time element between the present and the future judgments of God. To point out present judgment he wrote, 'You judge' and to distinguish the future from the present he later added, 'He shall judge.' I have now offered sufficient proof by reason, examples and authority of God's care for us, also of His governance and judgment, especially since the books that are to follow will be concerned with the same proof. If I now receive from God, whose business I am transacting, strength to complete my task, I will attempt to bring to light and, at the same time, refute the arguments commonly proposed by my adversaries.

---

22 Ps. 9.5.
23 Ps. 95.13.

BOOK THREE

IT IS WELL: the foundations have been laid for a work, begun with holy motive and undertaken through love of a sacred duty. They have neither been laid on shifting sand nor built of stone that does not last; they are made solid through the arrangement of sacred materials and strengthened by the skill of the divine architect. These foundations, as God Himself says in the Gospel, can neither be shaken by violent winds, nor undermined by river floods, nor washed away by down pouring rains.[1] Since the hands of Holy Scripture, so to speak, erected the building and its joiners' work made it solid, the building must be as strong, through the aid of the Lord Jesus Christ, as they who built it. The building received the essence of its structure from its makers and cannot be destroyed so long as they who made it are sound. Since one cannot ever destroy the walls of ordinary buildings without tearing apart their stones and mortar, in like manner, before destroying this house which we have built, one must first destroy the materials used in its erection and completion. But since it cannot ever be destroyed, we may rightly presume the safety of that structure whose strength is insured by immortal aid.

This being so, the question is asked why, if everything in this world is controlled by the care, governance and judgment of God, the external aspects of life among the barbarians are very much better than ours; why even among us the lot of good men is more difficult than that of the bad? Why should upright men be cast down while reprobates grow

---
[1] Matt. 7.25.

strong? Why does the whole world come under the sway of authorities, for the greater part unjust? I could answer with reason and with sufficient constancy: 'I do not know,' because I do not know the secret councils of God. The oracle of the heavenly Word is sufficient proof for me in this case. God says, as I have proved in the previous books, that He regards all things, rules all things and judges all things. If you wish to know what you must believe, you have Holy Scripture. The perfect explanation is to hold with what you read.

I do not want you to ask me why God does as He does in the instances of which I have been speaking. I am a man. I do not understand the secrets of God. I do not dare to investigate them. I am also afraid to pry into them, because, if you desire to know more than you are allowed to know, that in itself is a kind of sacrilegious rashness. Let it suffice for you that God testifies that He Himself performs and ordains all things. Do you ask me why one man is greater and another less, one man is wretched and another happy, one man strong and another weak? Why God does these things I do not know, but my demonstration that this is done by Him should suffice for a full explanation. Just as God is greater than all human reason, in like manner it should mean more to me than reason that I recognize that all things are done by God. There is no need to listen to anything new on this point. Let God alone, the Creator, be sufficient over the reasoning of all men. It is not proper to say of the actions of the divine judgment this is right and this is wrong, because whatever you see and are convinced is the work of God, that you must confess is more than right.

This can be said with alacrity and certainty about the governance and judgment of God. I need not prove by arguments what God Himself proves by His own words. When we read that God says He perpetually sees the entire earth, we prove thereby that He does see it because He Himself says He sees it. When we read that He rules all things He has created, we prove thereby that He rules, since He testifies that He rules. When we read that He ordains all things by His immediate judgment, it becomes evident by this very fact, since He confirms that He passes judgment. All other statements, said by men, require proofs and witnesses. God's word is His own witness, because whatever uncorrupted Truth says must be the undefiled testimony to truth.

I shall not be silent on whatever God willed to be known and preached by His followers, since our God wished us to know certain things through the Scriptures, which are, as it were, from the recesses of His mind and spirit because, in a way, the very words of Holy Scripture are the mind of God. I wish to know one thing before I begin to speak. Must I speak with Christians or with pagans? If with Christians, I do not doubt that I will prove my point. If with pagans, I will disdain proof, not because I lack proof, but because I have little hope that they would profit from my words. It is fruitless and futile labor where a perverse listener will not accept proofs. I will deal with Christians because I think that there is really no man bearing the name of Christian who does not wish to appear a Christian. However many there may be of pagan and impious unbelief, it is sufficient for me to present my proofs to Christians.

(2) You are presenting the case why we Christians who believe in God are more wretched than all others. The words of the Apostle to the Churches could supply me with the proper answer in this instance: 'no man should be moved in these tribulations; for you yourselves know that we are appointed thereto.'[2] Since the Apostle says that we are placed

---
[2] 1 Thess. 3.3.

by God in this world to bear hardships, miseries and sorrows, what is strange about it if we who fight for the sake of sustaining all adversities should suffer all manner of evil? Many do not understand this and think that Christian men should receive these things from God as tribute, as it were, for their faith. They think that, since Christians are more religious than all other peoples, they should also be stronger. Let us agree with their opinion and their way of expressing it.

Let us see what it is to believe in God with faith. We who wish our reward for belief and faith to be so great in this world should consider what the quality of that belief or faith must be. What is belief or faith? I think a man has faith who believes faithfully in Christ, that is to say, he is faithful to God who observes faithfully the commandments of God. As the slaves of the rich or as the administrative agents of government, to whom expensive furnishings or well-stocked warehouses are entrusted, doubtless cannot be styled faithful if they have wasted the things entrusted to them, in the same way, indeed, Christians also are unfaithful if they have abused the goods granted them by God.

You ask, perhaps, what are the goods which God grants to Christians? What, indeed, unless all those things by which we believe, that is, all those things by which we are Christians. First there is the Law, then the Prophets, the Gospels, the Epistles of the Apostles, lastly the gift of being reborn anew, the grace of holy baptism and the anointment with holy oil. As with the Hebrews of old, God's chosen and own people, when the dignity of the judges had grown into royal authority, God called the most approved and select men to rule as kings, after they were anointed with oil. Thus it is that all Christians, who, after baptism in the Church, have observed all the commandments of God, shall be called to Heaven to receive the reward of their labor.

Since these are the foundations of faith, let us see who keeps these great bonds of faith in such a way that he is judged faithful. As I have said, he is necessarily unfaithful who does not keep the faith entrusted to him. Indeed, I do not ask that a man perform all that is ordered by the Old and New Testaments. I take away the severity of the Old Law and I take away the words of doom preached by the prophets. I take away also all those things that cannot be altogether taken away, that is, the most severe instructions of the books of the Apostles or the teachings, replete with the highest perfection, of the books of the Gospel. I ask who complies, at least, with very few of God's commandments.

I do not mean those things from which so many flee that they are almost accursed. Of such value are the honor and reverence due to God held among us that we consider worthy of scorn those things which are done with devotion. Finally, who deigns to listen to the Saviour prohibiting us to take thought of tomorrow?[3] Who accepts when He ordered us to be content with one coat? Who, when He ordered us to walk unshod, thinks that that should be done or even expected of us? Therefore, I pass over this. That we judge superfluous those precepts which the Lord wished for our salvation is proof that the faith by which we believe falls short. The Saviour said:[4] 'Love your enemies: do good to them that hate you: and pray for them that persecute you and calumniate you.' Who lives up to these commands? Who would deign to act towards his enemies as God has ordered? I do not mean merely in his prayers, but in his conversation.

If a man forced himself to act as God ordered, his lips would do the acting and not his mind. He would be performing the function of his voice, but would not change the dis-

---
3 Matt. 6.34.
4 Matt. 5.34.

position of his mind; therefore, although he forces himself to say a prayer for his enemy, he speaks but he does not pray. It would be overlong to discuss all these things in detail. But let me add one thing, so that we may understand not only that we do not obey all the words of God, but that we obey practically none of them. The Apostle cried out:[5] 'for if a man think himself to be something, whereas he is nothing, he deceives himself.'

We add this to our crimes that we believe ourselves good and holy, whereas we are guilty in all things. Thus, the offenses of our guilt are piled high because of our assumption of self-righteousness. The Apostle said:[6] 'Whosoever hates his brother is a murderer.' We can understand from this that there are many murderers who regard themselves as innocent, because, as we see, murder is committed not only by the hand of him who kills, but by the mind of him who hates. This is why the Saviour completed the pattern of this command by a decree that was still more severe:[7] 'Whosoever is angry with his brother, without cause, shall be guilty of the judgment.' Anger is the mother of hatred. Thus, the Saviour wished to shut out anger lest hatred be borne therefrom.

If not only hatred but even anger makes us guilty of God's judgment, we know clearly that, as nobody is fully immune from being prone to anger, so nobody will be fully immune from guilt. God traces, as it were, the fibers of that precept and cuts to the core all its roots and branches when He says:[8] 'And whoever shall say, You fool, shall be guilty of Hell fire: and whoever shall say to his brother, Raca, shall be in danger of the council.' Many are ignorant of the nature of the insult contained in the word, Raca, but in their folly

---
5 Gal. 6.3.
6 1 John 3.15.
7 Matt. 5.22.
8 *Ibid.*

they know very well that it is said with hostile intent. Men, using their knowledge rather than their ignorance, thus prefer the expiation of their guilt in the divine fires, a form of censure they know, to expiation through human councils, a mode they do not know.

(3) Since such is the case and since the Lord's commandments are never obeyed by us, and are practically reversed, when shall we observe His greater commandments? The Saviour Himself said:[9] 'he who does not renounce all that he possesses cannot be my disciple,' and[10] 'he that takes not up his cross and follows Me is not worthy of Me.' He who calls himself a Christian must himself walk as Christ walked.

It is certain that not only those who seek after worldly pomp and pleasure, but even those who abandon worldly ties, do not fulfill these requirements. They who apparently renounce their wealth do not do so in such a manner that their renunciation seems complete. They who apparently carry their cross carry it in such a way that they receive more honor in the name of the cross than pain in the sufferings of Christ. Even if all these men should fulfill one of these precepts in good faith, none, doubtless, would herein accomplish the degree of perfection of proceeding along the way of life as the Saviour proceeded. The Apostle said:[11] 'He who says he abides in Him ought himself also to walk as He walked.'

(4) Perhaps some think that the precepts of the Apostles are severe. Indeed, they should be considered severe if the Apostles demanded from others more duties than they took on themselves. However, if they demanded much less from others than from themselves, they must be adjudged, not

---

9 Luke 14.33.
10 Matt 10.38.
11 1 John 2.6.

only as serious-minded teachers, but as the most indulgent of parents, who take on themselves through love of God the burdens which, in their misplaced love, they take away from the shoulders of their children. What did one of them say to the listening congregation?[12] 'My little children, of whom I am in labor again, until Christ be formed in you.' And again:[13] 'Be you followers of me, as I am also of Christ.'

He who had ordered himself to be an imitator of Christ hereby orders us to follow himself. And, indeed, no one doubts that he himself imitated Christ. Christ subjected Himself to the world for us; so did he for Christ. Christ bore weariness and heavy toil for us; so did he for Christ. Christ suffered insults for us; so did he for Christ. Christ endured suffering and death for us; so did he for Christ. Therefore, not without reason and conscious of his own merits did he say:[14] 'I have fought a good fight. I have kept the faith. As to the rest, there is laid up for me a crown of justice.'

Since the Apostle so imitated Christ, let us see which of us seems to be an imitator of the Apostle. Of himself he writes first of all that he never gave offense to anybody,[15] but in all things he showed himself as the minister of God in much patience, in affliction, in want, in blows, in imprisonments and in stripes.

Elsewhere comparing himself with others, he says:[16] 'Wherein if any man dare (I speak foolishly), I dare also. I speak as a fool, I am more; in many more labors, in prisons more frequently, in stripes above measure, in deaths often. Of the Jews five times did I receive forty stripes save one. Thrice was I beaten with rods: once I was stoned; thrice I suffered

---
12 Gal. 4.19.
13 1 Cor. 11.1.
14 2 Tim. 4.7.
15 2 Cor. 6.3-5.
16 2 Cor. 11.21-27.

shipwreck.' Certainly, if we completely omit the Apostle's other virtues of which he speaks, yet in the one instance where he suffered shipwreck three times, we can outdo him. We have been shipwrecked not merely three times; almost our whole life is a shipwreck. Everyone lives in such great wickedness that there is hardly a Christian who is apparently not being shipwrecked continuously.

(5) Perhaps some one says we should not endure for Christ in this day and age what the Apostles endured in their day. It is true there are no longer pagan princes nor persecuting tyrants. The blood of the saints is not shed, nor is faith tried by torture. Our God is content that we serve Him in peace, that we please Him by the very purity of righteous deeds and the holiness of an unsullied life.

Our faith and devotion are all the more due Him because He demands less and gives more. Our princes are Christian; there are no persecutions and religion is not disturbed. Thus, we who are not forced to prove our faith by more severe trials should, at least, all the more seek to please God in lesser things. He by whom the smaller things are well done will, in case of necessity, prove himself a capable performer of greater things.

(6) Let us omit, therefore, the sufferings of most blessed Paul. Let us even omit what we have read in religious books written later on about the sufferings of all the Christians who, mounting to the doors of their heavenly palaces by the steps of their tortures, fashioned the stairs, so to speak, from wooden racks and scaffolds. Let us see if we can try to fulfill the Lord's commandments in those practices of religious devotion, the lesser and more common of which we Christians can perform peacefully and at all times. Christ has ordered us not to be litigious. Who obeys this command?

He not only ordered that, but He went so far as to order us to relinquish those things which are in dispute, so long as we get out of the law suit. He has said:[17] 'If a man will contend with you in judgment and take away your coat, let go your cloak also unto him.'

I ask who there are who yield to spoliation at the hands of their enemies? I ask, furthermore, who there are who try not to rob their enemies? So far are we from leaving them other things in addition to our coats that, if we possibly can do it, we take away the coats and cloaks of our enemies at the same time. Indeed, so ardently do we obey the Lord's commandments that we are not satisfied with refusing the least part of our garments to our enemies, unless, if circumstances permit, we can rob them of everything to the best of our ability.

To this command there is another and similar command added, in which the Lord says:[18] 'if one strikes you on the right cheek, turn to him also the other.' How many, do you think, would calmly listen to this command, or if they seemed to listen, would agree to it in their hearts? And how many are there who, if they receive one blow, do not return many for that one? So far is he from turning his other cheek to him who strikes him that he thinks he is winning when he has overcome his adversary, not by beating, but by knocking him down.

The Saviour has said:[19] 'all things whatsoever you would that men should do to you, do you also to them.' There is a part of this thought we know so well that we never omit it. There is a part we omit as if we were wholly ignorant of it. We know quite well what we wish done for us by others,

---
17 Matt. 5.40.
18 Matt. 5.39.
19 Matt. 7.12.

but we do not know what we ourselves should do for them. Would that we did not know! Our guilt would be less if we could claim ignorance, according to the saying:[20] 'he that knows not the will of his Lord shall be beaten with few stripes, but he that knows and does not do according to the will of his Lord, shall be beaten with many stripes.' With us, the offense is greater, because we like a part of the holy command since it is to the advantage of our affairs, but we omit a part of it to the injury of God.

The Apostle, Saint Paul, in his function of preaching also amplified this word of God:[21] 'Let no man seek his own, but that which is another's.' And again:[22] 'each one not considering the things that are his own, but those that are other men's.' You see how faithfully Saint Paul executed the precept of Christ. As the Saviour ordered us to take thought for others in the same manner as for ourselves, the Apostle ordered us to look more to the affairs of others rather than to ourselves. He was, indeed, a good servant of a good Master and an outstanding imitator of a singular Teacher. He so walked in the footprints of his Master that he somehow made by his own feet those of his Master more distinct and prominent. Which of these precepts do we Christians fulfill: that of Christ or of Paul? I think we obey neither. We are so far from doing something for the affairs of others that would work to our own disadvantage that we all give first consideration to our own affairs, no matter what discomfort it entails for others.

(7) Perhaps I seem to single out certain greater commandments which no one fulfills and which, as the Christians themselves think, cannot be fully fulfilled, and to disregard

---
20 Luke 12.47.
21 1 Cor. 10.24.
22 Phil. 2.4.

others which can be and are fulfilled by all. As to the first point, it should be considered that no slave is allowed to choose arbitrarily which of his master's orders he will or will not execute. Neither does he with insulting arrogance choose to do what pleases him and rejects what displeases him. Human masters certainly are of the opinion that slaves who heed a part of their orders and disdain the remainder can in no way be tolerated with equanimity, that is, those slaves who, according to their own fancy, do what they think should be done and treat with contempt what they think should be so treated.

If slaves obey their masters according to their own judgment, they are not obedient even when they obey. When a slave performs only those of his master's commands which he likes to perform, he is not following his master's will, but his own. If we who are but weak little men do not wish to be held entirely in contempt by our slaves whom their slavery makes our inferiors but whom their humanity makes our equals, how unjust it is for us to despise our heavenly Master? Yet we, being human beings, do not think that we should be despised by men who are also human beings. Perhaps we are of such great wisdom and deep intelligence that we, who are unwilling to bear insults from our slaves, wish God to be subject to insults from us. Perhaps we believe that God should benignly tolerate those things which we ourselves know are undeserving of human tolerance.

For this reason, and to return to what I have already said, if there are any who think that I am speaking of the greater and keeping silent on the lesser of God's commandments, they must understand that their complaint is uncalled for. There is no just reason for singling out some commandments, when all should be performed. I have already said that it is in no way permitted to the slaves of masters in this world to choose which of their master's commands they shall or shall not execute. In like manner we, who are the slaves of the Lord, must realize that it is absolutely improper either to do what pleases us according to our whims, or in an abusive indulgence of pride to trample under foot what displeases us.

(8) Let me come to an agreement with those who do not wish me to speak of God's greater commandments because they think, perhaps, they are fulfilling the lesser precepts. It is not sufficient for our salvation to perform the lesser and scorn the greater, according to that saying:[23] 'and whosoever shall keep the whole law, but offend in one point, is become guilty of all.' Because of this, although it is not sufficient for us to observe the commandments relating to small and little things, yet I agree to talk only of the smaller, so that I may point out that the majority of Christians have not lived up to even the little and smallest of the commandments.

Our Saviour ordered Christians not to swear. You will find more men who perjure themselves more frequently than you will find men who do not swear at all. He also commanded that nobody should curse. Who speaks without cursing? Curses are forever the first outbursts of anger, and whatever we cannot accomplish in our weakness we hope for in our anger. Thus, in every beat of our angry hearts we make use of evil desires instead of actual weapons. Therefore everyone very visibly shows that whatever he hopes will happen to his enemies, he would do them if he could.

We all disobey God's commands by lightly putting our tongues to this improper use, and, therefore, we think God regards it lightly. God's orders were, says Holy Scripture:[24]

---
23 James 2.10.
24 1 Cor. 6.10.

'cursers shall not possess the kingdom of God.' From this we can understand how grievous and ruinous it is to curse when by itself this excludes a man from Heaven even though all his other actions are good.

Christ ordered that envy be far from us. On the contrary, we envy not only strangers but even those most near to us. We sprinkle with malice not only our enemies but even our friends. This is the ruling vice in the hearts of almost all. Our desire of feasting has its limits, but our desire of slander has none. We are ever sated by food, but never by detraction.

Perhaps the punishment for this fault is slight. Holy Scripture says:[25] 'the slanderous man shall be rooted out.' This is indeed a heavy and fearful statement, but it does not correct us. While nobody ceases to mutilate another, he considers it so valuable that he does not spare even himself. The retribution for this vice is visibly suitable, since it pursues the author only. He who is slandered is not really injured, but only he is punished from whose mouth the slander originated.

By repeating these things, I suppose I appear deranged, and I take it upon myself to seem deranged. Was the Lord deranged when He ordered, as says the Apostle:[26] 'let all complaint be put away from you, with all malice.' Both of these faults remain constantly with us, but malice more than complaint. Complaint is not always on our lips, but malice is always in our hearts. Thus, I am of the opinion that, were complaint to cease among us, malice would still remain.

Our God has also ordered us to live without murmurings and complaints.[27] When during the lifetime of the human race have these not been in existence? If it is hot, we complain

---

25 Rom. 1.30; Prov. 21.28.
26 Ephes. 4.31.
27 Phil. 2.1-18.

of drought. If it rains, we complain that we are overcome by floods. If it is a bad crop-year, we complain of want. If a good year, we complain of low prices. We desire to obtain abundance and complain when we have obtained it. What could be more wicked or more insolent than this? And so we complain of God's mercy because He gives us what we ask.

God ordered His servants that all scandal occasioned by the eyes should be removed completely. Therefore He said:[28] 'if anyone whosoever shall look on a woman to lust after her he has already committed adultery with her in his heart.' Hence, we can fully understand how chaste the Saviour wished us to be, who forbids us licentiousness of the eyes. Knowing that our eyes are, to an extent, the windows of our minds and that all evil desires enter the heart by using the eyes as natural underground passageways, God wished to destroy these evil desires while they were still outside, lest they gain strength within the mind and their deadly fibers grow if they once were germinated in our eyesight.

The Lord said that the lewd glances of the lusting man do not fall short of the crime of adultery, thereby making it clear that he who would truly avoid adultery must guard his eyes. The Saviour, wishing His followers to cultivate a perfect and pure holiness, ordered them to avoid with the greatest circumspection even the least of these faults. As the pupil of the eye is pure, so is the life of the Christian man. Just as the eye could not receive a speck of dust without damaging the eyesight, so our life should not have a speck of immodesty in it.

Hence, also, what God says in the following:[29] 'if your eye scandalizes you, pluck it out: if your hand scandalizes you, cut it off. It is better for you that one of your members per-

---
28 Matt. 5.28.
29 Mark 9.46; Matt. 5.29-30.

ish, than your whole body be cast into Hell.' If therefore, according to the word of God, we are dragged into Hell through scandal, it is indeed right that we amerce our hands and eyes, if by so doing we can escape Hell. Not that any man should deprive himself of his limbs, but we, because certain intimacies of domestic relationships have become so necessary to us that we use them sometimes as hands and eyes, rightly remove the functions of their present services lest we suffer the torments of eternal fire. When it is a question of service or life, it is more right for the Christian to lack service rather than life.

(9) In all these commandments of which I have spoken, our Lord has ordered our obedience. Where are they who obey all God's commandments or even a very few of them? Where are they who love their enemies or do good to those who persecute them, or overcome evil by good? Where are they who turn their cheek to those who strike them, who yield their property without litigation to those who despoil them? Where is he who is completely free from detracting? Where is he who injures nobody by his reproaches? Where is he who imposes silence on his lips lest they burst forth into acrimonious curses. Who is it who keeps these little commandments, and I will not mention the greater ones of which I spoke a little while ago?

Since this is so, and since we fulfill none of God's commands, why do we complain about God who has more reason to complain about all of us? What is our reason for saying in sorrow that God does not heed us, when we ourselves do not heed Him? What is our reason for muttering that God does not look down towards earth, when we ourselves do not look up towards Heaven? What is the reason for being annoyed that our prayers are disdained by God, when we ourselves disdain His commandments?

Make us the equals of our Lord, what room is there for just complaint when each suffers according to his deeds? There is this exception which I can easily prove, namely, we never suffer in proportion to our deeds and God deals with us much more leniently than we deal with Him. But, in the meantime, let me prosecute the case according to the law with which I began. Thus spoke the Lord Himself:[30] 'I have cried unto you and you have not heard Me: and you shall cry unto Me and I shall not hear you.' What is more suitable and just than this? We have not heard; therefore, we are not heeded. We have not looked; therefore, we are not noticed.

Who, I ask, among masters in this world is content to treat his slaves according to the following rule, that he will despise them only in proportion as he himself is despised by them? We scorn God more grievously than worldly masters are usually scorned by their slaves, because the slave's greatest show of contempt is not to do what he is ordered. We, however, not only expend all our zeal and labor in the nonexecution of orders, but we act contrary to them. God commanded us to love one another, but we mutilate each other in mutual hatred. God commanded that all contribute to the upkeep of the needy, but almost all plunder the goods of others. God commanded all Christians to keep their eyes pure, but how many are there who do not roll about in the mire of fornication?

What more can I say? I am about to speak on a grave and lamentable subject. The Church herself, which should be the appeaser of God in all things, what is she but the exasperator of God? Beyond a very few individuals who

---

30 Prov. 1.24; Jer. 11.11.

shun evil, what else is the whole assemblage of Christians but the bilge water of vice? How many will you find in the Church who are not either a drunkard or a beast, or an adulterer, or a fornicator, or a robber, or a debauchee, or a brigand or a murderer? And, what is worse than all this, they do all these things almost unceasingly.

I ask all Christians to examine their consciences. Of these crimes and misdeeds which I have just now enumerated, who is not guilty of some or who is not guilty of all? You could more easily find a man guilty of all than of none. Because what I have said may seem too gravely censorious, I shall say in addition that you could more easily find men guilty of all these crimes than of some; that you could more easily find men guilty of the greater than of the lesser crimes. That is, it is more easy to find those who have perpetrated the greater along with the lesser than find those who have committed the lesser without the greater.

Almost the whole commonalty of the Church is reduced to such a low degree of morals that, among all Christians, it is the general norm of holiness to be less corrupt than others. Some regard the churches, or rather the temples and altars of God, with less reverence than the home of the least important municipal judge. All do not presume to step over the threshold of illustrious potentates or even of presidents and provosts. They enter when called by the judge, or to transact business, or when the greatness of their office permits them entrance. Should anyone enter contrary to the rules, he is beaten, or put out, or punished in a manner which brings shame and humiliation to him.

But to the temples, or rather, to the altars and shrines of God, all men, filthy and dissolute, rush at random, entirely without reverence for the holy dignity of the temples. All should hasten to pray to God, but he who enters for the sake of being reconciled to God should not depart to arouse His anger. The same function should not ask for indulgence and provoke anger at the same time.

It is a new kind of monstrous deed that men constantly do what they lament having done, and that they enter the house of God to weep for their old sins and then go out [and commit new ones]. Why do I say they go out? They are setting their crimes in motion in the midst of their prayers and supplications. While their lips do one thing, their hearts do another. While they bewail their past evils with words, they are meditating future evils, and thus their prayers are originators of crimes rather than winners of pardon by entreaty. The curse contained in Scripture is truly fulfilled in them, so that from prayer they depart condemned and their prayer is become a sin.[31]

Finally, if anybody wishes to know what men of this kind think of in church, let him see what follows. When the solemn rites are over, they all immediately scurry to their wonted pursuits, some to steal, others to get drunk, others to commit fornication, others to highway robbery. It seems to be clear that while they were inside the church they planned what they would do, once they were outside.

(10) Many think that all these evils and depravities in vice, which I have already mentioned, must refer to slaves or the most degraded of men, and that the freeborn are not besmirched by the stain of such disgraceful acts. But what else is the life of all men engaged in business but fraud and perjury? What is the life of the *curiales* but injustice? What is the life of government officials but slander? What is the life of all connected with the army but pillage? Perhaps you think that such crimes are permissible in men of this sort.

---

31 Ps. 108.7.

You say that their acts are their professions and that there is nothing strange, therefore, if they practice what they profess. This is like saying that God wishes man to do or profess evil, or like saying that it is really no offense to the Sacred Majesty of God that the lower classes seem to commit the greatest crimes, especially when by far the greater portion of the human race belongs to this group. Doubtless, where the throng of sinners is greater, there also the injury to God is greater. You say that all those of noble birth are free from these crimes.

This, indeed, is not enough, because all the nobility in the world seems like nothing but one man in a great mob of people. Let us see if even this small group is without crime. Let us first consider what Holy Scripture says about men of this sort. The Apostle, addressing the people of God spoke thus:[32] 'Hearken, my dearest brethren: has not God chosen the poor in this world, rich in faith and heirs of the kingdom which God has promised to them that love Him? But you have dishonored the poor man. Do not the rich oppress you by might? Do they not blaspheme the good name that is invoked upon you?'

Serious is this testimony of the Apostle, unless the nobility think themselves immune from the Apostle's strictures, inasmuch as he referred only to the rich? But, if the nobles are identical with the rich, or if they are rich but outside the noble class, then they are almost noble, because so great is the distress of our day that nobody is considered nobler than he who has the most wealth. Whether the Apostle was speaking of one, or the other, or both, makes little difference. It is of little interest which side he had most in mind, because his words certainly apply to both.

---

32 James 2.5.

Who among the nobility or the rich has ever abhorred crime? Here I am mistaken, because many do abhor it, but few avoid it. They abhor in others what they themselves constantly commit, being in a way the accusers and perpetrators of the same crimes. They denounce in public what they practice in secret, and because of that, when they think they are condemning others, they condemn themselves all the more by their own reproaches.

Let me leave to one side the question of who is the more guilty. Who, indeed is the rich man or noble who either retains his innocence or keeps his hands clean from crime of all sorts? How superfluously of me to have said, 'of all sorts.' Would that they were free of the greatest sins, because the socially great wish to have, so to say, the privilege of committing the lesser crimes, as of their right. I say nothing about their lighter sins. Let us see if any among them is free from the two capital sins, that is, homicide and lewdness. Which of them is not covered with human blood or stained with the foulness of impurity? Even one of them suffices for eternal damnation, but there is hardly a rich man who has not committed both.

(11) Perhaps one of them is thinking in this manner: 'I am not doing these things now.' I praise you if you are not, but perhaps you did them in the past and to have ceased is not to have ever done them. If this were the case, what is the profit of one man ceasing from crime and so many continuing in it?

The conversion of the one does not correct the crimes of the many, nor does it suffice for the appeasement of God that one man ceases to sin while the whole human race continues to offend Him, especially when he who is converted for the purpose of escaping eternal death receives a great reward for his conversion. Even though he evades eternal death, it is never possible for him to remove the punishment of damnation from others. It is a crime, unbearably conceited and enormously wicked, that anyone should think himself so good that he supposes the wicked can be saved through him.

God, speaking of a certain land and a sinful people, said:[33] 'If these three men, Noe, Daniel and Job shall be in it, they shall deliver neither sons or daughters; but they only shall be delivered.' I think that nobody would be so presumptive as to dare to compare himself with such men. Though a man try to please God in this world, it is a kind of the greatest unrighteousness to boast of his own righteousness. Hereby is removed all hope in that false opinion by which we believe that a countless multitude of the damned can be saved by the intercession in this world of a few good men.

Since no one is equal to those of whom I have already spoken, what hope is there for anybody that a large number of men, who are both evil and unknown to them, can be saved by a few good men? These [three] holy men so intimate with God, did not even deserve this of the Lord, that they could save their members in their children, as it were. And rightly so. Though all children are apparently members of their parents, they must not be regarded as members of those whose love they have begun to discard, because the endowments of nature perish in the depravity of degenerate morals. Thus it happens that even we who are called Christians lose the force of that great name through the vice of depravity.

It is of no advantage whatsoever to have a holy name and no morals, because a life that does not harmonize with our profession cancels the dignity of a glorious title through the baseness of unworthy deeds. Since we see hardly a portion

---

33 Ezech. 14.14.

among all Christians, and hardly a corner of all our churches that are not filled with all manner of offense and with the stain of all manner of deadly sins, why do we flatter ourselves with the name Christian? Herein we are all the more guilty because of this most sacred of names which our lives belie. We offend God all the more under the name of religion because, having been placed in religion, we continue to sin.

BOOK FOUR

ET US put to one side the prerogative of the name of Christian, of which I have already spoken. On the basis of that prerogative we think that, because we are more religious than all other peoples, we must also be stronger. For, as I have said, since the faith of the Christian is to believe with faith in Christ and this faithful belief in Christ is to keep His commandments, it follows, without doubt, that neither does he possess faith who lacks faith nor does he who tramples on the mandates of Christ believe in Him. Therefore, the whole question turns on this, that he who does not perform the work of a Christian does not appear to be a Christian, because the name without practise and functions is as nothing. As a certain man has said in his writings:[1] 'What is high office without its due and attached high honors but an honored title without a man who possesses it? What is dignity in an unworthy subject but an ornament placed in the mud?'

So, to use the same words myself, what is a holy appellation without merit but an ornament set in the mud? The Holy Scriptures have testified to this in writing:[2] 'a golden ring in a swine's snout, a woman fair and foolish.'' And in us the appellation Christian is like a golden ornament. If we use it unworthily, we seem to be swine with an ornament.

In short, whoever wishes to know more fully that words without substance are as nothing, let him observe the count-

---

1 Salvian, *Ad Ecclesiam* 305-306.
2 Prov. 11.22.

less peoples who, when their merit ceased, lost even their names. The twelve Hebrew tribes, when they were chosen by God of old, received two holy names, being called the People of God and the People of Israel. Thus we read:³ 'hear, O my People, and I will speak. O Israel, and I will testify to you.' At that time the Jews bore both names; now they bear neither. They who have long since put aside the worship of God cannot be called the People of God. Neither can that people be said to see God who have denied the Son of God, as it is written:⁴ 'Israel has not known me, and my People has not understood.'

For this reason, our God spoke elsewhere about the Hebrew people to the prophet, saying: 'Call His Name, Not Beloved,' and again to the Jews themselves. 'You are not my people, and I am not your God.'⁵ But He Himself showed clearly elsewhere why He said this about them, for He said:⁶ 'They have forsaken the Lord, the vein of living waters,' and again:⁷ 'for they have cast away the word of the Lord and there is no wisdom in them.'

Indeed, I fear that what could be said of them then, the same can be said of us now, because we do not obey the words of the Lord. And we who do not obey His words have altogether no wisdom in us, unless, perhaps, we believe we are wise in spurning God, and judge that the very fact of holding Christ's commandments in contempt is the apex of prudence.

Indeed, there is reason to believe that we think in this manner, because we all pursue sin with such unanimity as if we were transgressing according to an extremely well-plan-

---

3 Ps. 49.7.
4 Isa. 1.3.
5 Osee 1.9.
6 Jer. 17.13.
7 Jer. 8.9.

ned conspiracy. Since this is so, what reason is there for us being deluded by the false notion, thinking that, because we are called Christians, the good name can aid us in the midst of the evils we commit, when the Holy Spirit says that not even faith without good works can profit Christians? It is of much more account to have the faith rather than the name because the name is a man-made word, whereas faith is the fruit of the soul. That this very fruit of faith is barren without good works is the testimony of the Apostle, who said:[8] 'Faith without good works is dead,' and again:[9] 'even as the body without the spirit is dead: so also faith without good works is dead.' He also added certain more harsh sayings for the confusion of them who flatter themselves by their false claims to the Christian faith.

(2) Some one says: 'You have faith and I have works. Show me your faith without good works and I will show you my faith by my good works.' By this he points out that good acts are, as it were, witnesses to the Christian faith, because, unless a Christian performs good works he absolutely cannot give proof of his faith. Since he cannot prove that he has faith, it must be considered as wholly non-existent. That the Apostle thought that such a faith must be considered as valueless he immediately showed in his additional words, saying to the Christian:[10] 'You believe that there is one God. You do well: the devils also believe and tremble.'

Let us consider the Apostle's meaning in this instance. Let us not be angry at the divine testimony, but agree with it. Let us not contradict it, but profit by it. 'You believe,' said the Divine Word to the Christian, 'that there is one God. You do well: the devils also believe and tremble.' Was the

---
8 James 2.20.
9 James 2.26.
10 James 2.19.

Apostle in error by comparing the Christian faith with the devil? Certainly not. He wished to point out what has been said above, that without good works a man in his pride of faith should appropriate nothing to himself. For this reason, he says, the devils also believe in God. He means that as the devils, though they believe in God, continue in their wickedness, so there are men who have a belief like unto the devils' in that they keep on asserting their belief in God but do not cease doing evil.

The Apostle also adds for the shame and condemnation of sinful men that the devils not only believe in the name of God, but even fear and tremble before Him. This is to say: 'Why do you flatter yourself, O man, whoever you may be, for your belief which is as nothing without fear and obedience to God. The devils have something more. You have only one thing; they have two. You have belief, you do not fear. They have belief and also fear.' Are you surprised when we are punished? Are you surprised when we are chastised, when we are delivered over to the law of the enemy, when we are weaker than all others?

Our miseries, infirmities, destruction, captivities and the punishment of wicked slavery are proofs that we are bad servants of a good master. How are we bad servants? Because our suffering is in proportion to our merit. How are [we bad servants] of a good master? Because He points out to us what we deserve, but He does not punish us as we deserve. He prefers to correct us by the most clement and kindly chastisement rather than to have us perish. But we, insofar as our crimes are concerned, are worthy of the penalty of death. On the other hand, God, being more merciful than severe, wishes more to correct us lovingly by tempering His censure than to cut us down with a stroke of just chastisement.

I know very well that it is unpleasant for us when we are struck down. Why are we surprised that God scourges us when we sin, when we ourselves flog our little slaves who transgress? We are unjust judges. We, little men, do not wish to be flayed by God, when we ourselves whip men who are of our own status. I do not wonder that we are unjust in this matter. In us, nature and wickedness are both servile. We wish to sin, but not to be punished. Herein we have the same attitude as our slaves. We all wish to sin with impunity. Finally, I call on all men to witness whether I lie. I deny that there is anybody, no matter how guilty of a great crime, who will admit that he should be punished.

From this it can be realized how wickedly and improperly severe we are on others, but how indulgent with ourselves. We are most harsh to others, most lenient with ourselves. We punish others, but forgive ourselves for the same crime—an act of intolerable arrogance and presumption. We are unwilling to acknowledge guilt in ourselves, but we dare to arrogate to ourselves the right to judge others. What can be more unjust and what more perverse? The very crime we think justifiable in us we condemn most severely in others. Not without reason, therefore, did the Apostle cry out to us:[11] 'Wherefore you are inexcusable, O man, whosoever you are who judge. For wherein you judge another, you condemn yourself. For you do the same things which you judge.'

(3) Some among the rich say: 'We do not do the same things that slaves do. Slaves are thieves and runaways, slaves are constantly catering to their palates and stomachs.' It is true that these are the vices of slaves, but the masters, not all of them, though, have more and greater vices. Certain of them, but very few, must be excepted. I do not name

---
11 Rom. 2.1.

them, lest by doing so I may seem less to praise them than to blame others by not naming them.

First of all, if slaves are thieves, they are perhaps forced to steal through want. Even though the customary allowances[12] are given, these allowances satisfy custom rather than sufficiency and thus fulfill the law without fulfilling the need. Their indulgence makes their fault less blameworthy, because the guilt of the thief who is unwillingly forced into the theft is excusable. Holy Scripture seems to excuse in part the offense of the needy when it says:[13] 'the fault is not so great when a man has stolen; for he steals to feed his hungry soul.' He steals to fill his hungry soul. For this reason, they who are excused by the Divine Word are not very well to be accused by us.

What has been said of theft by slaves, the same can be said about their running away. This much can be said more correctly about their flight, that they are driven to flight, not only by their wretched condition, but by their punishments. They dread their drivers, they dread the confidential domestic servants, they dread their stewards, so that, in the midst of all these overseers, they are almost nobody's slaves, rather than their real master's. They are beaten by all; they are tread upon by all. What more can be said? Many of them take refuge with their masters in fear of their fellow slaves. We should place responsibility not so much on those who flee as on those who force them to flee. They endure violence most unhappily. They long to serve, but are compelled to flee. They are really unwilling to depart from the service of their masters, but they are not permitted to continue serving by the cruelty of their fellow slaves.

They are also said to be liars. Nevertheless, they are com-

---
12 Cod. Just. 12.23.
13 Prov. 6.30.

pelled to lie by the brutality of impending punishment. Indeed, they lie because they wish to escape torture. What is strange that a slave, in his fear, should prefer to lie rather than to be flogged? They are accused of being greedy of gullet and stomach, but that is nothing new. A man who has often endured hunger has a greater longing for a full stomach. Granted, he may not be hungry for bread, yet he may hunger after tasty morsels, and, therefore, must be pardoned if he seeks all the more avidly what he is constantly without.

But you, the noble and rich, who have an overflow of all good things, who, because of this, should honor God by your holy works because you enjoy His blessings unceasingly, let us see whether your actions are, I do not say holy, but at least harmless. And, as I have said before, who among the rich, with a few exceptions, is not tinged with all manner of crime? And when I except a few, would that it were permissible to except a greater number, and even all. The innocence of the many was the salvation of all. I speak now about none, except him alone who knows that what I say applies to himself. If what I say is outside his conscience, my speech will in no way injure him. If he knows in his heart what I speak about, let him realize these things are not spoken by my tongue, but by his own conscience.

First of all, I shall speak about the vices of slaves. If a slave is a runaway, so are you also, O rich and noble, for all who forsake the Law of their Lord are runaways from their Master. Rich men, what fault do you find in the slave? You do the same as he. He is a runaway from his master and you from yours. But you are more blameworthy than he, because he, perhaps, flees from a bad master, and you from a good one. You accuse the slave of inordinate gluttony. It is a rare fault in him, arising from want, but it is a daily fault in you by reason of abundance.

Hence, you see the scathing words of the Apostle apply above all to you and, in fact, to you alone:[14] 'Wherein you judge another, you condemn yourself. For you do the same things which you judge.' Indeed, not the same, but much greater and worse. In the slave you punish even an infrequent over-indulgence of his stomach, yet you are constantly distended with undigested food. You also think theft is a vice of the slave, but you, too, O rich man, commit theft when you encroach on things forbidden by God. Indeed, all commit theft who commit unlawful acts.

(4) Why did I go into such minute details about these things and speak, as it were, allegorically, when not only the thefts but the highway robberies of the rich are acknowledged in the most open of crimes? Where can you find any one who is not poor, whether actually or by status, who is safe living beside a rich man? By the encroachments of the powerful the weak lose their belongings, or even themselves along with their belongings.[15] Not unrightly does the Holy Word apply to both when it says:[16] 'the wild ass is the lion's prey in the desert: so also the poor are devoured by the rich.' For, not only the poor, but almost the whole human race, is suffering from this tyranny.

As regards people in high places, of what does their dignity consist but in confiscating the property of the state? As regards some whose names I do not mention, what is a political position, but a kind of plunder?[17] There is no greater pillaging of poor States than that done by those in power. For this, office is bought by the few to be paid for by ravaging the many. What can be more disgraceful and wicked than this?

---
14 Rom. 2.1.
15 Cod. Theo. 10.1.16.
16 Eccli. 13.23.
17 Sidonius Apollinaris, Ep. 1.7.3.

The poor pay the purchase price for positions which they themselves do not buy. They are ignorant of the bargain, but know the amount paid. The world is turned upside down that the light of a few may become illustrious. The elevation of one man is the downfall of all the others. The cities of Spain know all about this, for they have nothing left them but their name.[18] The cities of Africa know it—and they no longer exist.[19] The cities of Gaul know it, for they are laid waste, but not by all their officials.[20] They still hold a tenuous existence in a very few corners of the land, because the honesty of a few has temporarily supported those provinces which the ravages of the many have made void.

(5) I have been compelled by sorrow to wander from my subject. Therefore, let me return to my former topic. What slave-vices are there with which the nobles are not stained, unless, perhaps, it is that those sins, for which they punish slaves, they themselves commit, as though they were allowed? A slave is not allowed to have access to those ravages which the above-mentioned nobles perpetrate. It may be that I am exaggerating, because certain slaves, having become noble, committed equal or greater crimes. But it can by no means be imputed to slaves as a body, that the servile condition turned out so happily for those few.

Murder is rare among slaves because of their dread and terror of capital punishment, but it is common among the rich because of their hope and trust in impunity. Perhaps we are wrong in putting in the category of sins what the rich men do, because, when they kill their slaves, they think that it is legal and not a crime.[21] Not only this, they abuse

---
18 Orosius, *Adversus Paganos* 7.41.
19 See Salvian's account of Capture of Africa, 172-173.
20 Sidonius Apollinaris, Ep. 3.6.3.
21 Cod. Just. 9.14.1.

the same privilege even when practicing the filth of unchastity. How few among the rich, observing the sacrament of marriage, are not dragged down headlong by the madness of lust? To how few are not home and family regarded as harlots? How few do not pursue their madness toward anybody on whom the heat of their evil desires centers? It was about such men that the Divine Word said:[22] 'they are become as stallions rushing madly on the mares.' What is it but a proof of what has been said that they want complete physical union with whomsoever they have looked upon with desire?

It seems unjust to speak of concubines because, in comparison with the aforementioned vices, it is a kind of chastity to be content with a few consorts and to put a bridle on lust by limiting themselves to a certain number of wives. I say 'wives,' because the affair has reached such shamelessness that many consider their maid-servants their wives.

Would that they would have those only as consorts who are looked upon as wives! But, what is more loathsome and abominable, certain men who have contracted honorable marriages take additional wives of servile status, thereby debasing the dignity of marriage by the debasement of degenerate cohabitation. They do not blush to become the husbands of their maid-servants, tearing down the loftiness of marriage with their own social equals for the sake of the filthy beds of their servants. Indeed, they are worthy of the status of those women of whose company they regard themselves worthy.

(6) Doubtless, many of those who are nobles or who wish to appear as nobles listened with haughtiness and contempt to a consideration of these things of which I have spoken, namely, that some slaves are less dissolute than their masters.

---

[22] Jer. 5.8.

When I predicate this not about all of them but only about those it fits, no one should be angry who nowise recognizes himself as such, lest by the fact that he is angry he himself appear one of them. Rather, any nobleman who detests these evils should be angry at these men, because they defile the name of nobility by their base crimes. Though such men weigh heavily on all Christians, they especially defile by their baseness those who are said to belong to their class.

Therefore I have said that certain nobles are worse than slaves, and I have spoken objectionably, if I do not prove my statements. From the following crime, a very great one, almost the whole slave class is immune. Which of the slaves has a crowd of concubines? Which of them is defiled by the crime of having many mistresses, and, like dogs or pigs, thinks that he can have as many such as he can subject to his lust?

The answer seems to be that it is not lawful for slaves to do those things; indeed, they would if they could. I believe this, but, what I do not see being done, I cannot hold as being done. No matter how base his mind, no matter how evil his desires, nobody is punished for a crime of which he is not guilty. Certainly, slaves are bad and worthy of contempt. However, the freeborn and nobles are the more to be reproached if, in their more honored place in society, they are worse [than the slaves]. Hence it happens that it is necessary to arrive at the conclusion not that slaves are to be absolved from the guilt of their wrong-doing, but that the majority of the rich are more to be condemned than the slaves.

For, who can be eloquent about freebooting and crime because the Roman State is dying or already dead or certainly drawing its last breath? In that one section where it still has a semblance of life, though strangled by the chains of taxation as if by the hands of brigands, there is still to be found a great number of rich men whose tax impositions the poor have to pay,[23] that is, there is found a great number of rich whose taxes kill the poor. I said that many can be found. I am afraid I could more truly say all. So few, if there are any at all, are free from this crime that we can find almost all the rich in that category in which I said there were many.

Consider the remedies recently given to some cities. What have they done but make all the rich immune and pile more taxes on the wretched poor? In order that the old taxes should be remitted the former, they have imposed new taxes on the latter. The cancellation of all semblance of taxation has enriched the former; the corresponding increase has made the latter suffer. The rich have become richer by lessening the obligations which they bore lightly; the poor are dying from the multiplication of the burdens which they were already unable to bear. Thus, the great remedy most unjustly exalted the one and most unjustly killed off the other: to one it was a most wicked reward, to the other a most wicked poison. Hence it is I make the observation that there is nothing more vicious than the rich who are destroying the poor by their remedies, and none more unfortunate than the poor whom those things kill which are given as a remedy to all.

(7) Indeed, what is this, what state of affairs exists, when a noble, if he begin to be converted to God, immediately loses his rank among the nobility? In what account is the honor of Christ held among a Christian population where religion socially degrades a man? For, immediately that one of them tries to live a better life, he is abused by the scorn of worse men. Because of this all somehow are compelled to be evil, lest they be considered of non-noble birth. It is

---

23 Cod. Theo. 11.13.1, to alleviate the poor.

not without cause that the Apostle cried out:[24] 'the whole world is seated in wickedness.' And this is true, for all is said to be evil where the good can have no place in it. Indeed, the whole world is so filled with iniquity that either all who exist are evil, or all who are good are tortured by the abuse of the many.

Thus, as I have said, if anyone of higher rank give himself to religion, on that account he ceases to be honored. When a man changes his garments, he immediately changes his rank.[25] If he were of high rank, he is become worthy of contempt. If he were most exalted, he is become most base. If he were completely honored, he is become altogether wretched. Yet certain worldly and unbelieving men wonder why they are afflicted by God's anger and wrath, when they persecute Him in the person of all His holy men. All things are awry, all things are changed to their opposites. If any man is good, he is spurned as being bad; if he is bad, he is honored as being good. It is not strange, therefore, if we who are leading worse lives daily suffer worse punishments daily. Men daily commit new evils and do not put aside the old; fresh crimes spring up, but the old are not repudiated.

(8) What room is there for further argument? No matter how bitter and calamitous our suffering, we suffer less than we deserve. Why do we complain that God deals harshly with us? We treat God much more harshly. We provoke him by our impurities, and force Him against His will to punish us. Though the mind and majesty of God are of that nature that He is moved by no passion of anger, yet

---

24 I John 5.19.
25 Most likely Salvian is referring to that clause in the *Codex Theodosianus* 12.1.59 which decreed that the *Curialis*, on entering Holy Orders, should either relinquish his entire wealth to the State or bequeath it to another who would be liable for taxes to the State.

so great is the irritation of our sins that, because of us, He is forced to anger. As I might say, we do violence to his kindness and, in a way, lay our hands on His mercy. In His gentleness He wishes constantly to spare us, but He is forced by our wickedness to punish the crimes we commit.

As is the practice with those who attack well-defended towns or attempt to capture and undermine their citadels, to lay siege to them with all kinds of machines and missiles—in like manner for attacking the mercy of God we fight with every crime of monstrous sin as if we, too, were using every kind of missile. We think God is unjust to us, when we ourselves are most unjust to Him. Every fault of every Christian is an offense against His divinity.

When we do those things forbidden us by God, we trample on the commands of Him who forbids. Thereby, we wickedly blame the severity of God for our calamities, when we should blame ourselves. When we commit the sins for which we are punished, we ourselves are the authors of our torments. Why, then, do we complain about the harshness of our punishment? Each one of us punishes himself. Thus was it spoken to us by the prophet:[26] 'Behold, all you that kindle a fire, encompassed with flames, walk in the light of your fire and in the flames you have kindled.' The whole human race is rushing headlong into eternal punishment in the very order mentioned by Scripture. First, it lights the fire, then it adds strength to the flames, and lastly it enters the fire it has prepared.

When did man first light the eternal fire for himself? Truly, when he first began to sin. When does he add strength to the flames? When he heaps sin on sin. When will he enter the eternal fire? When he has completed the irremediable sum

---
26 Isa. 50.11.

total of all his sins, by the excess of his ever increasing transgressions, as our Saviour said to the Jewish leaders:[27] 'fill you up the measure of your fathers, you serpents, you generation of vipers.' They were not far from the apex of sin to whom God Himself spoke thus, that they completed their sins in such a way, doubtless, that while they were no longer worthy of salvation, they filled the number of their iniquities through which they perished.

Whence it is that, when the Old Law recalled that the sins of the Amorreans were complete, the angels thus spoke to Lot:[28] 'whosoever are yours, lead them out from the city, for we will destroy this place because their cry is grown loud before the Lord who has sent us to destroy them.' For a long time, indeed, that most sinful people had been kindling the fire by which they perished and thus, when their iniquities were complete, they were burned in the flames of their own crimes. They merited so ill of God that they suffered in this world the Hell that will come with judgment in the next.

(9) But some say there are none worthy of that end [Gomorrah], because none are to be compared with them in the perpetration of impurities. Perhaps that is so. However, how do we account for the fact that the Saviour Himself has brought to mind that all who spurned the Gospel were worse? Finally, to Capharnaum He said:[29] 'if in Sodom had been wrought the miracles that had been wrought in you, perhaps it would have remained unto this day. But I say unto you that it shall be more tolerable for the land of Sodom in the day of Judgment than for you.' If He says the people of Sodom are less worthy of damnation than all those who neglect the Gospels, then it is most certainly reasonable that

---
27 Matt. 23.32-33.
28 Gen. 19.13.
29 Matt. 11.23-24.

we, who neglect the Gospels in most things, should have all the more fear. This is especially so because we are unwilling to be content with sins to which we are already long accustomed and, as it were, on daily familiarity.

Many are not satisfied with the customary crimes, with litigation, with slander and plunder, with wine-bibbing and over-indulgence at feasts, with forgery and perjury, with adultery and homicide. They are not satisfied with all these crimes, although they continue in the most inhuman atrocities, which by themselves pertain to injuries against human beings, but they raise the blasphemous hands of their mad minds even against God, and as it is written about the unholy:[30] 'they have set their mouth against Heaven and their tongue has passed through the earth.' And they said: 'How doth God know? And is there knowledge in the Most High?' And again:[31] 'The Lord shall not see: neither shall the God of Jacob understand.'

To such men the word of the prophet can be applied most fittingly:[32] 'The fool said in his heart, there is no God.' They who say that nothing is seen by God almost deprive Him of eyes and even take away substance from Him. For, when they say He sees nothing, they say He does not exist at all. Although no evil deed is based on reason, because crime cannot be joined with reason, there is no sin, I believe, more irrational or senseless. What is madder than for anybody, who does not deny that God is the Creator of the universe, to deny His governance? How does he admit that God created the world and neglects what He created? As if, indeed, He took pains in creating all things so that He would neglect what He had made!

---
30 Ps. 72.9-11.
31 Ps. 93.7.
32 Ps. 52.1.

I am proving that He had such care of His creatures that He cared for them before He created them. Creation itself makes this evident. He would not have created, without intending to care before He ever created, especially since among human beings there is certainly none so dull who would make and perfect something in order not to take care of it when it is finished. He who tills a field tills it for the purpose of keeping it cultivated. He who plants a vineyard plants it for the purpose of keeping it planted. He who gathers the firstling of a flock does so in order to devote his care to increasing it. He who builds a house or lays its foundation, although he has not yet prepared it for habitation, intertwines his very struggles with the hopes of his future home.

Why do I say this about man, when even the lowliest in the animal kingdom do everything with an eye to the future? Ants, hiding various kinds of grain from the fields in underground storerooms, drag and lay them away, because, in their desire of life, they love what they hoard. The bees, when they posit the fundaments of the honeycomb or extract their offspring from flowers, why do they seek out the thyme unless it is in their pursuit and desire of honey? Or why do they seek out certain other little flowers, unless from the love of the little bees that are to come.

God, therefore, He who has instilled this love of their own offspring into the least of living beings, has alone deprived Himself of the love of His creatures, especially since all affection for good descends on us from His good love! He Himself is the fountain and source of all things, because as it is written,[33] 'in Him we live and move and are.' From Him we have also received all the love wherewith we love our offspring. The whole world and the whole human

---

[33] Acts 17.28.

race are the offspring of their Creator. By this very love with which He made us love our offspring, He wished us to understand how much He loves His offspring.

For, as we read:[34] 'the invisible things of Him are clearly seen, being understood by the things that are made.' In this way He wished His love towards us to be known through that love which He gave us for our offspring. As it is written, that He wished all fatherhood in Heaven and on earth to be named after Him, so He wished us to acknowledge paternal love in Him.[35] Why do I say paternal love? His love is much greater than that of a father. The voice of the Saviour in the Gospel proves this by saying:[36] 'for God so loved the world as to give His only begotten Son for the life of the world.' But the Apostle also says:[37] 'God spared not even His own Son but delivered Him up for us all. How has He not also, with Him, given us all things.'

(10) Therefore, as I have already said, God loves us more than a father loves his son. It is very clear that God loves us more than a father loves his sons, because He did not spare His own Son for our sakes. And what else? I add, He did not spare His just Son, His only begotten Son, His Son who is God. What more can be said? And all this for us, that is, for us the wicked the unjust and the most unholy.

Who can appraise that love of God for us, unless it is that His justice is so great that in Him there is nothing unjust? Inasmuch as it concerns human reason, any man would be acting unjustly if he caused his own son to be killed for the sake of his worst slaves. Because of this, the love of God is all the greater and more wonderful, so that the magnitude

---
34 Rom. 1.20.
35 Eph. 3.15.
36 John 3.16.
37 Rom. 8.32.

of His justice cannot be understood by man. Insofar as human weakness is concerned, the magnitude of His justice seems almost a kind of injustice.

And therefore the Apostle, to indicate somewhat the immensity of the divine mercy, said:[38] 'and why did Christ, when as yet we were ungodly, according to the time, die for the ungodly? For scarce for a just man will one die.' In this one sentence he showed us, indeed, the love of God. For, if scarcely anyone takes on himself to die for the sake of the greatest justice, by His death for our wickedness Christ proved His greatness. Why the Lord did this is taught in the following:[39] 'but God commends His charity towards us, because when as yet we were sinners, Christ died for us. Much more therefore, being now justified by His blood, shall we be saved from wrath through Him.' By this very fact He commends His love to us because He died for the wicked. A benefit is of greater value when given to the unworthy. Therefore, He says, 'God commends His charity towards us.'

How does He commend it? He gave it to those who did not merit it. If He had given it to holy and well-deserving men, He would not seem to have given what was not due them, but to have returned what He owed them. What have we given in return for all this, or rather, what should we give? First of all, there is that which the most blessed prophet testifies he owes and will give, when he said:[40] 'What shall I render to the Lord for all the things that He has rendered me? I will take the chalice of salvation and I will call upon the name of the Lord.'

This is the first repayment, that we pay back death for

---
38 Rom. 5.6.
39 Rom. 5.8-9.
40 Ps. 115.12-13.

death and that we all die for Him Who died for us, even though our death is of much less value than His. Hence it happens that, even though we take death upon ourselves, we do not pay the debt. But, because we are unable to pay Him more fully, we seem to be paying back the whole if we pay back all we can. This, then, is the first repayment, as I said.

The second is, if we do not pay back our debt by death, let us repay it by love. The Saviour Himself, as says the Apostle, wished by dying for us to commend His love to all of us, and by the example of His love lead us to make a fitting return for such great love. And just as those marvelous natural gems, when in close contact with even the hardest iron, hold that iron suspended by a seemingly living attraction, so also He, that is, the greatest and most brilliant gem in the Kingdom of Heaven, wished to descend from Heaven so that He would attract us, despite our hardness, to Himself and move us as if by the hands of His love. And thus, when we recognize His gifts and benefits, we may understand what we should do for so good a Master who had done so much for His wicked slaves. Thus would be fulfilled the saying of the Apostle,[41] 'that we should be killed all the day long for His love, and neither tribulation, nor hardships, nor persecutions, nor hunger, nor nakedness, nor the sword should be able to separate us from the love of God which is in Christ Jesus, our Lord.'

(11) Since it is very clear that we are thus indebted to God, let us see what we actually pay in return for what we owe. What but that sum total of which I have already said, that is, that which is indecent, unbecoming and pertaining to the injury of God, wicked acts, bad morals, drunken

---

41 Rom. 8.35-39.

feasts, bloody hands, foul lusts, mad passions and whatever more that conscience rather than words can contain? The Apostle says:[42] 'those things that are done by them in secret, it is shameful even to speak of.' Nor is this all, for this is an old saying and is as applicable at the present day as it was in the past.

What is more serious and saddening, we add new sins to the old. These sins are not only new, but they have a certain pagan and monstrous quality hitherto unseen in the churches of God. We hurl profanity and arrogant blasphemy at God, saying that God is indifferent, God is not watchful, God is negligent, God does not govern and that, because of this, He is unmerciful, callous, inhuman, harsh and hard. For He who is called unmindful, indifferent and negligent what is left but that He be called harsh, hard and inhuman? O blind impudence! O sacrilegious rashness! Is it not enough for us that we are bound up in our uncountable sins and guilty in all things before God, without being also God's accusers? And I ask what hope will there be for a man who by judging his judge, brings charges against him?

(12) They say, therefore, if God watches over human affairs, if He cares for and loves and rules, why does He permit us to be weaker and more wretched than all other peoples? Why does He allow us to be conquered by the barbarians? Why does He allow us to be subject to the law of the enemy? Very briefly, as I have said before, He allows us to bear these evils because we deserve to suffer them. Let us look at the baseness, vices and those crimes of the Roman commonalty which we have already spoken of, and we will understand whether we deserve protection when we live in such impurity.

---

42 Eph. 5.12.

Therefore, by arguing that we are wretched and weak, because, as very many say, human affairs are not looked after by God, what do we deserve? If He allowed us, living in so great vice and so great wickedness, to be most strong, prosperous and happy, perhaps there could be a suspicion that God, who allowed such evil and abandoned men to be happy, did not see the crimes of the Romans. Since, indeed, He orders such vicious and evil men to be abject and wretched, it is most manifestly clear that we are looked after and judged by God, because we are suffering what we deserve.

But we, without doubt, do not think that we deserve judgment, and hence we are the more guilty and criminal, because we do not acknowledge what we deserve. Indeed, the greatest accuser of evil men is one who, in arrogance, takes advantage of innocence. Among many guilty of the same crimes none is more criminal than he who does not think himself guilty. Thus we can add this particular crime to our evils, that we judge ourselves not guilty.

Someone says, let it be! Certainly, we are sinners and evil. What cannot be denied is that we are better than the barbarians. By this also it is clear that God does not watch over human affairs, because, although we are better, we are subject to those who are worse. We will now see whether we are better than the barbarians. Certainly, there is no doubt that we should be better. For this very reason we are worse, if we who should be better are not better. The more honorable the position, the more criminal the fault. If the person of the sinner is the more honorable, the odium of his sin is also greater.

Theft in all men is an evil crime, but, without doubt, a Senator who steals is more to be condemned than one of the lower classes. Fornication is forbidden to all, but it is much more serious if it is done by one of the clergy than by one of the people. And so we who are said to be Christian and Catholic sin more gravely, if we commit sins like the impurities of the barbarians. We sin more seriously under the profession of a holy name. Where the prerogative is higher, there is the fault greater. The religion which we profess itself accuses our errors. The lewdness of him who vowed chastity is more criminal; more foul is he who drinks while putting on a front of sobriety.

Nothing is more vicious than a philosopher pursuing obscene vices, because, besides that baseness which vices have themselves, he is all the more in the public eye through the the name of wisdom. We, among the whole human race, have professed Christian philosophy. Because of this we must be believed and considered worse than all other peoples, because we live under the name of such a great profession and, being placed in the midst of religion, we continue to sin.

(13) I know it seems unbearable to many if we are said to be worse than the barbarians. And what can we do, because it profits our case nothing, if it seems unbearable to us? We aggravate our case all the more if we are worse and and believe we are better. The Apostle says:[43] 'for he who thinks he is something when he is nothing, deceives himself. But let every man prove his own work.' We should place our trust in work, not in opinion; in reason, not in lust; in truth, not in inclination.

Therefore, because some men think it is unbearable that we are judged worse, or not even much better than the barbarians, let us see how, and of which barbarians we are better. For there are two kinds of barbarians in every nation: heretics and pagans. I say we are incomparably better than all these, therefore, insofar as it pertains to divine Law.

---

43 Gal. 6.3-4.

In what pertains to life and the acts of life, I sorrow and weep that we are worse.

However, as I have said before, I should not really say that about the whole body of the Roman people. In the first place, I exempt all religious and those laymen who are equal to the religious, or, if that is too much, those who are like the religious by a certain uprightness of honest acts. I say that all the others, or almost all, are more guilty than the barbarians. This means that to be worse is to be more guilty. Therefore, because some think it irrational and absurd that we are adjudged worse or even not much better than the barbarians, let us see, as I have said, how we are worse and to which barbarians.

For I, excepting only those Romans whom I have already named, say that the rest or almost all are more guilty and criminal in their lives than the barbarians. Perhaps you who read these charges are angry and, in addition, condemn what you read. I do not avoid your censure. Condemn me if I lie. Condemn me if I shall not bring proofs. Condemn me if I shall not demonstrate that the Sacred Scriptures have also said what I have asserted. Therefore, we think ourselves much better than all the other nations in the world. I myself who say the Romans are worse in most things do not deny that they are better in some things. For, as I have said, we are worse in our lives and in our sins, but better, without comparison, because of the Catholic Law. But the following point must be taken into consideration. That the Law is good is naught of merit to us. That we live bad lives is our doing. It profits us nothing that the Law is good if our life and way of life are not good. That the Law is good is a gift of Christ, but that our life is bad is the product of our own sin. By this we are all the more blameworthy if we follow a good Law and are evil doers. Far worse, we are not even followers if we are evil, because an evil doer cannot be called a worshipper. Neither does he follow who does a holy thing in an unholy manner; because of this, the Law itself which we follow is our accuser.

(14) Having put aside the prerogative of the Law, which either helps us not at all or condemns us by a just condemnation, let us compare the pursuits, morals and vices of the barbarians with ours. The barbarians are unjust, and so are we. The barbarians are avaricious, and so are we. The barbarians are unfaithful, and so are we. The barbarians are greedy, and so are we. The barbarians are lewd, and so are we. The barbarians have all manner of wickedness and impurities, and so do we.

Perhaps someone will answer: If we are equal to the barbarians in viciousness, why are we not their equals also in strength? Since the wickedness is alike and the guilt the same, either we should be as strong as they or they should be as weak as we. It is true; the conclusion is that they who offend more are the more weak. How do I prove this? Because, as I have said before, we have proved that God does all things as a judgment. If, as it is written,[44] 'the eyes of the Lord are in every place and behold the good and evil' and, according to the Apostle,[45] 'the judgment of God is, according to the truth, against them that do such things,' we, who do not cease to do evil things, see that we suffer the punishment of evil through the judgment of a just God.

But, you say, the barbarians commit the same evils, yet they are not as wretched as we. There is this difference. If the barbarians do the same things as we do, we, however, sin with a greater displeasure to God. For ours and the vices

---
44 Prov. 15.3.
45 Rom. 2.2.

of the barbarians can be equal, but in these same vices our sins must be greater. Since all the barbarians, as I have already said, are either pagans or heretics, I shall discuss the pagans first, for theirs is the prior mistake. The Saxons are savage. The Franks are treacherous. The Gepidae are ruthless. The Huns are lewd. In short, the life of all barbarian nations is corruption itself.

Do you think their vices have the same guilt as ours? Is the lewdness of the Huns as blameworthy as ours? Is the perfidy of the Franks as reprehensible as ours? Is the drunkenness of the Alemanni as blameworthy as the drunkenness of Christians? Is the rapacity of the Alani as much to be condemned as the greed of Christians? What is stranger if a Hun or Gepid cheats, he who is completely ignorant of the crime of cheating? What will a Frank who lies do that is new, he who thinks perjury is a kind of word and not a crime?

And what is strange, if the barbarians who do not know the Law and God believe thus, when well nigh the greater portion of Romans think the same way and know they are sinning? So that I will not speak of any other race of men, let us consider only the crowds of Syrian merchants who have occupied the greater part of nearly all cities.[46] Let us consider whether their life is anything other than plotting artifice and wearing falsehood thin. They think their words are wasted, so to speak, if they are not profitable to those who speak them. So great among them is the honor of God, who prohibits oath-taking, that they think all perjury is a particular gain for them.

---

46 There are relatively few references in the *Codex Theodosianus* to the pursuit of trade. However, the Roman merchant of the later Empire was practically taxed out of existence and his place taken by the Syrian trader who laid the foundation of the late mediaeval Levantine commerce.

What wonder is it that the barbarians lie, they who are ignorant of the crime of falsehood? They do nothing in contempt of heaven-given commandments, being ignorant of the Lord's command, because he who is ignorant of the Law does nothing against the Law. Therefore, this is our own particular crime, we who read the divine Law and ever violate the legal writings, we who say we know God and trample underfoot His orders and commands. Therefore, the fact that we spurn Him whom we think and boast we worship is in itself an insult, because it is made to appear as worship.

(15) Lastly, to say nothing about our other sins, who is there among all laymen, except a few, who does not always have the Name of Christ on his lips in order to swear. Thus, almost among noble and baseborn this is the oath publicly known: 'by Christ I am doing this because. . .'; 'by Christ I am acting thus because. . .'; 'by Christ I will not say anything else because...'; 'by Christ I will not do anything else because....' And what else? The affair has been fetched to this point, that, just as I have said before about the pagans and barbarians, Christ's Name does not now seem to be a sacred oath, but a word.

For, among most people this name is considered of so little value that some never think less of doing anything than when they swear they will do it 'by Christ.' While it is written, 'Thou shalt not take the name of the Lord in vain,'[47] to that stage has the reverence of Christ fallen that, among all the other vanities of the world, nothing seems to be almost more meaningless than the name of Christ.

Finally, some swear in the name of Christ, not only that they will do trivial and foolish things, but that they will commit certain crimes. Here is their usage of speaking: 'by Christ I

---

47 Exod. 20.7.

shall steal that...'; 'by Christ I am going to knock that man down...'; 'by Christ I shall kill that man.' It has come to this, that when they have sworn by the name of Christ they think they are committing crimes endorsed by religion.

Lastly, I will tell what happened to myself. A short time ago, being overcome by the entreaty of a certain poor man, I begged a certain influential person and implored him not to take away goods and substance from the poor and needy man, not to take away the reserve and stake on which his poverty rested. Then he who had gobbled the goods of the poor man and had devoured his prey with expectation and longing trembled and cast his ferocious eyes at my mouth, as if he thought I would take something from him which he had not taken from the other. He answered that he could never do as I requested, as if he were doing it by a true order or by the sacred writing which he could never fully disregard.

And when I asked the reason why he insisted this could not be done, he said a most violent thing which could not be altogether contradicted. He said, 'I have sworn that I must take that man's goods. See, therefore, whether I could or should not do what I said I would do, even with the insertion of Christ's name.' Then I withdrew, having heard the reason for his crime based on a very religious motive. What more could I do, I, to whom the affair was shown to be so just and holy?

(16) Here and now I ask all who are of sound mind: Who would ever believe that the insolence of human greed would proceed to this insult of God, so that men say they will do in the name of Christ that very thing by which they injure Him? What an incalculable and monstrous crime! What have wicked minds not dared! They arm themselves

for highway robbery with the name of God and, since Christ is the forbidder and avenger of all evils, they say they are doing what they do on His behalf. And we bewail the injustice of the enemy and say that pagans, in their barbarity, swear falsely.

With how much less sin do they transgress who swear falsely by demons than we who swear by God! How much less a crime it is to make sport of the name of Jove than of Christ! In their case, they invoke the name of a dead man. In our case, we swear falsely by a living God. In their case, it is not even a man. In our case, it is the Most High God. In our case, since we swear by the greatest pledge, the guilt and perjury must also be the greatest. In their case, since there is hardly an oath, it stands that there is no perjury, for, since the god through whom they swear does not exist, it is not perjury when they swear falsely.

He who wishes to know how true this is let him listen to the blessed Apostle Paul preaching these very things which I am saying. This is what he says:[48] 'But we know that what things so ever the Law speaks, it speaks to them that are in the Law.' And again:[49] 'for where there is no law, neither is there transgression.' In these two statements he clearly proposed that there are two parts of the human race, those placed outside the Law and those living within the Law. Who, therefore, are they who are now placed within the Law? Who but the Christians? Just as was the Apostle himself who says of himself:[50] 'I am not without the Law, but am in the Law of Christ.'

Who are they without the Law of Christ? Who but pagans who know not the Law of God? Therefore, he says of them:[51]

---
48 Rom. 3.19.
49 Rom. 4.15.
50 1 Cor. 9.21.
51 Rom. 4.15.

'where there is no Law, neither is there transgression.' He certainly showed by this one statement that Christians only, when they have sinned, are transgressors of the Law, but that pagans who know not the Law sin without transgression, because nobody can be a transgressor of something of which he is ignorant. Therefore, only we are transgressors of the divine Law who, as it is written, read the Law, but do not execute it. Because of this our knowledge is nothing but guilt, we who knew the Law only for this that we sin with greater offense, because what we know by reading and in our heart we trample underfoot in lust and scorn.

And most justly was that apostolic word said to every Christian:[52] 'You who make your boast of the law, by transgression of the law dishonor God. For the name of God through you is blasphemed among the Gentiles.' It can be understood from the fact that they defame the name of God, of how great a crime are Christians guilty. And although it has been written for us that we are to do all things for the glory of God,[53] we, on the contrary, do all things to the injury of God. Although our Saviour Himself calls out to us daily,[54] 'so let your light shine before men that the sons of men may see your good works and glorify your Father Who is in Heaven,' we live contrariwise, so that the sons of men see our evil works and blaspheme our Father who is in Heaven.

(17) Since this is so, we may well flatter ourselves with the greatest prerogative of the name of Christian: we who act and live in such a way that by the very fact that we are said to be a Christian people we seem to be a reproach to Christ. But, on the contrary, which of these evils similar to

---
52 Rom. 2.23-24.
53 1 Cor. 10.31.
54 Matt. 5.16.

those I have described prevail among pagans? Can it be said of the Huns: 'Behold what kind of men are they, who are said to be Christians?' Can it be said of the Saxons or Franks: 'Behold what they do, who assert they are worshippers of Christ?'

Can one holy Law be blamed for the savage customs of the Moors? Do the most revolting rites of the Scythians or Gepidae bring curses and blasphemy on the Name of God? Can it be said of some of them: 'Where is the Catholic Law in which they believe? Where are the commandments of holiness and chastity which they learn? They read the Gospels and are unchaste. They listen to the Apostles and get drunk. They follow Christ and plunder. They live a dishonorable life and they say they have an honorable law.' Can these indictments be made of any of these nations? Certainly not. But all these indictments are made about us. They are made against us in whom Christ suffers reproach. They are made against us in whom the Christian Law suffers reproach.

What I have said above is said of us: 'Behold the kind of men who worship Christ. It is clearly false when they say they learn good things. It is false when they boast they keep the commandments of the holy Law. For, if they learned good things, they would be good. Such, indeed, is a school as are its pupils. They are, doubtless, what they are taught to be. Thus it appears that the prophets whom they have teach impurity, that the Apostles whom they read have sanctioned wickedness, and the Gospels with which they are imbued preach those evils which they themselves do.

'In a word, holy deeds would be done by Christians if Christ has taught holy things. He who is worshiped can be judged by His worshippers. For how is a teacher good whose pupils we see are so evil? From this viewpoint, they are Christians; they listen to Him, they read Him. It is easy for all to understand the teaching of Christ. See what the Christians do and you clearly see what Christ teaches.'

Finally, the most cruel questions of the savage persecutors teach how depraved and wicked have always been the opinions of pagans about the sacred mysteries of the Lord. The pagans believed that in Christian sacrifices there is nothing done beyond certain impure and abominable acts. Some thought the origins of our religion have sprung from the two greatest crimes: first, from murder; then from incest, graver still than murder. Not from murder and incest alone, but something that is more criminal than incest itself and murder, the incest of the most sanctified mothers and the murder of innocent little children whom they thought not only to be killed by the Christians but, what is more abominable, even to be devoured by them. All these things were for appeasing God, as if He could be more offended by any crime; for purging sin, as if any other sin could be greater; for the commending of sacrifices, as if God could more abhor any other thing; for gaining eternal life, as if, indeed, even could He be won over by such offerings, it would be worthwhile to attain eternal life through such monstrous crimes.

(18) We can therefore understand what qualities, in pagan belief, the Christians have who worshipped God with such sacrifices. We also can understand their notion about God who taught these sacred mysteries. And why is this so? Why, indeed, unless because of those who are said to be Christians but are not: Christians who by their rascality and baseness defame the name of religion; Christians who, as it is written, confess that they know God, but deny Him by their acts since they are detestable and unbelieving, and to

every good work reprobate;[55] through whom, as we read, is the way of truth blasphemed and the most holy name of the Lord God violated by evil speech of sacrilegious men.[56]

How particularly difficult it is to atone for the evil deed of handing over the name of the Lord to the blasphemy of the heathen, we are instructed by the example of the most blessed David who, because of the intercession of his acts of justice, deserved to evade eternal punishment for his offenses through one confession only. Yet he, with penance as his protector, was unable to obtain full pardon for his sin. When Nathan the prophet had said to David, who was confessing his own sins to him, 'the Lord has taken away your sin, you shall not die,' he added immediately, 'nevertheless, because you have given occasion to the enemies of the Lord to blaspheme, for this word, the child that is to born to you, shall die.'[57]

And what happened next? Having laid aside his crown and put away his jewels, all splendor of royal dignity being removed, he was relieved of the purple. For all his sins he shut himself up alone, weeping, filthy in sackcloth, soaked in tears and soiled with ashes, and sought the life of his little child with the voice of many lamentations and beat upon the Most Holy God with great fervor of prayer. Thus asking and imploring, he believed he could in this manner obtain what he sought from God. Yet he was unable to obtain his request through what is the most forceful aid to those who ask.

From this it can be understood that there is no crime deserving of greater guilt than to give to the heathen a reason for blaspheming. For, whoever has erred gravely without giving cause for blasphemy to others brings damnation to himself

---

55 Titus 1.16.
56 2 Peters 2.2.
57 2 Kings 12.13-14.

only, but he who makes others blaspheme drags many to death with himself. He will, of necessity, be guilty for as many as he shall have drawn into guilt. Not only this, whatever sinner so sins that he does not cause others to blaspheme by his sin, his sin is injurious only to him who sins, but does not insult the Holy Name of God with the sacrilegious curse of those who blaspheme. But he who, by his sin, causes others to blaspheme, his sin is, of necessity, beyond the measure of human crime, because he has done unthinkable harm to God through the curses of many.

(19) As I have said, this evil is peculiar only to Christians, because through them only, in a way, is God blasphemed. They learn good and do evil who, it is written, confess God by words and deny Him by deeds.[58] They, as the same Apostle says, repose in the Law and know its intent and approve of those things that are the more profitable.[59] They have the form of knowledge and of truth in the Law. They preach that they must not steal, yet they do steal. They read that they must not commit adultery, yet they commit it. They glory in the Law, yet by transgression of the Law they dishonor God. Therefore, for this very reason, Christians are worse because they should be better. They do not practice what they preach, and they struggle against their faith by their morals. All the more blameworthy is evil which the label of goodness accuses, and the holy name is the crime of an unholy man. Hence, the Saviour also said in the Apocalypse to the lukewarm Christian:[60] 'Would that you were cold or hot. But now because you are lukewarm, I will begin to vomit you out of my mouth.' The Lord orders every

---

58 Titus 1.16.
59 Rom. 2.17-18.
60 Apoc. 3.15-16.

Christian to be fervent in faith and in spirit. For, thus it is written,[61] 'that we be fervent in spirit, serving the Lord.'

In this fervor of spirit, the ardor of religious faith is shown. He who has the greatest ardor is recognized as fervent and faithful; he who has none at all is understood as cold and a heathen. But he who is between, or is neither, is a lukewarm Christian and hateful to the Lord; therefore it is said to him, 'would that you were hot or cold. But now, because you are lukewarm, I will begin to vomit you out of my mouth.' This is to say, 'would that you had either the fervor and faith of good Christians or, certainly, the cold and ignorance of pagans. For your warm faith either would make you pleasing to God, or certainly, for the present, your ignorance of the Law would excuse you somewhat. But now, because you have already known Christ and neglect Him whom you have known, you, who, as it were, have been taken into the mouth of God through the acknowledgment of faith, are thrown out because of lukewarmness.'

The blessed Apostle Peter also made this plain when he was speaking of the vicious and lukewarm Christians, that is, to those who lived bad lives:[62] 'For it had been better for them not to have known the way of justice than, after they have known it, to turn back from the holy commandment which was given to them. For that of the true proverb has happened to them: the dog is returned to his vomit: and the sow that was washed to her wallowing in the mire.' That we may understand that this is said about those who live under the Christian name in the dirt and impurities of the world, listen to what he says about them in the same passage. He says:[63] 'for if, fleeing from the pollutions of the

---
61 Rom. 12.11.
62 2 Peter 2.21-22.
63 2 Peter 2.20.

world, through the knowledge of our Lord and Saviour Jesus Christ, they be again entangled in them and overcome, their latter state is become unto them worse than the first.'

This indeed, the blessed Apostle Paul said in the same manner:[64] 'Circumcision profits indeed if you keep the Law, but if you be a transgressor of the Law, your circumcision is made uncircumcision.' He himself teaches very plainly that by circumcision must be understood Christianity, when he said.[65] 'for we are the circumcision, who in spirit serve God, and do not confide in the flesh.' Therefore, we see that he compares bad Christians to pagans; not only compares, but almost puts them behind them, when he said:[66] 'but if the uncircumcised keep the justices of the law, shall not this uncircumcision be counted for circumcision? And shall not that which by nature is uncircumcision, if it fulfill the Law, judge you who by the letter and circumcision are a transgressor of the Law?'

And by this we understand, as I have said above, that we who have and spurn the Law of God are much more culpable than those who neither have it nor know it at all. Nobody despises things which are unknown to him. The Apostle has said:[67] 'I did not know concupiscence if the Law did not say: you shall not covet.' For neither do they transgress the Law who do not have the Law because, as it is written,[68] 'where there is no Law, there is no transgression.' Therefore, if they do not transgress the Law which they do not have, neither do they scorn the statutes of the Law which they do not have, because nobody, as I have said, can despise what he does not know. But we are scorners as well as transgressors

---

64 Rom. 2.25.
65 Phil. 3.3.
66 Rom. 2.26-27.
67 Rom. 7.7.
68 Rom. 4.15.

of the Law and, accordingly, are worse than the pagans, for they do not know the commandments of God and we do. They do not have them, but we do. They do not follow commands which are unknown to them, but we trample underfoot what we know. Therefore, ignorance among them is transgression among us, because it is being guilty of a lesser crime to be ignorant of the commandments of God than to spurn them.

BOOK FIVE

I KNOW THAT some men, altogether without faith and devoid of the divine Truth, advance the following argument against what I have said: If the guilt of the unfaithful Christians is so great that they sin more by disregarding the commands of the Lord which they know, than do pagan nations because they do not know, therefore ignorance of the Law is more beneficial to them than knowledge, and, to a degree, knowledge is a hindrance to those who know the truth. To these my answer must be that it is not the truth but vices which impede. It is not the Law but our behavior that is injurious. In short, if our behavior is good, the ordinances of the Law are in our favor; take away vices, the Law profits us. The Apostle says:[1] 'for we know that the Law is good, if a man use it lawfully.' Use the Law lawfully and you yourself have made the Law good for yourself. 'For we know,' he says, 'that the Law is good if a man uses it lawfully. Knowing this: that the Law is not made for the just man.'

For this reason, begin to be just and you shall be free from the Law, because a law which is already contained in morals cannot contravene morals. The Apostle says:[2] 'for we know that a Law is good if a man uses it lawfully. Knowing this: that the Law is not made for the just man but for the unjust and disobedient, for the criminal, ungodly and sinners, and if there is anything else contrary to sound doc-

---
1 1 Tim. 1.8-9.
2 1 Tim. 1.8-10.

trine.' Therefore, O man, the Law is not so much against you as you are against the Law; nor does the Law by ordering good act against you, but you act against the Law by your evil life.

Indeed, the Law is on your side, but you are against it. It gives you counsel by speaking holy things, but you contravene it by doing base things. You are not so much against it as against yourself. By this very fact that you are against it you are against yourself, because in it are your salvation and life. Therefore, when you desert the divine Law, you abandon your own salvation. We do not complain about the Lord's Law otherwise than an impatient invalid is wont to complain about the best doctors. We are like the sick man who, when he has his disease grow worse through his own vices, blames the incompetence of the doctor. As if, indeed, prescriptions can cure any illness if the sick man does not obey them, or as if an observance which the doctor orders can cure anyone if the patient does not fulfill it for himself.

What good does bitter wormwood do the stomach, if sweet drinks are taken immediately thereafter? What benefits does the silence of bystanders do a delirious man whom his own raving is killing? Or, of what profit can be an antidote, if poison is poured over it?[3] For us, therefore, the Law is the antidote and wickedness is the poison. The antidote of the Law cannot cure us whom the poisons of our vices are killing. But I have already spoken sufficiently about these vices in the foregoing pages, and, if occasion shall demand it, I shall also speak again about them with the Lord's help.

---

3 Cf. Saint Jerome: 'Cautery and the knife are the only remedies when mortification has set in. Poison is the only known antidote for poison' (*Nicene and Post-Nicene Fathers* 2.6.216).

(2) I have already mentioned above that there are two kinds of sects of barbarians: pagans and heretics. Since I think I have said enough about the pagans, let me add, as the exposition demands, something also about the heretics. Someone may say: 'Although the divine Law does not demand from pagans that they keep the commandments of which they are so ignorant, certainly the divine Law does demand their observance from heretics, who are not ignorant. It can be said they read the same things we read. They have the same prophets of God, the same Apostles, the same Gospels as we. Therefore, the Law is not less neglected by them than by us, or it is even much more so, because, although they read the same Scriptures as we, they do worse things than we.' Let us look at both sides.

You say they read the same writings which are read by us. How are those writings the same which are badly interpolated and badly translated by authors formerly evil?[4] Therefore they are not the same, because those things cannot be said to be whole which are corrupted in any part. Writings which have lost their fullness are lacking in perfection, and those writings do not preserve their complete value which are deprived of the power of being holy. Only we, therefore, have the Sacred Scriptures full, uncorrupted, and complete. We either imbibe them at their source or assuredly drink them drawn from the purest source through the medium of correct translation. Only we read them well, and would that we fulfilled them as well as we read them!

But I am afraid that we do not observe them well, do not read them with attention either, because there is less guilt in not reading the Holy Scriptures than in violating them after having read them. To be sure, the other nations either

---
4 The first attempt to translate the Scriptures into Gothic was made by the Semi-Arian Bishop Ulfilas (c. 311-383).

do not have the Law of God, or they have it in a weakened and maimed way, and, therefore, as I have said, they have it in such a manner that they do not have it at all. For, if there are any barbarian nations who in their books seem to have the Holy Scriptures less interpolated or torn into shreds than others, nevertheless they have them as they were corrupted by the tradition of their old teachers. Therefore, they have tradition rather than Scripture. They do not keep what the truth of the Law teaches, but what the wickedness of a bad tradition has inserted.

Indeed, the barbarians, being deficient especially of Roman more than educational tradition, know nothing unless they hear it from their teachers. Thus, they follow what they hear, and they who are ignorant of all literature and knowledge and know the mystery of the divine Law by teaching rather than by reading must necessarily retain the teaching rather than the Law. Thus, to them, the tradition of their teachers and their long-standing teaching are, so to say, law for them because they know only what they are taught.

Therefore, they are heretics, but not heretics knowingly. Indeed, with us they are heretics, but in their own opinion they are not. So much do they judge themselves Catholics that they defame us with the title of heresy. What they are to us, therefore, we are to them. We are certain that they do injury to the divine begetting because they say the Son is less than the Father. They think we injure the Father because we believe the Father and Son are equal. We possess the truth, but they think they have it. We honor the Godhead, but they think their belief is the honor of His divinity.

They are unobservant of their obligations, but to them this is the highest duty of their religion. They are ungodly, but they think that is true godliness. Therefore, they are in error, but they err with a good heart, not in hatred but in love of God, believing that they honor and love God. Although they possess not the true faith, they think they possess the perfect love of God. In what manner, for this erroneous and false belief, they are to be punished on the day of judgment, nobody can know but the Judge.

I think God bears patiently with them in the meantime because He sees that, although their belief is incorrect, they err through the acceptance of a seemingly correct opinion. He knows that they act in this manner because they are ignorant. However, He knows that our people neglect their own beliefs. Therefore, the barbarians sin through the wickedness of their teachers, but we through our own wickedness. They sin through ignorance; we, through knowledge. They do what they think is right; we, what we know is wrong. Therefore, with just judgment the patience of God sustains them, but reproachfully chastises us, because ignorance can be overlooked for a time, but contempt does not deserve pardon. For so is it written:[5] 'the servant who knows not the will of his Lord, and does not do it, shall be beaten with few stripes. But he who knows and does not do it, shall be beaten with many stripes.'

(3) Accordingly, let us not wonder that we are beaten with many stripes. We sin not in ignorance, but in rebellion. We know good, but do not do good. We understand the difference between right and wrong, but pursue the wrong. We read the Law and trample on lawful things. For this only do we learn the decrees of the holy commandments that we may sin the more gravely after being forbidden. We say that we worship God, yet we obey the devil.

And after these transgressions we want to receive good things from God, while we always add evil to evil. We de-

---
5 Luke 12.47-48.

sire our own will to be done by God, while we are unwilling to do God's will. We act, as it were, as God's superiors. We want God to obey our will, while we all struggle constantly against His will. But He is just, although we are unjust. He chastises those whom He thinks should be chastised. He has patience with those with whom He thinks He should be patient. He wishes His patience and chastisement to be useful for one and the same end, so that His chastisement may curb among Catholics the lust for sin. He wishes that in time His patience may make the heretics know the full truth of faith, especially when He knows that, when their lives are compared, they whom He sees excelling the Catholics are, perhaps, not unworthy of the Catholic faith.

But all those of whom I speak are either Vandals or Goths. I say nothing about the Roman heretics, of whom there is a huge multitude. Nor do I compare the latter either with the other Romans or the barbarians, because they are worse than the Romans through their lack of faith and more base than the barbarians in the foulness of their lives. This not only does not help us, but, even beyond that, it grieves us that we are hurt by our own people, because those whom I say are like this are Romans. Hence, we can understand what the whole Roman state deserves when one group of the Romans offend God by their way of living, another by their lack of faith as well as their way of living. Furthermore, even the very heresies of the barbarians at one time stemmed from the perverseness of a Roman teacher; hence, it is even our crime that the barbarian peoples began to be heretics.[6]

(4) Furthermore, insofar as it pertains to the way of life among the Vandals and Goths, in what way are we

---

6 Orosius, *Seven Books of History Against the Pagans* (trans. Irving Woodworth Raymond, Columbia University Records of Civilization 26, New York 1936) 375.

better than they, or can even be compared with them? First, let me speak of their love and charity which the Lord teaches is the chief of virtues and which He not only commends throughout Sacred Scriptures but even in His own words:[7] 'by this shall it be known that you are my disciples, that you love one another.' Almost all barbarians, at least those who are of one tribe under one king, love one another; almost all Romans persecute each other.

Who is there who does not envy his fellow citizen? Who gives complete love to his neighbor? Indeed, all are distant in affection from each other, although they are not distant in location; although they are proximate in living, they are remote in mind. Although this is really a great evil, would that it were true only of citizens and neighbors! More serious is the fact that relatives do not respect the bonds of relationship. Who behaves toward those nearest to him as he should? Who gives what he knows he owes to charity or to his name? Who, in his heart, lives up to his name? Who feels as closely related in his heart as he is by blood? Who is he in whom the yellow jealousy of ill-will does not burn? Who is he whose senses have not been invaded by spite, whom another's good fortune is not his own ill-fortune, who does not believe that the good of another is his own evil, to whom his own happiness so suffices that he also wishes another to be happy? There is now a new and immeasurable evil among most men: it is not enough for anyone to be happy himself, unless another is unhappy.

What kind of situation is this; how cruel, how deep-rooted in wickedness, how foreign to barbarians but how familiar to Romans that they proscribe one another with exactions? Indeed, not each other, for this would be almost more tol-

---

[7] John 13.35.

erable if each would endure what he inflicts on others. It is a more serious situation that the many are proscribed by the few, to whom public requisitions are their private booty, who make the bills of the fiscal debt into private gain.⁸ And not only the highest officials, but often the least officials do this; not only judges, but even the underlings of the judges.

What towns, as well as what municipalities and villages are there in which there are not as many tyrants as *curiales*.⁹ Perhaps they glory in this name of tyrant because it seems to be considered powerful and honored. For, almost all robbers rejoice and boast, if they are said to be more fierce than they really are. What place is there, as I have said, where the bowels of widows and orphans are not devoured by the leading men of the cities, and with them those of almost all holy men? For, they consider the latter as widows and orphans because they are either unwilling to protect themselves in their zeal for their profession, or they cannot protect themselves because of their simplicity and humility. Not one of them, therefore, is safe. In a manner, except for the very powerful, neither is anyone safe from the devastation of general brigandage, unless they are like the robbers themselves. To this state of affairs, indeed, to this crime has the world come that, unless one is bad, he cannot be safe.¹⁰

(5) Since there are so many who despoil the good, perhaps there are some who bring aid in this despoliation, who,

---

8 *Codex Theodosianus* (ed. Th. Mommsen, Berlin 1912) 11.7, 16, 20.
9 The *curiales*, were the provincial officials and the tax-gatherers. When society was 'frozen' into its respective classes by Diocletian, the officials and their heirs became permanent officials. Imperial law forbade their entrance to the clerical status. They were personally liable to the State for tax-levies and, when the amount collected was insufficient, the deficit was necessarily made up from the resources of the *curiales*.
10 Brigandage was particularly rife in Gaul from the third century onward. The large-landed estates of the wealthy fostered the unrest because they were places of refuge for the disturbed population.

as it is written,[11] snatch the needy and poor from the hand of the sinner. 'There is none who does good, there is almost not even one.'[12] The prophet said 'almost not even one' because, such is the rarity of good men, there seems to be scarcely one of them. Who gives help to the distressed and those that labor, when even the Lord's priests do not resist the violence of wicked men?

Either most of them are silent or, even though they speak, they are like those who are silent, and many do this not from lack of resolution, but, as they think, with considered discretion. They are unwilling to mention the manifest truth because the ears of wicked men cannot bear it. They not only flee from the truth, but they hate and curse it and in no way revere or fear it. When they hear it, they also condemn it in the hostility of their prideful stubbornness. Therefore, even they who can speak are silent while, in the meantime, they spare those very evil men. Nor do they wish to publish openly the force of truth to them, lest they make them worse by truth repeated more pointedly.

All the while, the poor are despoiled, the widows groan, the orphans are tread underfoot, so much so that many of them, and they are not of obscure birth and have received a liberal education, flee to the enemy lest they die from the pain of public persecution.[13] They seek among the barbarians the dignity of the Roman because they cannot bear barbarous indignity among the Romans. Although these Romans differ in religion and language from the barbarians to whom they flee, and differ from them in respect to filthiness of body and clothing, nevertheless, as I have said, they prefer to bear among the barbarians a worship unlike

---
11 Ps. 81.4.
12 Ps. 13.3.
13 *Codex Theo.* 11.1,7.

their own rather than rampant injustice among the Romans.

Thus, far and wide, they migrate either to the Goths or to the Bagaudae,[14] or to other barbarians everywhere in power; yet they do not repent having migrated. They prefer to live as freemen under an outward form of captivity than as captives under an appearance of liberty. Therefore, the name of Roman citizens, at one time not only greatly valued but dearly bought, is now repudiated and fled from, and it is almost considered not only base but even deserving of abhorrence.

And what can be a greater testimony of Roman wickedness than that many men, upright and noble and to whom the position of being a Roman citizen should be considered as of the highest splendor and dignity, have been driven by the cruelty of Roman wickedness to such a state of mind that they do not wish to be Romans? Hence, even those who do not flee to the barbarians are forced to be barbarians. Such is a great portion of the Spaniards and not the least portion of the Gauls, and, finally, all those throughout the whole Roman world whom Roman wickedness has compelled not to be Romans.

(6) I am now about to speak of the Bagaudae who were despoiled, oppressed and murdered by evil and cruel judges. After they had lost the right of Roman citizenship, they also lost the honor of bearing the Roman name. We blame their misfortunes on themselves. We ascribe to them a name which signifies their downfall. We give to them a name

---

14 The *Bagaudae* were the organized peasants who were victims of the tax-gatherers. They became a serious threat to the Empire, and Maximian, co-emperor with Diocletian, led an army into Gaul to crush the peasant revolt. The peasants had elevated two usurping emperors, Allianus and Amandus, as claimants to supreme power in the State. In 458 Emperor Majorian utilized their strength to fight the Vandal king, Genseric.

of which we ourselves are the cause. We call them rebels. We call those outlaws whom we compelled to be criminal.

For, by what other ways did they become Bagaudae, except by our wickedness, except by the wicked ways of judges, except by the proscription and pillage of those who have turned the assessments of public taxes into the benefit of their own gain and have made the tax levies their own booty? Like wild beasts, they did not rule but devoured their subjects, and feasted not only on the spoils of men, as most robbers are wont to do, but even on their torn flesh and, as I may say, on their blood.

Thus it happened that men, strangled and killed by the robberies of judges, began to live as barbarians because they were not permitted to be Romans. They became satisfied to be what they were not, because they were not permitted to be what they were. They were compelled to defend their lives at least, because they saw that they had already completely lost their liberty. What else is being done today than was done then, for example, those who are not up to now Bagaudae are now compelled to be? Insofar as force and injuries go, they are now driven so that they want to become Bagaudae, but they are prevented by weakness so that they are not. Thus, they are as captives oppressed by the yoke of the enemy. They bear torture out of necessity, not out of choice. In their hearts they desire liberty, but undergo the greatest of slavery.

(7) In like manner, therefore, the same thing is happening to almost all the lower classes, for they are driven by one cause to two very different choices. The highest force demands that they wish to aspire to liberty, but the same force does not permit them to be able to do what it compels them to wish to do. Perhaps it can be charged against

them that they wish to be men who desire nothing more than not to be forced to wish for liberty. Their greatest misfortune is what they wish for. For, it would be much better for them if they were not compelled to wish for it.

But what else can these wretched people wish for, they who suffer the incessant and even continuous destruction of public tax levies. To them there is always imminent a heavy and relentless proscription. They desert their homes, lest they be tortured in their very homes. They seek exile, lest they suffer torture. The enemy is more lenient to them than the tax collectors. This is proved by this very fact, that they flee to the enemy in order to avoid the full force of the heavy tax levy. This very tax levying, although hard and inhuman, would nevertheless be less heavy and harsh if all would bear it equally and in common. Taxation is made more shameful and burdensome because all do not bear the burden of all. They extort tribute from the poor man for the taxes of the rich, and the weaker carry the load for the stronger. There is no other reason that they cannot bear all the taxation except that the burden imposed on the wretched is greater than their resources.

They suffer from envy and want, which are misfortunes most diverse and unlike. Envy is bound up with payment of the tax; need, with the ability to pay. If you look at what they pay, you will think them abundant in riches, but if you look at what they actually possess, you will find them poverty stricken. Who can judge an affair of this wretchedness? They bear the payment of the rich and endure the poverty of beggars. Much more serious is the following: the rich themselves occasionally make tributary levies which the poor pay.

But, you say, when the assessment due from the rich is very heavy and the taxes due from them are very heavy, how does it happen that they wish to increase their own debt? I do not say that they increase the taxes for themselves. They increase them because they do not increase them for themselves. I will tell you how this is done. Commonly, new envoys, new bearers of letters, come from the imperial offices and those men are recommended to a few well-known men for the mischief of many.[15] For them new gifts are decreed, new taxes are decreed. The powerful levy what the poor are to pay, the courtesy of the rich decrees what the multitude of the wretched are to lose. They themselves in no way feel what they levy.

You say they who were sent by our superiors cannot be honored and generously entertained otherwise. Therefore, you rich men, you who are the first to levy, be the first to give. Be the first in generosity of goods, you who are the first in profusion of words. You who give of mine, give of thine. Most justly, whoever you are, you who alone wish to receive favor, you alone should bear the expense. But to your will, O rich men, we the poor accede. What you, the few, order, we all pay. What is so just, so humane? Your decrees burden us with new debts; at least make your debt common to us all. What is more wicked and more unworthy than that you alone are free from debt, you who make us all debtors?

Indeed, the most wretched poor thus pay all that I have mentioned, but for what cause or for what reason they pay, they are completely ignorant. For, to whom is it lawful to discuss why they pay; to whom is permitted to find out what is owed? Then it is given out most publicly when the rich get angry with each other, when some of them get indignant because some levies are made without their advice and handling.

---

15 *Cod. Theo.* 8.11,1.

Then you may hear it said by some of them, 'What an unworthy crime! Two or three decree what kills many; what is paid by many wretched men is decreed by a few powerful men.' Each rich man maintains his honor by being unwilling that anything is decreed in his absence, yet he does not maintain justice by being unwilling that evil things be done when he is present. Lastly, what these very men consider base in others they themselves later legalize, either in punishment of a past contempt or in proof of their power. Therefore, the most unfortunate poor are, as it were, in the midst of the sea, between conflicting, violent winds. They are swamped by the waves rolling now from one side, now from the other.

(8) But, surely, those who are wicked in one way are found moderate and just in another, and compensate for their baseness in one thing by goodness in another. For, just as they weigh down the poor with the burden of new tax levies, so they sustain them by the assistance of new tax reliefs; just as the lower classes are oppressed by new taxes, so they are equally relieved by tax mitigations. Indeed, the injustice is equal in taxes and reliefs, for, as the poor are the first to be burdened, so they are the last to be relieved.

For when, as has happened lately, the highest powers thought it would be advisable that taxation should be lessened somewhat for the cities which were in arrears in their payments, the rich alone instantly divided among themselves the remedy given for all. Who, then, remembers the poor? Who calls the poor and needy to share in the common benefit? Who permits him who is first in bearing the burden even to stand in the last place for receiving redress? What more is there to say? In no way are the poor regarded as taxpayers, unless when the mass of taxes is imposed upon them; they are not reckoned among the number of taxpayers when the tax-reliefs are portioned.

Do we think we are unworthy of the punishment of divine severity when we thus constantly punish the poor? Do we think, when we are constantly wicked, that God should not exercise His justice against all of us? Where or in whom are evils so great, except among the Romans? Whose injustice so great except our own? The Franks are ignorant of this crime of injustice. The Huns are immune to these crimes. There are no wrongs among the Vandals and none among the Goths. So far are the barbarians from tolerating these injustices among the Goths, that not even the Romans who live among them suffer them.

Therefore, in the districts taken over by the barbarians, there is one desire among all the Romans, that they should never again find it necessary to pass under Roman jurisdiction. In those regions, it is the one and general prayer of the Roman people that they be allowed to carry on the life they lead with the barbarians. And we wonder why the Goths are not conquered by our portion of the population, when the Romans prefer to live among them rather than with us. Our brothers, therefore, are not only altogether unwilling to flee to us from them, but they even cast us aside in order to flee to them.

Except for one reason only I might well wonder that all the poor and needy taxpayers do not flee in a body to the barbarians. They do not do it, because they cannot carry with them their few little possessions, households, and families. For, when many of them would leave behind their little plots of land and cottages in order to avoid the full force of taxation, how could they not wish to take with them, if there were any possibility of doing so, those things which they are compelled to leave behind? Therefore, because they are incapable of doing what they really prefer, they do the one thing of which they are capable. They give themselves to the upper classes in return for care and protection.[16] They make themselves the captives of the rich and as it were, pass over into their jurisdiction and dependence.

However, I would not consider this serious or unbecoming, indeed, I would rather thank this public spirit of the powerful to whom the poor entrust themselves, if they did not sell these *patrocinia,* if, when they say they are defending the poor, they are contributing to humanity and not to greed. It is harsh and severe that the poor seem to be protected by this law in order to despoil them, and they defend the poor by this law in order to make them more wretched by defending them. For, all those who seem to be defended give to their defenders almost all their goods before they are defended; thus, in order that the fathers may have defense, the sons lose their heritage. The safety of the parents is secured by the penury of the offspring.

Behold those things which are the aids and *patrocinia* of the upper classes! They give nothing to those whose care they undertook, but only to themselves. By this agreement some temporary aid is given to the parents so that in the future the whole may be taken away from the children. Therefore certain rich lords sell, and for the highest price, everything they offer to give. Because I have said they sell, would they would sell according to the accustomed and common usage! In that case something, perhaps, would remain to

---

16 The power of the noble landed aristocracy in the West was the subject of many imperial laws. They were so powerful that they were debarred from command in the army. Their estates afforded an asylum for lawbreakers. They themselves refused to pay taxes, kept their own little armies, and exercised their own justice independent of the State. They either cast into prison those who were in their debt or they appropriated their belongings. The victims thus became *coloni,* or sub-tenant farmers, on the large estates or *latifundi.*

the buyers. Indeed, this is a new kind of buying and selling.

The seller gives nothing and receives all; the buyer receives nothing and loses all completely. Almost every contract has in it seemingly evil desire in the buyer and want in the seller, because the buyer purchases to increase his substance, the seller sells to diminish his. This is an unheard kind of trading, whereby wealth is added to the sellers and nothing remains to the buyer except beggary alone. An affair of the following kind is intolerable and monstrous. It is one which human minds could hardly, I will not say bear, but not even hear. Most of the poor and wretched, despoiled of their few possessions and evicted from their little plots of land, must, even when they have lost their property, bear the taxes for the things they have lost. Though possession has gone from them, the tax assessment has not. They lack property, but are crushed by taxes!

Who can estimate the extent of this evil? The invaders have nested in their property and the poor pay the taxes for the invaders. After the death of the father, the sons do not have the little plots of land in accordance with their rights and are killed off by duties due on their fields. What else is done by crimes such as these, except that those who are stripped naked by private invasion die from public exaction, those from whom plunder has taken their property lose their lives through taxes? Accordingly, some of those of whom I speak are either wiser or necessity has made them wise. When either they lose their homes and fields to the invaders or flee as fugitives from the tax collectors, because they cannot hold their land, they seek out the estates of the rich and become their *coloni*.[17]

---

[17] The *colonus adscriptus* was the sub-tenant farmer on a large estate. Toil on the land was at once his heritage, duty, and obligation. Local custom fixed the dues paid to master and these could not be arbitrarily

Just as they who, when driven by the terror of the enemy flee to the forts, or they who, when their status of immunity is lost, flee in desperation to some asylum, in like manner the poor, because they are unable to protect further either the seat or dignity of their birthplaces, give themselves over to the yoke of being *inquilini*.[18] They are reduced to this necessity that they are not only driven from their wealth, but even from their social status. They are exiled not only from their property, but even from themselves. They lose with themselves all their goods and thus are without property and lose the rights of citizenship.

(9) Indeed, because unhappy necessity thus compels them, their extremely straitened lot would be bearable to a certain extent, if there were not something more extreme. What is more grievous and bitter is that a more cruel evil is added to this evil. They are received as newcomers. They become natives[19] by the mere legal fiction of a dwelling place and, following the example of that commanding evil-doing woman who was said to change men into beasts, so all these men who are received within the estates of the rich are changed, as it were, by the transformation of Circe's cup. Those whom the rich receive as outsiders and newcomers they begin to consider as their own. Those who were known to be freemen are turned into slaves.

---

increased by the lord. On the other hand, he could not become a cleric or a runaway. He could not be sold without his land and his land could not be sold without him. He was 'tied to the soil.' He owed his lord certain days of work on the lord's land, and the lord owed him and his family protection.

18 The *coloni inquilini* were entitled to retain for their own use all they could gain from the soil beyond the value of a yearly payment which they had to make to the owner of the soil.

19 The word *nativi* was the mediaeval word for serfs, those native or born on the estate. Cf. F. A. Gasquet, *Parish Life in Mediaeval England* (London 1929) 72; also, Ducange, *Glossarium*, under title *Nativus*.

And we wonder why the barbarians capture us when we make our own brothers captives. There is nothing strange that there are invasions and the destruction of states. We have for a long time been striving toward this by the oppression of the many, so that by capturing others even we ourselves have begun to be captives. For we feel, although much later than we deserve, we feel at length those things which we have done to others, and according to the words of Holy Scripture we are eating the labor of our own hands,[20] and under a just Judge, God, we are paying back what we owe.

Indeed, we have not been merciful to the exiled, and behold, we ourselves are exiles. We defrauded wanderers; behold, we ourselves are wanderers and are cheated. We circumvented men of freeborn status by taking advantage of the ruinous circumstances of the times; behold, we ourselves have recently begun to live on foreign soil and we already fear the same ruinous circumstances. How great is the faithless blindness of evil-minded men! We are carrying out the condemnation of a God who judges, but we do not acknowledge that we are being judged.

And some holy men wonder that others who as yet have not borne any such punishment are not reformed by our misfortune. Not even we ourselves are corrected by the torments due our iniquities, we who are already being punished by God. O pride not to be tolerated! Many visibly suffer the punishment of their sins, yet nobody deigns to understand the causes of punishments.

But the cause of this pride is clear. Though we are already suffering some punishment, we are not yet suffering what we deserve. So great is the mercy of God that, al-

---

20 Ps. 127.2.

though He wishes us to make some atonement for our sins, He is, however, unwilling to tolerate everything. The fact that He chastises the wicked is not returning evil for evil. He wishes us to acknowledge rather than sustain our sins, so that He shows us by loving and salutary stripes the ones we deserve to bear. Nevertheless, He does not inflict on us what we deserve, according to that saying of the blessed Apostle, who says:[21] 'Do you not know that the goodness of God leads you to penance? But according to your hardness and impenitent heart, you are treasuring up for yourself wrath against the day of wrath.'

Truly are we acting in the manner said by the Apostle. God calls us to repentance, but we treasure up wrath. God invites us to pardon, but daily we heap up offenses. We do violence to God by our sins: we ourselves arm the divine wrath against us. We force an unwilling God to punish the enormities of our crimes. It is almost that we do not allow Him to spare us. For, though no sign of injustice can ever fall on or be apparent in Him, we act in such a way that if He did not punish the enormities of our crimes He would seem to be unjust.

(10) You say someone who was once a sinner is perhaps no longer a sinner. Is there any limit to wrongdoing? Do not men first give up life itself rather than wickedness? Who is he who does not die with his sins and, in a way, is buried with and in his crimes? Of them truly can be said most fittingly that saying of the prophet:[22] 'their sepulchres are their homes forever, and are compared to foolish cattle and are like unto them.' And would we were like cattle! It would indeed have been better to have gone astray through

---
21 Rom. 2.4-5.
22 Ps. 48.12-13.

bovine folly. Our transgression is made worse and more criminal because they have sinned, not in ignorance, but in contempt of God.

Is this true of laymen only, and of none of the clergy? Is this true of men of the world only, and not of few among the religious also who are given over to wordly vices under the appearance of religion? These, after the lewdness and crime of their past sins have taken on themselves the title of sanctity. Others, not by their way of life but by profession, have changed only their name and not their lives. They think that the height of divine worship consists in their costume rather than in action, and have cast off their garments, but not their minds.

For what reason do those men think they are less guilty of evil desire who, when they are said to have done a kind of penance, do not put aside their old way of life just as they put aside their costume? They do almost everything in such a way that you would think they have not so much done penance for their sins committed beforehand as they repent afterwards of having done penance. They seem not so much to have repented that they lived bad lives formerly than that they promised to live good lives afterwards. They know I am telling the truth and they give testimony to me in their own consciences. I am speaking especially about the many religious who, after accepting the reputation that accompanies one who has done penance, are candidates for new honors and purchasers of power far more ample than they previously possessed.

They wish to be not men of the world only, but even something more than that. They are not satisfied with what they were before, unless they are greater afterwards than they were formerly. How, therefore, do men such as these not repent of having done penance, just as they do not repent of having thought a little about conversion and God? They abstain from their own wives, but do not abstain from the invasion of other men's property; they profess bodily continence, but are debauched by incontinency of heart.

This is certainly a new kind of conversion. They do not do what is lawful, and they commit acts against the law. They abstain from lawful sexual intercouse, but not from plunder. What are you doing in your foolish delusions? God forbade sin, not marriage. Your deeds do not' agree with your inclinations. You should not be the friends of crime, you who call yourselves strivers after virtues. What you do is absurd. This is not conversion, but aversion. Cease from your sins, you who, as the rumor is, have long since given up the burden of lawful marriages. It is indeed right that you cease from all crime. However, if you think that it is difficult and impossible to refrain from all, then certainly refrain from the greatest and unnatural.

Grant, whoever you are, that your neighbors are unable to abide near you. Grant that the poor are unable to live near you. Grant that you are the persecutor of many needy persons and the destroyers of the wretched. Grant that you are the scourge of all, as long as they are outsiders. I ask at least spare your own, and if not all of them, because you perhaps think it burdensome and difficult to spare all your own, then at least spare all those of yours who preferred you not only to their other relatives and kinsmen, but even to those persons most near to them and their own very loved children. And why do I speak of children and sons? They have preferred you almost over their hearts and hopes. They did not act praiseworthily indeed and whoever even acted in this way recognized his own error. You, who received advantage from the error, what do you care? You are especially indebted to him, because he sinned in an excess of love for you. He was, indeed, blind in his love for you, and for this he is pointed out and blamed by all. For this very reason you have become more harmful to him because he made himself blamed by all out of love of you.

(11) What do you find similar to this among the barbarian Goths? Which of them injures those who love him, attacks him who likes him, and cuts the throat of his friend with his dagger? You persecute those who love you; you cut off the hands of those who offer gifts; you kill your nearest loving ones. And do you not fear? Are you not frightened? What would you do if you had not felt the immediate judgment of God in the scourging you are now getting? On top of this, you add and constantly pile up new crimes on your former evils. Consider what punishments remain for you who commit graver sins when even lesser faults are customarily punished by devils.

Be content now, I say, with the robberies of friends and comrades. Let it suffice that the poor were harried. Let it suffice that beggars were despoiled by you. Hardly anybody near you can be without fear, hardly anybody near you can be secure. Torrents gushing out of the Alpine crags or fires fanned by the wind are more easily borne. And, I might say, the sailors who are devoured by the whirlpool of Charybdis or, as they say, by the dogs of Scylla do not die such a death.

You evict your neighbors from their little holdings and your relatives from home and property. As it is written:[23] 'shall you alone dwell on the earth?' This is indeed the one thing which you cannot obtain. However much you seize all, however much you invade all, you will always find a neighbor. I ask, look at others whom, whether you wish it or not, you yourself even regard favorably. Look at others whom, whether you wish it or not, you yourself even admire. They are higher than

---

23 Isa. 5.8.

the rest in honor and equal in esteem. They are greater in power and less in their humility. You know perfectly well, you to whom I am now speaking, about whom I am speaking. You, the same man about whom I now complain, should recognize whom I am honoring by this praise.

And would that there were many who might be praised. The goodness of many might be the salvation of all. Grant that you are unwilling to be worthy of praise. Why do you, I ask, wish to be worthy of damnation? Why is nothing dearer to you than injustice, nothing more pleasurable than avarice? Why is nothing more cherished than rapacity? Why do you judge nothing more precious than wickedness, nothing more profitable than plunder? Learn the true good from a pagan, who says:[24] 'we should be fenced around by charity and goodwill, not by arms.' Therefore, your way of thinking leads you astray; the wickedness of a base and blind mind deceives you. If you wish to be upright, powerful, and great, you must excel all others in honesty, not in ill will.

I once read somewhere, 'no one is evil but a fool: for if he were wise, he would prefer to be good.' And you, therefore, if you can at this point return to sanity, cast aside wickedness if you wish to possess wisdom. For, if you desire to be wise or sound-minded at all, you must change and free yourself from yourself completely. Deny yourself, therefore, lest you be denied by Christ; disown yourself, in order that you may be received by Christ; lose yourself, lest you perish. As the Saviour says,[25] 'For whosoever shall lose his life for My sake shall gain it.' Therefore, love this so profitable loss that you may obtain true gain. You will not be completely set free by God unless you yourself denounce yourself.

---

24 Pliny, *Panegeric 49.*
25 Luke 9.24.

BOOK SIX

I PERSONALLY have been speaking for a long time and seem to have overstepped the rules of disputation. Doubtless, he who reads (if there is anyone who, on account of Christ, reads these words written for the love of Christ) is perchance thinking of saying about me, 'Since the subject he pursues is a general one, what does it add to his argument that he heap up so much evidence against one person. Grant that such a person—as you have thought—about whom he spoke exists as he is described. But how does one man's crime thwart another man's goodness, or, what is much more important, how is the cause of all injured by the crime of one?'

I can prove by definite examples that it is injured. Achar at one time took by theft 'something of the anathema,' and the crime of one man was the ruin of all.[1] David ordered the people of Israel to be counted, and the Lord punished his error by the destruction of the whole people.[2] Rapsaces said certain things that were an insult to God, and God struck down to the ground 185,000 men because the insolent tongue of one man spoke evil of Him.[3] Not unjustly does the blessed Apostle Paul order a pestilent fellow cast out of the church, and he showed why he so ordered by saying:[4] 'because a little leaven corrupts the whole mass.' Hence, we know clearly that very often one bad man is the destruction of many.

---

1 Jos. 7.1-5.
2 2 Kings 24.
3 Isa. 36.37. (Rabsaces)
4 1 Cor. 5.6.

Nor does this happen with injustice. Whoever reads this must understand that I have not said unnecessarily certain things about one bad man, because it is written that through one man the wrath of the divine majesty has very often been kindled. But I am not confining my arguments to this delimitation. Neither must we think that one man hinders all, since all mutually hinder one another. It is not right that we think all are jeopardized through one, since all jeopardize one another. In a way, all are rushing to destruction, or certainly, that I may say it more leniently, almost all.

Whence comes this good fortune to the Christian people, that the number of evil-doers would be less or even the same as the number of good? O lamentable misery! O mournful misery! How unlike, today, is the Christian people itself, that is, to what it formerly was! At that time, because they lied, Peter the chief of the Apostles punished Ananias and Saphira with death.[5] The most blessed Paul also expelled one evil man from the church, lest he make many evil by his presence.[6]

Today, we are even content with an equal number of good and evil men. Why do I say we are content? Rather, it would be right for us to exult and dance with joy if that parity should happen to us. Behold how much we have fallen back. Behold how much we have fallen behind that purity of the Christian people, that purity by which all were formerly untainted. Behold how much we have been reduced, when we think the Church would be happy if it had within it as many good as evil men. For, how could we judge the Church not blessed if it had half its members guiltless, the Church which we today lament is almost all sinful?

Hence, since this is the case, it was unnecessary, unnecessary indeed for me to speak so at length about one evil man.

---

5 Acts 5,1-11.
6 1 Cor. 5,6-7.

It was unnecessary for me to weep over one man's crimes, for all men's crimes or almost all must be wept for and lamented. There are many such evil men. Certainly, what is not less sinful, they desire to be such and they labor by their performance of evil works not to appear otherwise. Thus, although they commit lesser evils because they are capable only of lesser evils, they are, however, not less evil because they would not want to be less evil if they could.

In short, because they are capable of one thing, they are such by desire and their will does not lag behind. Insofar as their ability permits, they strive to excel. Although their rivalry is found in most dissimilar things, it is similar to that of good men. Just as good men wish to surpass all others in the honesty of their minds, so the evil desire to surpass in depravity. Just as it is the glory of the good to be better daily, so it is the achievement of all the evil to be worse. Just as the best men desire to ascend the heights for all virtues, so the worst men wish to win for themselves the palm for all vices.

This, indeed, is to our particular misfortune, that is, especially to us Christians, who, as I have said, think that wickedness is wisdom and about whom God particularly says:[7] 'I will destroy the wisdom of the wise and I will reject the understanding of the prudent.' And about whom the Apostle cried out:[8] 'if any man seems to be wise, let him become as a fool in order that he may be wise.' This means that, if any man wishes to be wise, let him be good, because nobody is truly wise unless he is truly good. We, on the contrary, through the imperfection of our evil minds, and, as God says, through 'our reprobate sense,'[9] reject goodness for folly and love levity

---
7 1 Cor. 1.19.
8 1 Cor.3.18.
9 Rom. 1.28.

for wisdom and we believe we are daily that much more prudent as we are worse .

(2) I ask: What hope of betterment is there for us, who are induced to evil not by error of belief, but who strive with the zeal of our evil purpose, so that we seem to be always worse? This is why I lamented a short time ago that we are much worse than the barbarians, because ignorance of the Law excuses them, while knowledge of the Law accuses us. They love evil over good through not having experienced truth, because they are ignorant of those things that are good. We since we possess the knowledge of the truth, know very well what things are good . . . .[10]

In the first place, there is almost no crime or vice which is not to be found at the games.[11] There it is the height of pleasure to see men die, or, what is worse and more cruel than death, to see them torn to shreds; to see the bellies of wild animals filled with human flesh; to see men eaten for the entertainment of those standing around; to see the pleasure of the onlookers, that is, to be devoured almost no less by the looks of men than by the teeth of beasts. And that this be done, there is a world of expense. With great care and pains are the preparations made. Hidden places are approached, impassable ravines are searched, impenetrable forests are wandered through, the cloudy Alps are climbed, the deep valleys are probed. In order that the bowels of men may be devoured by wild animals, nature is not allowed to hold anything in secret.

But, you say, these things are not done all the time. This is correct. That they are not always done is an excellent excuse for wrongdoing! As if, indeed, we should let acts which

---
10 Lacuna in text.
11 Cf. Tertullian, *De Spectaculis;* Ludwig Friedländer, *Roman Life and Manners under the Early Empire* (trans. J. H. Freese and Leonard A. Magnus, London 1913) 2.1-30.

injure God be done constantly, or let acts which are bad be done well because they are not done all the time. Murderers do not always kill. Yet they are murderers even when they are not killing, because all the while they are stained with murder. Robbers do not always rob. Yet they do not cease to be robbers, because even when they are not actually committing robbery they do not put the thoughts of robbery from their minds. In like manner, all those who delight in games of this sort are not mentally blameless of the guilt involved in looking at the games even when they are not looking, because they would always look if they could.

Nor is this the only sin. There are others greater. What are they? Are not hens fed by the consuls according to the custom of the old pagan profanations? Are not the auguries of the flying bird sought? Almost all those sacrifices are performed which the pagans of old thought foolish and laughable. When the very consuls do all those things, those men who give their names to the years and from whom the years themselves take their beginning, are we to believe that those years can proceed well for us which are begun with such ceremonies? Would that just as these things are done only for the consuls, so they would infect those only on whose account they are done.

It is most deadly and serious that, while these ceremonies are done with public contest, the honor of a very few becomes the crime of all, and thus, since two are placed in office each year, scarcely anyone anywhere escapes contamination.

(3) Let us presume that enough has been said about the games which, as you make excuse, are not performed all the time. However, let us speak about the daily obscenities. These the legions of devils have devised, of such a nature and so innumerable that even honest and upright minds can hardly overcome them all completely, although they can scorn and

tread underfoot some of them. Armies about to fight are said either to cut up with pitfalls, or fix with pilings, or sow with cavalary obstacles those places through which they know the enemy troops will come, so that, although some do not fall into all these traps, none fully escapes. In the same way, the demons have prepared so many alluring ambushes for the human race in this life that, even though one avoids most of them, he is, however, caught by one or another.

Indeed, because it would take long to speak about all these snares now, namely the ampitheaters, music halls, public processions, jesters, athletes, tumblers, pantomimes and other monstrosities, which disgust me to talk about, and because it is disgusting to have knowledge of such evil, I will speak only about the impurities of the circuses and theaters. Such things are done there that nobody can speak about them, let alone think of them, without being tainted.

For the most part, other vices claim for themselves particular portions of us: filthy thoughts affect our minds; immodest glances, our eyes; evil language, our ears. When one of these functions has gone astray, the rest can be without sin. But in the theaters none of our senses is free from guilt, because our minds are tainted by evil desires, our ears by hearing, our eyes by seeing. Indeed, all these scenes are so disgraceful that a person cannot even describe them and talk about them without shame. Who can talk about these imitations of evil things, these obscene voices and words, these base motions and foul gestures, and retain his sense of modesty intact? Thus we can understand how criminal are these sights when they forbid description. Indeed, some of the greatest crimes, such as murder, robbery, adultery, sacrilege, and others in the same vein, can be mentioned and argued about and the character of the speaker remains unimpaired. The impurities of the theaters are singular in that they cannot be honestly denounced in public.

Thus, there comes something new for the prosecutor when he discusses the baseness of these crimes, so that, although without doubt he who wishes to bring the charge is upright, he cannot speak and denounce these obscenities and his character remain whole. All other evils taint those who perform them, not those who see or hear them. Though you hear someone blaspheme, you are not tainted by the sacrilege because you mentally disagree. And if you come upon a robbery, you are not made evil by the act, because you abhor it in your mind.

The impurities of the game are unique, because, in a way, they make the crime one, both for those who perform them and those who watch them, For, while the spectators approve and gladly watch them, all perform them through sight and consent. Truly, that saying of the Apostle particularly falls not only on those who perform them, but even on those who consent to the performances, that they are worthy of death.[12] Therefore, in these representations of fornication the whole audience mentally commits fornication, and those who, perhaps, came in purity to the games, return from the theaters in adultery. For, not only do they commit fornication when they return home, but also when they come to the theater, for, by the very fact that anyone desires an obscene thing he is unclean while he hastens to uncleanliness.

(4) Since this is the case, behold what kind of acts either all, or almost all, Romans do. Yet we who do these things claim we are neglected by God. We say we are forsaken by our Lord, when we ourselves forsake the Lord. Let us suppose that our Lord is willing to watch over us, even though we do

---
12 Rom. 1.32.

not deserve it. Let us see if He can. See the countless thousands of Christians daily tarrying at the games where base performances are enacted. Can God watch over people like this? Can He watch over those who revel in the circuses and who commit adultery in the theaters?

Or, perhaps, do we wish and think it becoming that, when God sees us in the circuses and theaters, He also looks at those performances at which we look and at that wickedness on which we gaze? That He gazes at them with us, one or the other of the following must happen. If He deigns to see us, it follows that He must see those things where we are, or, if He averts His eyes from them, which is doubtless what happens, so He must likewise avert them even from us who are there. Nevertheless, we unceasingly do these things about which I have spoken.

Or do we think, perhaps, according to the custom of the old pagans, that we have a God of theaters and circuses? They made their theaters and circuses long ago because they believed that these were the delights of their idols. Why do we do these things, we who are certain that our God hates them? Certainly, if we knew that this wickedness pleases God, I would not forbid that we do them unceasingly.

If, indeed, we firmly belive that God abhors and hates these places, because in them there is just as much food for the devil as there is offense to God, how do we say that we worship God in church? We ever serve the devil in the obscenity of the games, and do this knowingly, understandingly and with well-considered deliberation. I ask, what hope shall there be for us before God, we who injure Him, not by chance or ignorance, but after the manner of those former giants whom we read to have attempted in their insane endeavors the heights of heaven and to have, as it were, climbed into the clouds?

In like manner, we, by the injuries which we constantly

inflict on God throughout the whole world, fight heaven as if by common agreement. To Christ, therefore (O monstrous madness), to Christ we offer circuses and mimes, and this in our day especially when we receive something good from Him, when some prosperity is granted by Him, or a victory is given by the Divinity over our enemies. And how do we seem to act otherwise in this affair than as one who injures a man bestowing a favor, or knocks down with violent reproaches the man who is kind to us, or pierces with a dagger the face of him who kisses us?

I ask all the powerful and rich of this world what punishment should be meted out to that slave who thinks up evil against a good and loving master, who hurls abuse at a well-deserving master, and returns insults for the freedom which he accepts. Doubtless, he who should not be allowed to return evil for evil and yet returns evil for good is considered guilty of the greatest of crimes. This, therefore, is what we do, we who are called Christians. We irritate God when He is merciful to us. We provoke Him by filthy impurities when He is favorably disposed, and we scourge Him with insults when He is kind to us.

(5) To Christ, therefore (O monstrous madness), to Christ we offer circuses and mimes, to Christ for His favors we return the indecencies of the theaters, to Christ we offer as sacrificial victims the vilest of games. Is this the teaching of our Saviour who became incarnate for our sake? Did He or His Apostles preach this? Was it on this account that he underwent the humility of human birth and undertook the shameful beginnings of earthly origin? Was it on this account He lay in a manger to whom angels ministered while He lay there? Was it for this He wished to be wrapped in swaddling clothes and ruled heaven while wearing them? Was it for this He

hung on a gibbet, whom the world feared as He hung there?

The Apostle says:[13] 'Who, on our account, though He was rich, became poor that you might become rich through His poverty.' The Apostle also says:[14] 'And being in the form of God, He humbled Himself even unto death, even unto the death of the cross.' Christ teaches us this when He bore these sufferings for us. We pay back a glorious substitute for His suffering, we who, when we receive redemption by His death, recompense Him with the most disgraceful lives. The most blessed Paul says:[15] 'For the grace of our Lord Jesus Christ has appeared, teaching us that denying ungodly lives and wordly desires, we should live soberly, justly and holy in this world; looking for that blessed hope and the coming of the glory of our Great God and our Saviour, Jesus Christ, who gave Himself for us in order that He might redeem us from all iniquity and cleanse a people acceptable to Himself, and followers of good works.'

Where are these men who do those things on account of which the Apostle says Christ came? Where are those men who flee the desires of the world and lead a life, just and holy? Where are they who in their good works show that they hope for the blessed hope, and, leading clean lives, prove thereby that they await the kingdom of God because they deserve to receive it? The Apostle says:[16] 'the Lord Jesus Christ came in order that He might cleanse a people acceptable to Himself, the followers of good works.'

Where is that cleansed people, where is that acceptable people, where are those followers of good works, where is that people of sanctity? Holy Scripture says:[17] 'Christ suffered

---
13 2 Cor. 8.9.
14 Phil. 2.8.
15 Titus 2.11-14.
16 *Ibid.*
17 1 Peter 2.21.

death for us, bequeathing us an example that we may follow in His footsteps.' We follow the footsteps of the Saviour in circuses, we follow the footsteps of the Saviour in theaters. Christ bequeathed us such an example, of whom we read that He wept, not that He laughed. Both are an example for us, because weeping is compunction of the soul, laughter the corruption of instruction. And therefore He said: 'Woe unto you who laugh because you will weep';[18] and 'blessed are you who weep because you will laugh.'[19] But we are not satisfied with laughing and rejoicing, unless we rejoice with sin and in madness, unless our laughter is mixed with impurities, unless it is mixed with disgraceful acts.

(6) I ask: What sort of misconception is this, what sort of foolishness? Can we not be constantly glad and laugh, unless we turn our laughter and our joy into a crime? Or, perhaps, do we think that simple joy is of no value and that there is no delight in laughter without crime? I ask: What evil is this or what madness? Let us laugh, I say, let us rejoice without stint and constantly, provided it is done innocently. What folly and madness that we do not consider laughter and joy to be valueless, unless they contain in themselves injury to God? Injury, indeed, and that the Greatest!

In the games there is a certain apostasy from the faith and a deadly deviation from the Creed and from the heavenly pledges. For, what is the first confession of faith of Christians in the saving baptism? What is it except that they profess they are renouncing the devil, his pomps and games and works. Therefore, according to our profession of faith, the games and pomps are the work of the devil.

How, therefore, O Christians, do you frequent the games

---
[18] Luke 6.25.
[19] Luke 6.21.

after baptism, the games which you confess to be the work of the devil? You have once renounced the devil and his games. You must know that when you return to the games you are returning knowingly and deliberately to the devil. For you have renounced both things, and at the same time you have said one is both. If you return to one, you resort to both. You say, 'I renounce the devil, his pomps, spectacles and works.'

What do you say next? You say, ' I believe in God, the Father Almighty, and in Jesus Christ, His Son.' The devil is renounced in order that God many be believed in, because he who does not renounce the devil does not believe in God. Therefore, he who goes back to the devil forsakes God. The devil is in his spectacles and in his pomps. Therefore, when we return to the spectacles of the devil, we forsake the faith of Christ. In this way, all the pledges of our faith are broken, and all that follows in the Creed sways to and fro and is overthrown. Nothing that follows is valid if the primary clause does not stand up.

Therefore, O Christian, tell me how do you think you are observing the commitments of the Creed, you who have lost the principles? Limbs without the head are of no value; all things look to their beginnings. The limbs, indeed, if they perish, drag all to the ground. When the root is taken away, the remains are either nonexistant, or, if they do live on, they are of no use, for nothing subsists without its head. Therefore, if to any man it seems a light crime to see the games let him look at all those things I have said, and he will see that in the games there is not pleasure, but death. What else is it than to incur death, to have lost the source of life? For, where the foundation of our faith is overthrown, life itself is strangled.

(7) Again, therefore, I must return to what I have often said: What is there like this among the barbarians? Where

among them are there circuses, where are there theaters, where the crime of different impurities; that is to say, the ruin of our hope and salvation? Even if they, being pagans, used these things, their sin and guilt would be less offensive to what is holy, because, although the sights would be impure, there would be no violation of the sacrament.

But we, what can we answer on our behalf? We hold and cast aside the faith, and we confess the gift of salvation equally as we deny it. Where, therefore, is our Christianity, we who receive the sacrament of salvation only for the purpose that we may sin afterwards with the greater crime of deviation from righteousness? We prefer stage plays to the churches of God. We spurn the altars and honor the theaters. We love things and worship things. God alone, in comparison with all other things, is vile to us.

Finally, besides other instances which prove it, one particular illustration establishes the point I am making. If, when it should happen—because it often does happen that on the same day on which an ecclesiastical feast occurs the public games are performed—I ask of everybody's conscience what place has greater crowds of Christian men: the spectators' benches at the public games or the entrance to the house of God? Do the crowds prefer the temple or the theater? Do they love more the teachings of the Gospel or the theatrical musicians; the words of life or the words of death; the words of Christ or the words of the mime?

There is no doubt that we love more that which we prefer. For, on every day of the fatal games, whatever feast of the Church it may be, not only do those who say they are Christians not come to the church, but, if any come perhaps unwittingly, if they hear the games being performed, while they are already in the church, they leave the church. They spurn the temple of God in order that they may run to the theater. They leave the church in order to fill the circus. We leave Christ at the altar and feed our adulterous eyes with the most impure visions and with the fornication of the vilest games. Very rightly, therefore, the Lord has said to us: 'on account of your dirt you have been expelled into banishment.' And again He says:[20] 'the altars of this laughter shall be banished.'

(8) But it can be answered that these performances are not enacted in all Roman cities. That is true. I also add that they are not now done in those places where they were done formerly. They are not now done in the city of Mainz, but that is because it is ruined and destroyed. They are not performed at Cologne, but that is because it is filled with the enemy. They are not done in the most excellent city of Trier, but that is because it is laid low by invasion, four times repeated.[21] They are not done in most of the cities of Gaul and Spain.

Therefore, woe to us and our iniquities; woe to us and our impurities! What hope is there for the commonalty of Christians in the sight of God, when these evils cease to exist in Roman cities only from that time when they began to be under the law of the barbarians? Vice and impurity are, as it were, native characteristics of the Romans, and are, as it were, their mind and nature. Wherever there are Romans, there is much vice.

Perhaps you think this is a serious and wrong accusation. It is serious indeed, if false. But you say, how is it not false, when the performances of which I have been speaking are now given in only a few Roman cities? You say that most of these cities are no longer polluted with the crime of these

---

20 I have been unable to locate these texts.
21 Alois Haemmerle, *Studia Salviana* 1.19-26, gives the years as 406, 411-13, 418, 438-39.

iniquities. Although those cities are the very sites and homes of former wickedness, nevertheless, those performances which were enacted there formerly are never done there now.

We must consider why these towns are still the sites and lodging places of the games, though the games have ceased to exist. They are still the sites and homes of vices because all manner of impure actions were done in them formerly. The games themselves are not now performed, since they cannot be peformed because of the misery and poverty of our time. That they were formerly enacted was due to depravity. That they are not enacted now is due to necessity.

The fall of the imperial fisc and the beggary of the Roman treasury do not allow the wide lavishing of expenses on unprofitable business. Let them still waste and cast as much money as they want, as it were, into the dirt. They cannot lose as much as formerly, because there is not as much to lose. Inasmuch as it pertains to our lewd desires and most impure pleasure, we would, indeed, wish to have more, if only we could convert more into this mire of wickedness.

This proves how much we would want to squander were we rich and powerful, when we, as beggars, spend so much. For, this is the crime and ruin of our present way of life that, when in our poverty we do not possess what we can spend, our wicked minds want still more money to cast away. We cannot flatter ourselves any of this account, so that we can say that these expenses which were formerly incurred are not now incurred in all our cities.

These things are no longer done in all cities, because the cities where these things happened no longer exist, or, if they were once done there, [the means] to do them [are lacking].[22] Where they used to be done, they cannot be done. Just so, God

---
22 Lacuna in text.

Himself spoke to sinners through His prophet, because 'the Lord remembered these things and,' he says, 'He ascended over His heart, and the Lord was not able to bear more because of the evil of your endeavors and the abominations which you have done; and your land is made into a desolation, a wonder and a curse.'[23] Through these things, therefore, it has already happened that the greater part of the Roman world is become a desolation, a wonder and a curse.

(9) Would that these shows had been performed only of old and that the Romans in their wickedness would cease at some time or other performing them. Perhaps, as it is written, God would be appeased for our sins, but in no way do we act so as to appease Him. Unceasingly, we add evil to evil and we heap sins on sins, and, though the greatest portion of us has already perished, we act so that we all will perish.

Who, I ask, does not fear for himself as he sees another man killed beside him? Who sees his neighbor's house burn and does not strive with all his might that he himself is not consumed in the fire? We not only see our neighbors burn, but the greatest portion of our own bodies is already on fire. What sort of criminal wickedness is this! We are aflame, we are aflame, and yet we do not fear the flames with which we are already aflame.

As I have said, that sins which were done formerly are not now done everywhere is the result of misery, not of being taught a lesson. I can easily prove this. Bring back the conditions of the old days, and immediately the old pleasures are restored to whatever they were wont to be. I add further. Insofar as it pertains to the desires of men, although the games are not everywhere, they still are everywhere because the Roman people wish them to be everywhere. When a man is restrained

---

23 Jer. 44.21-22.

from evil by sheer necessity alone, the very desire for a base act is condemned as the act itself.

If, as I have said, according to the saying of our Lord:[24] 'whosoever looks on a woman to lust after her is guilty of adultery conceived in his heart,' we can understand that, although necessity restrains us from committing base and culpable acts, we are still condemned for the very willing of base acts. And what shall I say about the will to do these acts? Almost all commit them at every possible opportunity. Finally, when the residents of any town come to Ravenna or Rome, a part joins the Roman people in the circus and a part joins the people of Ravenna in the theater. Therefore, let nobody think himself excused because of place or absence. All who are joined to each other in their will to do base actions are one in the baseness of their actions. We flatter ourselves especially on the probity of our way of life. We flatter ourselves on the rarity of our vices!

I say further that not only these corruptions of the infamous games which were formerly enacted are still with us, but that they are with us much more criminally than they were before. Then the members of the Roman world flourished intact; the public treasury had made the granaries adequate and citizens of all the towns were affluent in riches and delights. Scarcely could the authority of religion hold a censorship of morals amid such abundance of things.

Then, indeed, the authors of base pleasures feasted at will in most places, but all things were filled and stuffed to overflowing. Nobody thought of the State's expenses, nobody thought of the State's losses, because the cost was not felt. The State itself sought how it might squander what it was already scarcely able to acquire. The heaping up of wealth

---
24 Matt. 5.28.

which had already exceeded its limit was overflowing even into trifling matters.

But what can be said of the present-day situation? The old abundances have gone from us. The resources of former times have gone. We are already poverty-stricken, yet we do not cease to be spendthrift. Poverty is even accustomed to aid wasteful wards in that they cease to be wicked as soon as they have ceased to be rich. We are only a new kind of wastrels and profligates, in whom opulence ceases to exist, but in whom evil continues to endure. With us, therefore, the causes of corruption are not in enticements, as with other men, but in our hearts. Our wickedness is in our mind, so that the loss of our wealth does not move us to amend our ways of life. We proceed to sin through love for evil things.[25]

(10) Although up to this point I have made sufficient mention of how great are the vices of the Romans, vices with which the barbarians are not befouled, I shall yet add many things which are not yet told. Before I begin, let me remind you that any kind of fault which is injurious to God should in no way seem light to anybody. It is never to be allowed that a famous and illustrious man be dishonored by anyone. If anyone should dishonor him, he is adjudged guilty by legal decrees and the author of the insult is condemned by law. Since that is the case, how much more difficult is it for anyone to atone for the crime of being injurious to God? The guilt of him who commits the wrong always increases through the dignity of him who bears the injury, because the offense of him who commits the act is necessarily greater in proportion to the greatness of the person who is injured.

Hence, we read in the Law that even those who seem to have acted lightly against the sacred commandments have,

---
25 Text corrupt, but this according to Pauly's edition.

nevertheless, been punished most severely.[26] This is that we might understand that nothing which pertains to God must be considered lightly, because even what seems to be very little in fault is made great by the injury to God. What did Oza, the Levite of God, do against the heavenly command when he tried to steady the tottering ark of the Lord?[27] There was nothing on this point prescribed by the Law. Yet, immediately that he steadied the ark, he was struck down. Not that he was insolent in manner or undutiful in mind. Yet he was undutiful in his very act, because he went beyond his orders.

When a man of the Israelite community gathered wood on the Sabbath,[28] he was killed, and this by the judgment and order of God, a Judge most loving and merciful and who, doubtless, preferred to spare rather than kill him if the reason for severity had not overcome the reason for mercy. One man who was more unmindful perished, lest many be undone afterwards through lack of caution. And why do I speak of single individuals?

The whole Hebrew people, when they made their journey through the desert, lost some of their group because they longed for their customary flesh meats.[29] Indeed, lest they desire what had not been forbidden them, God wished, I believe, to further legally the observance of the law so that He might curb their rebellious longings. God so acted that the whole people would more easily know how much they should avoid the things He had forbidden by His heavenly writings, when even those faults provoked Him which He had not yet forbidden by law.

The same people also groaned at the hardships they under-

---
26 Exod. 31.12-18.
27 2 Kings 6.6-8.
28 Num. 15.32-36.
29 Num. 11.4-6.

went and on account of this they were punished by heavenly blows, not because it is unlawful for him who labors to groan, but their groaning was based on ingratitude, as it were, accusing God as the author of excessive work. From this we should understand how much we who enjoy the blessing of agreeable things should please God, when it is not even lawful to complain about those things which seem disagreeable.

(11) Perhaps you are asking what is the purpose of these examples? What else, without doubt, except that nothing which is offensive to God should be considered light. For we were speaking of the public games, the mockeries of our hope, the mockeries of our life. While we play in theaters and circuses, we perish according to that saying of the Sacred Word:[30] 'a fool works mischief as if it were a sport.' We, while we laugh among base and unbecoming things, commit crimes, and indeed not the smallest crimes, but crimes that are more punishable because, when they seem to be small in kind, they are the most deadly in their deadliness.

There are two evils which are greatest, namely, when a man destroys himself or injures God. Both are committed in the public games. Through criminal acts of baseness the eternal salvation of the Christian people is extinguished in them, and through sacrilegious belief the divine majesty is violated. There is no doubt that they injure God, since they are consecrated to idols.

Minerva is worshipped and honored in the gymnasia, Venus in the theaters, Neptune in the circuses, Mars in the arena, Mercury in the wrestling schools, and therefore the worship of superstitions is according to the inclination of those who worship. Whatever is of an impure nature is done in the theaters. Whatever is luxurious, in the wrestling schools. What-

---
30 Prov. 10.23.

ever is immoderate, in the circuses. Whatever is mad, in the arena pits.

Here there is wantoness, there lasciviousness. Here there is intemperance, there insanity. And everywhere, the devil. Moreover, in the particular sites of the games all kinds of devils are to be found, because they preside over the abodes dedicated to their worship. Therefore, in spectacles of this kind there is not allurement alone or vice alone. It is a kind of sacrilege for a Christian man to be associated with this superstition, because he shares in the worship of those devils in whose festivities he takes delight.

Although this is always serious, it becomes still more unbearable when beyond the accustomed habit of our life, adversities or exceedingly good fortune make our attitude all the more blameworthy, because God is to be appeased more when we suffer adversity and offended less when we enjoy prosperity. God should be appeased when He is angry; He should not be offended while He is being appeased. Adversities come to us through God's wrath; good fortune through His favor.

We, however, do everything backwards. You ask how? Listen. In the first place, if won over by His mercy (for we never live in such a way that we would deserve being heard), if, as I have said, won over by Himself alone, we are granted by God peaceful days and abundant harvests, tranquillity rich in all things and abundance increasing beyond our prayers, then we are corrupted by so great a prosperity of good fortune, we are corrupted by so great a depravity of insolent manners, that we completely forget God and ourselves.

The Apostle says that all the good to be obtained from God-given peace consists in this; 'that we lead a quiet and peaceful life in all godliness and chastity.'[31] Yet, for this only do we use

---
31 1 Tim. 2.2.

the peace given by God, that we live in drunkenness and luxury, in wickedness and in plunder, in all kinds of crime and wrong-doing. Indeed, we accept from a giving God the benefits of a given peace as a dispensation to infamy, and we accept an armistice for peace in order that we may sin more freely and safely.

Therefore, we are unworthy of heavenly gifts, we who do not put God's favors to good use and who make of the means of good works the material for being evil. Hence it happens that the peace itself which is thus treated by us is against us, nor does it help to accept a thing by which we are made worse. Who can believe this? We change the nature of things by our iniquities, and those which God made good by the gift of His love we make evil for ourselves by our vicious morals.

(12) But, of course, we who are corrupted by prosperity are corrected by adversity and we, whom a long peace has made profligate, strife makes us temperate. Have the peoples of the cities who were lewd in prosperity begun to be chaste in adversity? Has drunkenness, which increased with peaceful and abundant years, ceased immediately with the plundering done by the enemy?

Italy has already been laid waste by many calamities. Have the vices of the Italians ceased on that account? The city of Rome has been besieged and taken by storm.[32] Have the Romans ceased to be frenzied and blasphemous? Barbarian nations have overrun Gaul. Insofar as it pertains to evil living, are the crimes of the Gauls not the same as they were? The Vandals peoples have crossed into Spanish territory.[33]

---

32 The reference is to Alaric's capture of Rome (410).
33 The Vandals established themselves temporarily in Gaul about 406 and crossed over into Spain with the advent of the Visigoths in Southern Gaul in 411-412.

The lot of the Spaniards is indeed changed, but their wickedness is not changed.

Lastly, lest any part of the world be immune from fatal evils, wars have begun to cross over the seas.[34] They have laid waste and overthrown cities which were cut off by the sea in Sardinia and Sicily, the imperial storehouses. The vital blood vessels, as it were, being cut, they have captured Africa itself, which is, so to say, the heart of the Empire. And then what? When the barbarians entered these lands, did the inhabitants cease in their vices, perhaps in fear? Or, as even the worst of slaves are wont to be corrected for the moment, did terror immediately wrest modesty and restraint from them?

Who can judge the enormity of this evil? The barbarian peoples were sounding their arms around the walls of Cirta and Carthage and the Christian population of Carthage still went mad in the circuses and reveled in the theaters.[35] Some were strangled outside the walls; others were committing fornication within. A portion of the people was captive of the enemy without the walls and a portion was captive of vice within the walls.

I do not know whose lot was worse. The former were captive in the flesh outside, but the latter were captive in soul within. Of the two deadly evils, I think it is lighter for a Christian to bear captivity of the body rather than of the soul, according to that which the Saviour Himself teaches in the Gospel, that the death of souls is much more serious than the death of bodies.[36] Do we believe, perhaps, that that people was not captive in their souls who then rejoiced in the captivity of their own people? Was he not captive in heart and soul who laughed

---
34 The Vandals were not allowed to settle in Spain by the Visigoths. Between Visigothic pressure and the invitation of Roman factions in North Africa, the Vandals crossed the Mediterranean in 429.
35 Capture of Carthage (439) by Genseric.
36 Luke 9.24-25.

amid the punishments of his own people, who did not understand that he was being strangled in the strangulation of his own people, who did not think he was dying in their death?

As I have said, the noise of battle outside the walls and of the games within, the voices of the dying outside and the voices of the reveling within, were mingled. Perhaps there scarcely could be distinguished the cries of the people who fell in battle and the yelling of the people who shouted in the circus. When all these things were being done in this fashion, what else did such people accomplish, unless perhaps, since God was still unwilling to destroy them, they themselves exacted their own destruction?

(13) Why do I speak about things that are far away and are, so to say, removed into another world, when I know that in my own native country[37] and in the cities of Gaul almost all the more excellent men have been made worse by their misfortunes. Indeed, I myself have seen at Trier men, noble in birth and elevated in dignity, who, though already despoiled and plundered, were actually less ruined in property than in morality.[38] Though they were despoiled and stripped, something of their property still remained to them, but nothing whatsoever of self-restraint. They were more dangerous enemies in themselves than the enemy outside, so that, though they were overthrown by the barbarians from without, they were still overthrown more by themselves.

It is sad to refer to what I saw there. Honored old men, tottering Christians, the ruin of their city already imminent, tended slavishly to their palates and lusts. What is the first accusation here? That they were honored, that they were old, that they were Christians, or that they were in danger? Who

---

37 This is direct proof of Salvian's birth in Gaul.
38 Probably the first sack of Trier (406).

would believe that actions like these would be possible either by old men when life was secure, or by boys at a critical moment or ever by Christians?

The leading men in the city were laying down at banquets; they forgot honor; they forgot age; they forgot religion; they forgot the dignity of their name. They were stuffed with food, lax from wine-bibbing, frantic from shouting, frenzied with revelry. They were bereft of no less than their senses. Indeed, because they were almost constantly like this, they no longer had senses. Though these were the actual circumstances, what I am about to say is much worse. Not even the ruin of their cities put an end to this waywardness.

The wealthiest city of Gaul was taken by storm four times.[39] It is easy to know of which one I speak. The first captivity should have sufficed for amendment, so that the repetition of their sins would not renew destruction.

What followed? What I say is incredible. The continuance of calamities in that city caused an increase of crimes there. Like the serpentine monster which multiplied when killed, as the fables have it, so even in the most excellent city of Gaul crimes increased by the very blows with which crimes were checked so that you would think that the punishment of crime was, as it were, the mother of vice. What next? It has come to this, through the daily multiplication of corrupting evils, that it would be easier for that city to be without an inhabitant than for almost any of its inhabitants to be without crime. This, then, is the condition in that city.

What about another city, not far distant, but almost of the same magnificence?[40] Is there not the same destruction of both property and morals? Beyond the fact that the two common

---
39 Trier was the seat of the Praetorian Prefect and therefore the most important city in Gaul.
40 Probably Mainz.

evils, avarice and drunkenness, had there destroyed all, it came to this at least that the leaders of that very city, in their avid greed for wine, did not arise from their feasting when the enemy was entering the city. I believe God clearly wished to show them why they were perishing, since at the actual moment of perishing they were doing that very thing through which they had come to final perdition. I saw there tear-inspiring sights. It did not matter whether they were boys or old men. There was one buffoonery, one levity. All kinds of evil went on at the same time: luxury, drinking to excess, immorality. All were doing everything alike: they played, drank, and committed adultery. The old and honored men were wanton in their feasting. Those already too weak to live were imposing in their wine. Those too infirm to walk were robust in drinking. Those who staggered in their steps were quick in dancing.

What resulted from all this? Through all that I have said they were fallen so low that in them was fulfilled the saying of the Sacred Word:[41] 'wine and women make men fall away from God.' For, while they drink, gamble, commit adultery, and are mad, they begin to deny Christ. And we wonder after all these things that they have suffered the ruin of their own property, they who long before have gone to pieces mentally! Therefore, let nobody think that city perished only at the time of its own ruin. Where such things are done, the inhabitants had already [morally] perished long before they [physically] perished.

(14) I have spoken about the most famous cities. What about other cities in other parts of Gaul? Have they not fallen because of similar vices of their inhabitants? Their crimes possessed them in such a way that they did not fear danger. Their

---
41 Eccli. 19.2.

captivity was foretold them and they were not afraid. Indeed, fear was taken away from the sinners to obviate the possibility of caution. Thus, when the barbarians were located almost in plain sight of all, there was neither fear of men nor protection of cities. So great was the blindness of soul, or rather so great was the blindness of sins, that, without doubt, nobody wished to perish, yet nobody did anything to prevent his perishing.

Everything was carelessness and inactivity, negligence and gluttony. Drunkenness and sleep took hold of all, according to that which has been written about such men, 'because the sleep of the Lord had fallen on them.'[42] Indeed, a sleep flowed in upon them that ruin might follow. For when, as it is written, his measure of iniquities being full and the sinner deserves to perish, foreknowledge is taken away from him, lest he escape perishing.[43] I have said enough about these things. I think I have proved clearly enough what I proposed. This was that the vices of the citizens never ceased, even to the critical moment of destruction of their cities.

(15) Perhaps you are saying that these things happened in the past, or no longer exist, or will forever cease. If today any city or province is struck down by heavenly blows, or is overrun, humbled, converted, and corrected by a hostile population, if practically all peoples who bear the Roman name prefer to perish rather than be corrected, it is easy to see they prefer to die rather than live without their vices. This can be proved in a few words by the fact that the greatest city of Gaul was destroyed three times by successive captures, and, when the whole city had been burned, evil increased after its destruction.

---

42 1 Kings 26.12.
43 Gen. 15.16.

Those whom the enemy did not kill in the city's ruin, disaster overwhelmed after its ruin. They who escaped death in the city's destruction did not survive disaster after its fall, for wounds, struck deeply, killed some with lingering deaths. Others were burned by the flames of the enemy or even suffered the pain of torture after the flames were extinguished. Some died of hunger, some of nakedness, and some wasted away. Others were numbled with cold. Thus, they hastened through different ways of dying into a single door of death.

What followed? Other cities were also afflicted by the destruction of one town. Here and there—something that I myself have seen and experienced—lay the nude and torn bodies of both sexes, infecting the eyes of the city as they were torn to pieces by birds and dogs. The deadly stench of the dead brought death to the living. Death was breathed from death. And thus even those who escaped the destruction of the aforemetioned city suffered the evils of another destruction.

What happened after this, I ask? Who can judge this kind of madness? A few nobles who survived destruction demanded circuses from the emperors[44] as the greatest relief for the destroyed city. Would that there be given me here and now eloquence equal to the moment for presenting the indignity of this affair, that there would be as much power in my complaint as there is sorrow in its cause.

Who can decide what must be accused first in the events I have narrated: irreverence or foolhardiness, extravagance or madness? Everything is in these words. What is more irreverent than to demand something that is to the injury of God? What is more foolhardy than not to consider the merits of what you ask? What is more hopeless extravagance than to desire the things of luxury while in mourning? What is more

---

44 This probably refers to the reign of Honorius and Constantius in the West, 420-421.

obtuse than to be in the midst of evil and have no understanding of the evils? Of all these, madness is the least culpable, because the will does not intend crime where sin is committed in madness. But how much more blameworthy are those about whom I speak, because they acted as madmen, even though in their right minds.

O people of Trier, do you therefore long for circuses, and this when you are devastated and knocked out, after you have suffered disaster and bloodshed, punishment and captivity, after so many destructions have overrun your city? What is more tearful than this foolishness, what is more mournful than this madness? I confess, I believed you were most wretched when you were suffering destruction, but I see you are more wretched still when you asked for public spectacles. I thought that in destruction you had lost only your property and goods; I did not know you had also lost your senses and intelligence.

Do you ask for theaters and demand a circus from the authorities? I ask you: for what place, for what people, for what city? For a burned and destroyed city, for a people captive and slaughtered, a people that either has perished or is in mourning? For a people, for whom, if anything survives, it is only calamity; for a people who all are anxious in their sorrow, or exhausted in their tears, or prostrate in their bereavment; for a people of whom you almost often do not know whose lot is worse or harder, that of the dead or of the living? So great are the miseries of the living that they surpass the unhappy lot of the dead.

O citizens of Trier, do you, therefore, seek public games? Where, I ask, are they to be held? Over the funeral pyre and ashes, over the bones and blood of the dead? What part of the city is free from all these evils? Where has not a stream of blood been shed? Where not the bodies strewn? Where not the lacerated limbs of those who fell? Everywhere there is the appearance of a captured city. Everywhere the horror of captivity. Everywhere the image of death. The most unhappy remains of a people lie on the grave mounds of their dead, and you still ask for circuses? The city is black from fire and you usurp the face of festivity. All things weep and you are glad. Especially do you further provoke God by your most disgraceful enticements; and by the worst of superstitions you arouse the anger of God. I do not wonder at all, I do not wonder that the evils which took place have happened to you, for, since three destructions did not correct you, you deserve to perish by a fourth.

(16) All these happenings I have discussed somewhat more fully in order to prove that all these calamities which we have suffered have been borne, not by the lack of God's providence or through His neglect, but rather in justice and judgment, in a most uniform dispensation and worthy retribution. We have suffered them, because no portion of the Roman world or the Roman name, however gravely struck by heavenly punishment, was ever fully corrected. Therefore, we never deserve to enjoy prosperity, because we are not corrected by adversity. Good things are from time to time given to us, unworthy though we are, because the good Lord is, as it were, a most indulgent father. Though He never ceases to humble us for our sins, He does not, however, allow us to be afflicted for long. Therefore, He now punishes His people with adversity as a discipline, and then He favors them with peace as an indulgence.

The best and most skilled doctors give different cures for different diseases and aid some with sweet and others with bitter medicaments. They cure some by burning with cautery and some by soothing poultices. To some they administer difficult surgical amputations. On others they pour the soothing smoothness of oil. The same cure is sought, although by different methods. So also our God. When He compels us by more harsh blows, He cures, as it were, by cautery and amputation. When He favors us with prosperity, He is again comforting us, as it were, with oil and poultices. Through the application of varied medicaments, He wishes to lead us all to good health.

Even the worst of slaves whom punishment does not correct are wont to be corrected by flattery, and they are made submissive by kindness whom flogging did not make submissive to their masters. Children and stubborn little boys whom threats and the stick do not make obedient are often led to obedience by little cakes and flattery. Hence we must understand that we are more worthless than the most worthless slaves and more foolish than the most brainless children, we whom neither flogging corrects as it does bad slaves, nor flattery wins, as it does children.

(17) I think I have proved sufficiently how punishment has not corrected any people who bear the Roman name. It remains that I prove how neither the gifts nor complimentary words of God correct us. What are the gifts and kind words of God? What, indeed, but our peace and quiet and the tranquillity of prosperity which serves our desires and wishes? Therefore, let me say something special, since the case demands it. As often as we are in fear, in distress and danger, when our cities are besieged by the enemy or our provinces devastated and depopulated, or when the members of the State are wounded by various adversities, we implore with prayers the aid of a heavenly hand. If by the aid of divine mercy our cities are saved, or the depopulation is ended, or the hostile armies are put to flight and all fear is taken away by the gift of God, what do we do immediately after all that?

I believe we strive to compensate our Lord God in worship, honor and reverence for the benefits we have received from Him. This is in accordance with reason and it is the custom of human beings that thanks be given to the lenders of favors and that those bestowing gifts receive a return for their gifts. Perhaps we act in this manner and make human retribution at least to our God. When we receive good things from Him we return Him good things. We run immediately to the Lord's house. We prostrate our bodies on the ground. We beseech with joy mixed with tears. We decorate the sacred portals with votive offerings. We fill the altars with gifts. Because we ourselves are festive in His gifts, we also put on the face of our festivity in His temples, or certainly, what is not less pleasing to His heart, we renounce the former vices of our lives. We bring the offerings of good works. We offer sacrifices of our new conversion in return for our joys. Finally, we declare a holy war on all uncleanliness. We flee the madness of the circuses. We denounce the vileness of theatrical shows. We vow a new life to the Lord and make a sacrifice of ourselves to God in order to obtain His protection forever.

(18) Since these things I have enumerated should be done in return for God's recent favors, let us see what we actually do. We run directly to the games and take wings to their madness. The people flood the theaters and everybody revels in the circuses. God gives us good things that we be good. We, on the contrary, as often as we accept good, heap up our evils. God calls us by His favors to righteousness; we rush to unrighteousness. God by His favors calls us to repentance; we rush to destruction. God calls us to chastity; we rush to impurity.

Nobly do we respond to His sacred gifts. Nobly do we either acknowledge or honor His gifts, we who accept so many benefits from Him and compensate Him with so much injury. This very thing, is it not an injury to God, or can any injury be more unbecoming when there is much and great need for thanks?[45] Through the inveterate taint of all evils in us we can no longer be otherwise than evil, unless we completely cease to exist. I ask: What hope of good fruit is there in us?

They who sin in ignorance are corrected when they learn their error. They who are devoid of religion begin to change their way of life when they change their faith. Lastly, as I have said, they who are made evil by too great abundance or security cease to be bad when they cease to be secure. We do not fall through ignorance, nor are we ignorant of religion, nor are we corrupted by material prosperity and security. Everythings is just the opposite.

We know the true religion and are not excused by ignorance. We do not have the peace and wealth of former times. All things which were are either gone or changed. Only our vices alone have increased. Nothing is left of our peace and former prosperity except our crimes alone and in full. Our crimes which have ended our prosperity are left. Where are the old resources and dignities of the Romans? Formerly, the Romans were most strong; now they are without strength. The old Romans were feared; we are afraid. The barbarian people paid them tribute; we are tributary to the barbarians. The enemy sells us the enjoyment of daylight. In a way, our entire welfare is at a price.

O our misfortunes! To what have we come! And we are thankful to the barbarians from whom we buy ourselves for a price. What can be more abject or wretched for us? And we think we are still living, despite the conditions under which we actually live. We even make ourselves a laughing-stock;

---

45 Lacuna in text. Reading according to Pauly.

we call the gold which we pay, a benefit. We call what is really a ransom, a gift. But it is a price paid on the hardest and most miserable terms. All captives enjoy their freedom once they are redeemed. We are constantly being redeemed, but we are never free. The barbarians deal with us in the manner of those masters who hire out for a daily wage their slaves who are not necessary for their own service. Likewise, we are never free from this tax which we pay. We continually pay wages for the purpose of paying them forever.

BOOK SEVEN

IT IS POSSIBLE that I may seem at variance with my general undertaking when, in the closing passages of the last book, I spoke somewhat about the weakness and misery of the Romans. I know the Romans can say and give complete proof that God does not watch over human affairs, because, in the old days, the Romans as pagans conquered and ruled, but now as Christians they are conquered and enslaved. What I said a little while back about almost all pagan nations could suffice for the refutation of this charge. My argument is that they who know God's Law and neglect it sin more than they who, in their ignorance, do not act according to the Law.

However, with God's approbation, since I have arrived at that part of the undertaking where something should be said about the old Romans, I will prove clearly with God's help that His favors were as just to them in the past as His severity is just towards us in the present. I will prove, in addition, that His favor by which they were exalted was as deserved then as we are deserving of punishment now.[1]

Would that that punishment were profitable to us! It is much more serious and lamentable that there is no amendment after punishment. The Lord wishes to cure us by His chastisements, but healing does not result from cure. What sort of evil is this? Beasts and cattle are cured by surgery. The

---

1 This proof is not forthcoming.

diseased flesh of mules, donkeys, and pigs, when their flesh has been burned by cautery, acknowledge the benefit of the curative burning, and immediately, when the blemish of the infected bodies has been either burned or cut off, living flesh succeeds to the place of the dead flesh. We ourselves are burned and cut, but we are healed neither by surgical amputation nor by cauterization. Indeed, what is worse still, we are worse because of the cure. Accordingly, what is wont to happen to beasts and cattle which have incurable diseases is happening to us, and not without purpose. For, in all parts of the world, since we are not corrected by healing care, we find our end through death and massacre.

So that I will not repeat what I have said much further back, is our situation due to the fact, as I mentioned a little while ago, that we who live are equally miserable and pleasure-loving? Grant that these are the vices of the fortunate (although nobody can be evil and happy at the same time, because where there is not true uprightness there is not true happiness). Yet, as I have said above, grant that these are the vices which result from a long peace and opulent security. But why, I ask, are there vices in those places where there is neither peace nor security? Certainly, in all the Roman world peace and security do not exist.

Why do vices alone endure? Who, I ask, can bear lasciviousness in a man who is poverty-stricken? Indeed, luxurious poverty is more blameworthy and frivolous misery is more worthy of odium. The whole Roman world is both wretched and given to luxury. Who, I ask, is both poor and frivolous? Who thinks about the circus, while he is awaiting captivity? Who fears death, and laughs? We go to the games though we fear captivity. We laugh, though we are afraid of death. You would think the whole Roman people is soaked, so to speak, in Sardonic herbs.² It is dying, but continues to laugh. In almost all parts of the world, tears follow our laughter, and that saying of our Lord comes home to us even in the present world, 'woe to you who laugh because you will weep.'³

(2) Perhaps you are thinking that, since I have spoken at length about public games and public immorality, in this respect only are we worse than the barbarians, because they do not commit the sins we commit and they are not stained in the same way with the sin of carnal lust and the filth of deadly fornication. If you will, let me also compare the Romans with the other nations in respect to the latter. Indeed, I do not know that they are more rightly comparable to any other than to those barbarians whom, placed as possessors in the very bosom of the State, God has made the masters of the Roman soil. Hence although God's judgment can in no way be disputed, since He has taken from us the best portion of our right and given it to the barbarians, let us see whether He apparently acted according to a just judgment in this removal and bestowal.

Nobody doubts that the Aquitainians and the Nine Peoples⁴ possessed the best part of all Gaul. It is a land productive in its fertility, and not only fertility, but pleasantness, beauty, and luxury, which are sometimes preferred to fertility. In that part of Gaul the whole region is, so to say, interwoven with vines. Its meadows are flowered. Its fields are ploughed, or planted with fruit trees, or filled with delightful woods. The land is well watered with fountains, interspread with rivers, and rich in harvests. Truly, the holders and masters of that

---

2 The *herba Sardonica*, a species of *ranunculus* which grows in Sardinia. Those who eat it are afflicted with muscular spasm of the face, giving a horrible appearance of laughter.
3 Luke 6.25.
4 The Nine Peoples inhabited the extreme south-west corner of Gaul, bounded approximately by the Garonne River.

land seem to have possessed not so much a portion of that soil as an image of paradise.

With these blessings, what happened? Without doubt, the inhabitants should have been more dutiful to God, they whom God particularly enriched with the most abundant of His favors. What is more proper or what is more fitting than that they, whom the Lord by His gifts seemed to have wished to favor in a special manner, should also in like manner have more especially pleased the Lord by worship and religion, particularly since God demands nothing burdensome, nothing heavy from us. He does not call us to the plough or to the mattock, nor to digging the earth, nor to preparing the ground for planting the vines. In short, He does not demand those services from His slaves which we demand from ours.

What does He say—'Come to Me, all you who labor and are burdened and I will refresh you. Take My yoke upon you and learn from Me because I am meek and humble of heart and you will find peace for your souls; for My yoke is sweet and My burden light.'[5] Therefore, the Lord does not call us to labor, but to refresh ourselves. What does He demand from us, what does He order to be given Him by us, but only faith, chastity, humility, sobriety, mercy, and holiness? All these requests do not burden us. They adorn us.

Not only this, but they adorn our life in this world in order that they may adorn more our life in the next. O good, O holy, O Lord of inestimatable mercy! Who for this end gives us the gifts of religion in this life that He may later reward in us the gifts which He now gives. Such, without doubt, even all the Aquitainians should have been, and, indeed, as I have said, they should have been more especially such because they received special gifts from God.

What was the result of all these gifts? What was bound to

---
5 Matt. 11.28-30.

be the result? What, unless all things are otherwise than they should be? Indeed, in all Gaul, just as men are first in riches, so they are first in vice. Nowhere is pleasure more evil; nowhere is life more vicious; nowhere is discipline more corrupt. For these sacred gifts they gave this recompense to the Lord, that in proportion as He drew them by His favors to Himself for his own appeasement, they labored to provoke Him by their excesses.

(3) Are my statements false, and are they said, perhaps, in a spirit of envy rather than of truth? I shall not use that method of proof which others are wont to use in law suits. I will not bring in as witnesses those who are carefully chosen, or outsiders, or unsuitable to prove my point. Let me question those very men by whom these things have been done. I have spoken falsely if they refute me. Indeed, they acknowledge their faults and, what is more serious, they acknowledge them in such a way that they do not grieve when they acknowledge them. They still have the same attitude of mind when they confess as when they committed these faults. Just as they were not ashamed to commit evil deeds, so they do not now repent of having committed them.

However, exception must be made for a very few holy and distinguished men who, as one of their number has said,[6] 'have redeemed their crimes by scattering their wealth.' I say I am speaking about these exceptions who deserve to be corrected by God and whom we rightly believe were guilty of lesser crimes even in that almost general impure conflux of vices. He who is willing to make atonement does not completely injure his Lord. What else is there to say? I think that a man who looked to God even while sinning could obtain this from God that he would sin no more.

---

6 Paulinus of Nola, *Ep.* 33.3.

The remainder, and they are almost the majority, and mostly noble, are nearly all alike. The gluttony of nearly all is a raging vortex; the life of all is almost a brothel. Why should I speak about brothels? I even think that a brothel is less criminal [than the men whom I have in mind]. For the prostitutes who are in them do not know the marriage bond and therefore do not stain that of which they are ignorant. Indeed, their shamelessness is deserving of punishment, but they are not held guilty of adultery. Add to this, that brothels are few and there are few prostitutes who have condemned themselves to a most unhappy life in them.

But among the Aquitainians, what city, in its richest and most noble section, was not like a brothel? Who among the noble and rich did not live in the mire of lust? Who among them did not immerse himself in the abyss of the most sordid whirlpool of vices? Who among them gave to his wife the faith of a husband? Especially, insofar as it pertains to the promiscousness of lust, who among them did not reduce his wife to one of his maid-servants and so degraded the vows of holy marriage that no woman in his house seemed more vile by marital contempt than she who was the principal party by the dignity of marriage?

(4) Perhaps someone is thinking that my accusations are not altogether correct, because it is true that the mothers of households in Aquitaine exercised their rights and held the place of honor and power over their homes. Indeed, many had the full right of ruling the house, but almost none had her rights over marriage unsullied. Just now I am not inquiring into the power exercised by the wives, but how corrupt was the way of life of their husbands. I should say that the mothers did not even possess their power intact in that locality, because any woman who has not her rights of marriage inviolate and

safe does not possess intact the right of government over the household. The mother of the house is not far removed from the lowliness of female slaves when the father of the house is the husband of maids.

Who among the rich Aquitainians was not like this? Whom did not these shameless maids consider rightly their adulterers or husbands? As the Prophet says,[7] 'they had become as post-horses on the mares. Each one whinnied after his neighbor's wife.' They about whom we read these words sinned with a less crime and, as I think, with a less number of crimes and promiscuity [than the Aquitainians]. The Aquitainians were truly as post-horses not for a few only, but for all their young female slaves. They whinnied, as it were to their own flocks and in the manner of those beasts which are styled the stallions of the herd. They became wanton in the excesses of their heated lust. They overpowered whatsoever woman their burning shameful madness first laid hands on.

At this point I ask the wise men, since these were the actual circumstances, what kind of families were in Aquitaine where there were such fathers of families? How much corruption of slaves would there be where the corruption of the masters was so great? There is nothing healthy in a sick head, and no limb altogether performs its function where the main part is not functioning. In his own house, the master is as the head to the body and his life is the norm of life for all. The worst thing in this is that all pursue the worse things more freely, and a bad institution more easily degrades the good than a good institution corrects the bad.

Furthermore, even when good and upright fathers of the family cannot make their servants good, how great do we think was the depravity of the families in Aquitaine, where

---

7 Jer. 5.8.

the masters were examples of impurity? In that country this was not only a bad example, but, by a kind of enforced necessity, unwilling female slaves were compelled to obey their shameless masters. The lewdness of the masters meant the subjection of his female subjects. From this it can be understood how sordid was the mire of shamelessness where women, living against their will under the most impure masters, were not allowed to be chaste.

(5) You may be saying that it is difficult to prove these charges and that there are no traces extant of past turpitudes and vices. Look! Even now, many of these men, although they are without a homeland and live as paupers in comparison with their past opulence, are for the most part worse than they were. They are worse, not in one way, although they do the same things they did formerly; they are worse by the very fact that they do not cease from crime. Indeed, their evil deeds, although they are not greater in kind, are yet more numerous. In this way, although they do not increase the novelty of their crimes, their crimes are piled up in plurality.

As I have said, add that old men do these things, add that poor men do them. Both contribute an increase in crime. Indeed, it is less shocking for young men to sin and for rich men to sin. What hope or remedy is there for those who are recalled from their accustomed impurity neither by poverty-stricken misery nor old age? Grant that a foolish presumption of a long life or the hope of doing penance sometimes consoles some. Is it not a new kind of monster that some are evil even when they are about to die? Since this is the case, can anything more be said? However, I still add that many living even among the enemy do these things today. As captives they are in daily crises and fear. They were delivered by God to the barbarians on account of the very impurities of their lives, yet they do not leave aside their impurities even when they live among the barbarians.

(6) Perhaps the enemy in whose midst they commit these faults are such that their faults delight them and, since they are themselves unchaste, they would be seriously offended if they saw the Romans living chaste lives. If that were the case the wickedness of others should never cause us to be wicked. It is proper that every man excel in his own eyes in order that he may be good, rather than be evil for another. We should strive to please God by integrity, rather than men by impurity. Thus, even if anyone live among unchaste barbarians, he should observe the laws of purity which are for his own good rather than impurity which pleases his impure enemies. But what, above all else, increases our misdeeds?

Among chaste barbarians, we are unchaste. I say further: the very barbarians are offended by our impurities. Fornication of Goths is not lawful among the Goths. Only the Romans living among them can afford to be impure by prerogative of nation and name. I ask: What hope is there for us before God? We love impurity; the Goths abominate it. We flee from purity; they seek it. Fornication among them is a crime; with us a distinction and an ornament.

Do we think that we can face God, do we think that we can be saved, when every crime of impurity, every base and shameful act, is committed by the Romans and censured by the barbarians? Here and now I ask them who think we are better than the barbarians: Tell me which of these vices is committed even by a very few Goths, or which of them is not committed by the Romans or by nearly all Romans? And we wonder when the soil of the Aquitainians, or all of our own is given by God to the barbarians, since the barbarians are now cleansing by chastity those lands which the Romans polluted by fornication.

(7) Perhaps, this was the case in Aquitaine only. Let me cross over to other parts of the world, lest I seem to give all my attention to Gaul. Have not the same or perhaps greater vices destroyed Spain? Indeed, even if the heavenly anger had handed Spain over to any barbarian tribe, the enemies of purity there would have suffered tortures worthy of their crimes. But in addition, for a manifest condemnation of impurity that country was delivered to the Vandals, that is, to the most chaste among the barbarians.

By the captivity of the Spaniards, God wished to show in two ways how much He hated carnal lewdness and loved chastity, when He put the Vandals in command solely on account of their great chastity and subjugated the Spaniards solely on account of their great impurity.

Why did God act thus? Were there not in the whole world stronger barbarians to whom the Spaniards might be delivered? Doubtless, there were many stronger. Indeed, if I am not mistaken, all were stronger. God gave all to the weakest enemies to show that it was not the strength of numbers but the cause that conquered. He wished to show that neither are we being overthrown by the valor of our former slothful foes but we are right now being overcome solely by the impurity of our vices, so that that saying which the Lord said to the Jews may come home to us:[8] 'According to their uncleanliness and according to their iniquities have I done unto them, and I have turned away My face from them.' Elsewhere, He said to the same people: 'The Lord shall bring a people over you from afar'[9] and 'He said, "with the hoofs of their horses

---
8 Ezech. 39.24.
9 Deut. 28.49.

they shall tread your streets and they shall kill your people with the sword." [10] Everything spoken of by the Divine Word is fulfilled in us, and the punishment of all has fulfilled the force of the heavenly words.

(8) Since almost all barbarian nations have drunk Roman blood and torn apart our bowels, why is it that our God delivered the wealthiest State and the richest people who bear the Roman name to the most potent jurisdiction of enemies who were once most cowardly? Why? Unless that we may acknowledge, as I have said above, that it was a question of merit not of strength. Also that the fact of being handed over to the most craven would add to our confusion and punishment. Also that the fact of being subjected, not by the bravest, but by the most cowardly of the enemy, would compel us to acknowledge the blow of the heavenly hand.

We read that, when God wished it clearly understood that great deeds were done by Him, they were done through a few or through the lowliest, lest the work of His heavenly hand be attributed to human strength. In this way the leader Sisara, before whom the Hebrew army trembled, was laid low by a woman.[11] A woman's hand struck down Abimelech,[12] the stormer of cities, and the iron-clad battle array of the Assyrians fell through the work of a widow.

Lest I speak only of women, did not the Lord wish Benedad, King of Syria, whom, besides countless thousands of his own people, thirty-two kings and armies of the same number of kings served, to be conquered by a few foot soldiers of the Princes in order that He who was the Author of such victory would be acknowledged?[13]

---
10 Ezech. 26.11.
11 Judges 4.21.
12 Judges 9.53-54.
13 3 Kings 20.

Against the Medianites, also, who, as the Book of Judges relates, had filled all places like locusts, Gideon was ordered to lead a few men into battle. It was not that he did not have many in his army, but that he was forbidden to lead many into battle, lest the multitude might claim for itself some share of the victory.[14] Hence, when he had gathered 30,000 armed fighters, the Lord spoke thus to him:[15] 'the people with you are too many and the Medians shall not be given into their hands.'

What happened next? He left only 300 fighters to the man who was about to fight against countless thousands of barbarians. Indeed, He ordered the line of soldiers to be reduced to the smallest number in order that their fewness woud not permit them to realize any credit from the prosecution of the divinely waged war. Why the Lord acted thus, He Himself very clearly stated, saying:[16] 'lest Israel glory against Me and say, "I am saved by my own strength."' Let them hear, I say, let all the unjust and the presumptuous hear. Let all the powerful hear what God says when He says: 'Lest Israel glory against Me and say, "I am saved by my own strength."'

(9) I say, let them hear, all those who hurl blasphemies and statements contrary to the above, let them who place their hope in man hear these things. God says that all who presume they can be liberated by their own strength speak against Him. Who is there among the Romans who does not talk like this? Who is there among them who does not feel this way? Who is there among us who does not almost constantly blaspheme in this respect? It is common knowledge that there is no strength in the state, and, indeed, we do not acknowledge to whose favor we are indebted for being still alive.

---
14 Judges 7.
15 Judges 7.2.
16 *Ibid.*

When God gives us some measure of prosperity beyond our hope and merit, one man ascribes it to fate, another to chance, another to the plans of the leaders, another to foresight, another to the magistrates, another to his patron. Not one ascribes it to God. And we wonder if His heavenly hand does not give us something, He whom we detract for whatever He has given us. What else are we doing, since we deputize the good He gives us to the chance of events, to the qualities of the leaders, or to other frivolous causes?

If we follow this line of argument, it behooves us to render thanks to the earth that we reap yearly harvests, to the vines for our wines, to the sea because we catch fish, to the woods because we fell trees, to the sheep because we are clothed with garments, to the other beasts because our stomachs are filled with meat. What reasons is there for wanting to be grateful to God for His other gifts, from whom we detract the thanks for His most important favors? What man of our standing is happy when somebody thanks him for some gift received, when the recipient has not acknowledged the most excellent gift? Though we cannot fittingly thank God for anything, it would still not be enough if we wish to be grateful only for those things which He gives us for our daily sustenance. Situated as we are under the very yoke of the barbarians, yet we are without thanks for the fact that He comes to our aid in times of trouble, frees us from danger, and preserves us by His protection.

Not thus do the Goths behave, not thus do the Vandals act, though trained by evil teachers. They are better than we in this respect. I suspect some are offended by what I say, but, because truth must be considered more than offense, I will say and say it often. Not thus do the Goths behave, not thus do the Vandals act, who at moments of crises demand help from God and call their prosperity the gift of God.

In short, our misfortune in the last war proved this. When the Goths feared, we presumed to put our hope in the Huns; they in God. When they sought peace, we refused them peace. They sent bishops as intermediaries and we turned them away. They honored God even in foreign priests; we have contempt for Him even in our own. Accordingly, the end of the affair was in conformance with the action of both parties. To them, in their greatest fear, was given the palm of victory. To us, in our greatest confidence, was given confusion. Truly in us and in them was clearly proved that saying of our Lord,[17] 'For whoever exalts himself shall be humbled, and he who humbles himself shall be exalted.' To them, exaltation was given for humiliation; to us, dejection for elation.

(10) This the leader[18] of our forces learned, who, as a captive, entered that same enemy town which he had presumed he would enter that same day as a victor. He proved what the Prophet said:[19] 'for a man's way is not his own, nor is it in the power of man that he walk and direct his steps.' Since he thought he could find his way without guidance, he neither had the direction of his steps nor did he find the road to safety. As we read:[20] 'Contempt is poured upon the leader, he is led into pathless places and not on the road. He is brought to nothing even as the water which flows.'

In him, indeed, in addition to the unfortunate turn of affairs, there was made clear the immediate judgment of God. He himself has suffered all that he had in mind to do to others. Because he believed that he himself would capture the enemy without the help of the Divinity and the consent

---

17 Luke 14.11.
18 Litorius, a pagan, attacked Toulouse, capital of the Visigoths, and was defeated by them in 439.
19 Prov. 16.9; 20.24.
20 Ps., 106. 40; 57.8.

of God, he himself was captured. He presumed foreknowledge and wisdom, and incurred the greatest disgrace for his rashness. He himself had to bear the chains he had prepared for others.

I ask what more manifest judgment of God could there be than that he who had the confidence of a plunderer should become booty? He who presumed victory was defeated, surrounded, seized, and fettered. His arms were tied behind his back. Those hands, which he thought valorous, he saw bound. He became a public spectacle for boys and women. He saw barbarians making game of him. He bore the ridicule of those of both sexes. He who had had the great pride of a strong man was destined to die the death of a craven man.

Would that this were a speedy cure for his wrongs and not a long drawn out endurance. But, insofar as it pertains to the great punishments he endured, he was wasted by a long captivity and by long drawn out sickness in a barbarian convict-cell. He was reduced to such misery that he became an object of pity to the enemy. Most men think this is more difficult and bitter even than the punishment itself.

Why did all this happen? Why, doubtless, unless as I said, the enemy were humbled before God and we were rebellious. They believed that victory was in the hand of God. We believed that it was in our own hand, truly a sacrilegious and unholy hand. What is worse and more unpardonable than our attitude? Lastly, the enemy's king,[21] stretched on haircloth, insofar as the story is related and proved, poured out prayers up to the day of battle. Before the battle he threw himself on the ground in prayer. He rose from prayer to the battle. Before he took command in the battle he fought by prayer,

---

21 Theodoric I, King of the Visigoths. Theodoric was allied with Hunneric, King of the Vandals in Africa, but, when the latter repudiated Theodoric's daughter on a charge of infidelity, Theodoric allied his forces with the Emperor Maximus in an attempt to reconquer Africa.

and proceeded confidently to the fight because he had already merited victory by his prayers.

(11) The situation is not unlike this even among the Vandals. When our armies marched against them in Spain,[22] our forces had as much presumptive faith to crush them as even recently against the Goths. Our soldiers were brought low by a similar disdaining pride and by a like outcome. That saying of the Prophet was brought home to our army: 'the Lord shall cast aside your confidence and you shall not have prosperity.'[23] We were confident in our own wisdom and strength, contrary to the command of God, who says: 'let not the wise man glory in his wisdom nor the strong man in his strength, but let him who glories glory in this, to know and understand Me, because I am the Lord.'

Not without reason are we defeated, for the barbarians betook themselves to better aids than we. When we took pride in our armies and auxiliaries, the Book of the divine Law opposed us on the side of the enemy. The Vandals at that time in their fear and confusion took refuge especially in this help. They put a chain of heavenly speech against us, and against those who came they put, as fighters, the writings of the Sacred Book, as if they, in a way, unlocked the very mouth of God.

Here and now I ask: Who on our side ever acted like this? Who would not have been laughed at if he had thought it should be done? Laughed at indeed, just as almost all religious acts are laughed at by us. Therefore, what can that prerogative of a religious name profit us? That we call ourselves

---

22 A Visigothic force led by the Romans, Boniface and Castinus, would have defeated the Vandals in Spain were it not for the mutual distrust of the leaders.
23 Jer. 2.37.
24 Jer. 9.23-24.

Catholics? That we brag we are the faithful? That we despise the Goths and Vandals with the reproachful title of heretics, when we ourselves live in heretical depravity?

Most fittingly is that saying which the divine Word spoke to the Jews, trusting in the Law, applied to us: 'How do you say, "we are wise and the Law of the Lord is with us?" '[25] He says, 'trust not in lying words saying, "the temple of the Lord, the temple of the Lord, it is the temple of the Lord." For if you will amend your ways and inclinations, if you do not calumniate against the stranger, the orphan and the widow, nor shed innocent blood in this place, I will dwell with you in this place for ever and ever.'[26] This shows that, if we do these things, we flatter ourselves by presuming the name of Catholic.

Enough has been said here and above, and perhaps more still will be said later. There is no need for us to discuss this point further, since the judgment of God is evident. Events prove what God judges about us and about the Goths and Vandals. They increase daily; we decrease daily. They prosper; we are humbled. They flourish; we are drying up. Truly there is said about us that saying which the Divine Word spoke of Saul and David:[27] 'because David was strong and always growing more robust; the house of Saul grew less daily.' As the Prophet says:[28] 'For He is just, the Lord is just and His judgment is right.'

(12) We are judged by God with immediate judgment and therefore a most craven race has been raised up for our destruction and shame. This people wanders from place to place, passes from city to city, and destroys everything. First,

---
25 Jer. 8.8.
26 Jer. 7.4-7.
27 2 Kings 3.1.
28 Ps. 118.137.

they poured out of their own land into neighboring Germany, which was a country barbarous in name but under Roman authority. After Germany was ruined, the country of the Belgians burst into flame. Then it was the turn of the wealthy and rich Aquitainians, and after them the whole land of Gaul. However, the destruction of Gaul was still gradual, in order that while one part was struck down and destroyed, another might be amended by the example of the other.

But where among us was amendment or what part of the Roman world, no matter how afflicted, is corrected? As we read:[29] 'for all have declined, they have become useless at same time.' Therefore, the Prophet cries out to God and says:[30] 'You have struck them and they have not sorrowed; You have consumed them and they have refused to accept discipline; they have hardened their faces harder than a rock and were unwilling to return.' Present affairs show how truly this applies to us.

Gaul has been devastated over a long period of time. Has Spain, which is its neighbor, amended its ways? Because there was no fear whatsoever and no amendment, the Spaniards not undeservedly caught fire from the flames with which the Gauls were burning. The most criminal and serious side of this, as I have said before, is that when, figuratively speaking, the limbs of sinful men were burning, the vices of the sinners were not curbed. Our crimes compel God to scatter enemy blows from place to place, from city to city, and to dispatch nations and peoples, aroused from almost the very ends of the earth, across the sea to punish the crimes of the Africans.

Why has God done this? Having been brought from their own homeland, could the Vandals not have remained in Gaul? Whom did they fear so that they did not remain? They who

---
29 Ps. 13.3; 52.4.
30 Jer. 5.2.

were uninjured by us had up to that very time overrun everything. Grant that they were frightened while living among the Gauls. Why then, in Spain, when they even crushed our army in battle, why did they fear to stand and settle when they were already triumphant and victorious over our army? They had climbed to such a degree of arrogant bravery that they realized that, after trial in a long prepared for war, the strength of the Roman Empire, even with barbarian auxiliaries, could not equal theirs.

(13) They could have remained in Gaul and they were not afraid. Indeed, that heavenly hand which drew them to Spain to punish the sins of her inhabitants compelled them to pass on to Africa to devastate that country.[31] They themselves confessed that they were not doing their own will, for they say they were activated and driven by a divine command. From this we can understand how great are our evils, we for whose devastation and punishment the barbarians are compelled to go unwillingly, according to that saying of the King of the Assyrians, the devastator of the land of Israel:[32] 'Why have I ascended without the will of the Lord to this place? The Lord said to me, "go up to this land and destroy it."' Elsewhere, the Sacred Word says:[33] 'the God of Israel, the Lord of Hosts said thus, "behold I will send and take Nabochodnosor, the King of Babylon, my servant, and coming he shall smite the land of Egypt."'

Hence, we can indeed understand that all things which are afflicted are smitten by the judgment of God, yet, as I have often mentioned, they are overthrown because of their sins. Therefore, whatever has been done must be ascribed to our

---

31 Actually, the continuous pressure exerted by a numerically superior force of Visigoths forced the Vandals from Spain and into Africa.
32 Isa. 36.10.
33 Jer. 25.8-9; 43.11.

sins and not to God, because a deed is rightly ascribed to that cause which compelled its performance. A murderer, when put to death by a judge, is punished for his own crime. A robber or a sacrilegious person, when burned in the flames, is consumed for his own crimes.

Hence, the Vandals crossed over into Africa, not because of divine severity on the Vandals, but to cut off the sins of the Africans. By their grave and long-existing iniquity, they were drawing the Vandals long before the Vandals departed from their own land. We must understand that this sinful people received the punishment they had merited for some time for their misdeeds and crimes, but God's mercy had deferred the long overdue chastisement. Perhaps we are to believe that the Africans did not merit this. Indeed, no other people deserved it more, inasmuch as all kinds of depravities and impurities flourished at once among them.

Other peoples, although they are captive of some shameful vices, are not chained by other vices. Though they are not without drunkenness, they are without ill will. Though they are on fire with lust, they do not harbor greed. Though their bodily incontinence accuses many, their simplicity of mind commends them. But in almost all Africans, insofar as it pertains to both, that is, being equally good and evil, there is no balance, because almost the whole population is evil. After the purity of their original nature has been cut off, vice has created in them, as it were, another nature.

(14) With the exception of a very few servants of God, what was the whole land of Africa but one house of sin. It was like to that bronze vessel about which the prophet says:[34] 'O city of blood! the bronze vessel, in which there is a rust which does not go right out of it, because the blood shall not

---

34 Ezech. 24.6-7.

go out of it.' Thus we may see, he compared the city to a bronze vessel and iniquity to blood in order that we may understand that the iniquity of a people in the city is like bubbling blood in a bronze vessel. Not unlike this is the saying of the Sacred Word:[35] 'all the houses of Israel are made unto Me a mixture of brass and iron and tin and lead, in the midst of which there is a mixture of silver. Therefore say these things, "Thus spoke the Lord God: for this that you are all become one mixture. I will blow upon you and shall breathe upon you in the fire of wrath."

The Sacred Word mentioned kinds of metals different among themselves. How are different metals fused together in the same furnace? It is because by the variety of metals there is meant the dissimilitude of men. Even silver, which is a metal of more noble material, is treated in the same fires because men have condemned the gifts of a more noble nature by their degenerate lives. Thus we read that the Lord God said through His Prophet about the Prince of Tyre:[36] 'O son of man, take up a lament against the Prince of Tyre and say to him: "Thus speaks the Lord God: you have been a seal of likeness and a crown of becomingness among the delights of Paradise. You have been covered with all the best stones, the sardius, topaz and emerald." ' Again He says:[37] 'With silver and gold you have filled your treasuries, from the multitudes of commerce you have filled your warehouses.'

Were not all these things such that they seem to have been said particularly about Africa? Where were greater treasures, where greater commerce, where fuller warehouses? He said, 'with gold have I filled your treasury from the multitude of your commerce.' I add further: so rich was Africa at one

---
35 Ezech. 22.18-21.
36 Ezech. 28.11-13.
37 Ezech. 28.4-5.

time that it seems to me that the fullness of her commerce filled not only her own but even the treasuries of the world. And what were the rest of the words of the prophet? He says:[38] 'your heart is exalted in your beauty, because of the multitude of your sins I have cast you to the ground.'

How does this saying apply to the power of Africa, or in what way does Africa seem to have been cast to the ground? How, unless because, when she lost the height of her old power, she lost, as it were, heavenly dignity? The Prophet said:[39] 'and I will bring forth a fire from your midst and it will devour you.' What is more true than this? The fire of sin went forth indeed from the midst of their iniquity, a fire which devoured the good fortune of former times. He says:[40] 'and all who have known you among the people, shall be afflicted over you.' We might think that this saying did not apply to them, if the conquest of African soil were not the distress of the human race. He says:[41] 'you have become destruction and shall be nothing more for eternity.' It is well known that everything has already been brought to destruction in that land. I hope eternal evils shall not succeed and follow the punishment of present evils.

(15) May God, in His love and mercy, grant that this shall not be. Insofar as it pertains to what our crimes deserve, the condition is such that God could very well allow it. What manner of sins are not always being committed in Africa? Nor do I speak about all evils, because they are almost so great that they cannot be known and spoken of. I shall speak only about the greatness of their obscene impurities and, what is more grave, of their sacrileges. I pass over the madness of

---

38 Ezech. 28.17.
39 Ezech. 28.18.
40 Ezech. 28.19.
41 *Ibid.*

greed in some, that vice of the whole human race. I pass over the inhumanity of avarice, which is the evil proper to almost all Romans. Drunkenness is left aside, that vice common to high and low. I am silent about pride and bombast; these are the particular kingdom of the rich, and perhaps they might think that they are losing something that is their right if another person wished to claim part of it for himself. Finally, let all crimes of fraud, forgeries, and perjury be passed over. There never was a Roman city without these evils, although this was more especially the crime of all the Africans.

As all dirt flows into the bilge in the bowels of a ship, so vices flowed into the African way of life, as if from the whole world. I know of no baseness which did not abound there. Even though pagans and wild peoples have their own special vices, yet, all their crimes do not merit reproach.

The Gothic nation is lying, but chaste. The Alani are unchaste, but they lie less. The Franks lie, but they are generous. The Saxons are savage in cruelty, but admirable in chastity. In short, all peoples have their own particular bad habits, just as they have certain good habits. Among almost all Africans, I know not what is not evil. If they are to be accused of inhumanity, they are inhuman; if of drunkenness, they are drunkards; if of forgery, they are the greatest of forgerers; if of deceit, they are the most deceitful; if of cupidity, they are the most greedy; if of treachery, they are the most treacherous. Their impurities and blasphemies must not be mentioned here, because in the evils about which I have just spoken they have surpassed the evils of other races, but in impurity and blasphemy they have even surpassed themselves.

(16) I will speak about their impurity first. Who does not know that all Africa always burned with the obscene resinous tree of lust, so that you might think it was not a land and

site of men, but an Aetna of unchaste flames? Just as Aetna is naturally heated with certain inner burning fires, so that land is constantly heated by the abominable fires of fornication. Nor do I wish my assertations to obtain full credence in this matter. The testimony of the human race is required. Who does not know that almost all Africans are unchaste, with the exception, perhaps, of those converted to God, that is, those changed by faith and religion?

Chaste people are as rare and difficult to find as it seems rare that any Gaius is not a Gaius or any Seius is not a Seius.[42] It is so infrequent and unheard of that an African is not unchaste as it is novel and customary that an African is not an African. So general is the evil of impurity in them that whosoever among them would cease to be impure would apparently not be an African. Neither shall I discourse about the individual places, nor discuss all the cities, lest I seem to seek out and investigate with too great zeal what I am talking about.

I shall content myself with one city of all the cities in that land; the city that is the head and mother, as it were, of all the other cities there; that city, formerly the continual rival of the citadel of Rome in its arms and prowess, and afterwards in splendor and dignity. I am speaking of Carthage, the greatest adversary of the city of Rome and, as it were, a Rome in Africa. This city alone suffices as my example and witness, because she had completely within herself all the materials which are used for the provisioning, ruling, and governing of the State, anywhere in the whole world.

In that city were located all the agencies of public office, there were the schools of liberal arts, there the workshops of the philosophers, and finally all the schools for languages and ethics. There also the military stores and the military

---
42 The equivalent of our John Doe.

headquarters, there the proconsular dignity, there the daily judge and provincial ruler, a proconsul indeed in name, but a consul in power. There also were all the administrators and dignitaries differing among themselves in grade and title, the keepers, so to speak, of streets and crossroads, governing almost all parts of the city and members of the population.

Thus, I am content with this city as an example and witness of all other cities, in order that we may understand what kind were these cities which were under the administration of less honored officials, when we see what was the quality of that one city where there were always the highest officials. At this point I almost repent of my promise made above, which was to pass over almost all the vices of the Africans and speak chiefly about their impurities and blasphemies. For I see a city bubbling over, as it were, in vice; I see a city burning with every kind of iniquity; filled, indeed, with crowds, but more with iniquity; filled with riches, but more with vice; men surpassing each other in the villainy of their depravity; some struggling to outdo in rapacity; others to outdo in impurity; some drowsy with wine; others distended with too much food; some bedecked with flowers; others besmeared with oil; all wasted by varied kinds of indolence and luxury and almost all prostrate in the death of their sins. Not all were intoxicated from drinking wine, but all were drunk from their sins. You would think that the people were insane and not in their proper senses; whole neither in their mind nor in their step, falling against each other, as is the manner of drunken crowds.

Now, there is another evil of this kind, graver and, indeed, unlike it in kind, but not unlike it in inquity. Perhaps it is unlike in this respect, that it is greater. I speak about the proscriptions of orphans, the affliction of widows, and the torture of the poor. They groaned daily to God, praying for an end of their evils. What is most serious, in the force of their utter bitterness they sometimes even prayed for the coming of the enemy. They have obtained from God that at least all suffer in common from the barbarians the depredations which formerly they alone suffered at the hands of the Romans.

(17) Let us put these depravities to one side, because they are committed in almost all the Roman world. Besides, I had promised to say only a few words about them here. Would not the impurity and license about which I speak suffice for the destruction of the Africans? What portion of the city was not filled with indecency, what street or path within the city was not a brothel? The snares of lust were, so to speak, astride almost all crossroads and all streets and had spread their nets over them, so that even they who thoroughly abhorred this vice could scarcely avoid it.

They were like ambushing brigands who captured the spoils of the passing travelers. They were like those brigands who by the density of their frequent snares so fenced in almost all footpaths, all bends in the roads, all byways that scarcely anybody could be so cautious that he would not fall into some noose of their snares, even though he had disengaged himself from the greater part of them. As I have said, all citizens of that city stank from the mire of lust as they inhaled the unclean vapor of their mutual impurity.

Yet these horrible things were not horrible to them, because the same horror had infected all. You would think that city was one bilge-water of lust and fornication, like the mud collected from all the dirt of the streets and sewers. What hope could there be for that place where, with the exception of the Lord's temple, nothing but filth could be seen? Why do I except the temple of God? The temple belongs completely and solely to the priests and clergy. I do not discuss them, because I preserve reverence for the ministry of my Lord. Only those in the service of the altar, I think, were pure, just as we read that Lot was alone on the mountain while Sodom perished.

Furthermore, as to the people, who among such countless numbers was chaste? Do I say chaste? Who was not a fornicator, an adulterer, and this unceasingly and without end? It is necessary to cry out again: What hope could there be for that people where, since at one time one adulterer sullied the people of the church, if you were to search most diligently among all these thousands, you would scarcely be able to find one chaste man, even among the church-goers?

I will say much more. Would that the vices I have named were the only vices and that the impure men in that city would have been content to be defiled solely by the fornication of fallen women! More grave and criminal was the fact that those vices, about which the blessed Apostle Paul complained with the greatest lament of his soul, were almost all practiced in Africa. That is, men, having put aside the natural use of woman, burned in their desires for one another; men doing base things with men, and receiving to themselves the reward of their error which they should receive. Just as they do not approve of having God in their mind, God handed them over to a distorted mentality, so that they would do what was not usual.[43]

Did the blessed Apostle say this about barbarians and wild peoples? No indeed, but about us, that is, about the Romans in particular. The Africans, who formerly were never able to conquer the Romans in power and greatness, have now surpassed them in impurity, because they were capable of that one conquest. Whoever thinks he is rightfully angry with me

---
43 Rom. 1.27-28.

is angry more with the Apostle, because what I have said the Africans were, he has said the Romans, their masters, were.

(18) Perhaps the vice I am talking about was practiced in secret, or the curators of public order in the various parts of the city immediately took steps that these manifest crimes should not pollute the eyes of the citizens. If this had been done, however many there may have been who were sullied by the evil, not all would have been soiled in vision and mind. A vice that is very base is wont, when it is done in secret, not to be deserving of the full credence given a manifest crime. But it is a crime surpassing all censure for the greatest sins to commit a crime and have no shame for having committed it.

What more unnatural vice, I ask, could be done in Carthage? In a Christian city, in an ecclesiastical city, where the Apostles taught with their own teaching, where martyrs were crowned for their sufferings, men acted as women, and this without any protection of shame, without any cloak of modesty. Then, as if their fault would be light if only the authors of the evils were sullied by the evil, it became the sin of the whole city, because the public had knowledge of the vice. The entire city saw and allowed it to continue. The judges saw and were quiet. The people saw and applauded. Thus the fellowship of vice and crime was diffused throughout the entire city. Consent made it common to all, though its performance was not common to all.

You are saying, the evil was at last ended and the wrong corrected. Who could believe or even hear that men converted to feminine bearing not only their habits and nature, but even their looks, walk, dress, and everything that is proper to the sex or appearance of a man? Therefore, everything was put contrariwise, so that, since nothing should be more shameful to men than if they seem to have something feminine about them, in Carthage nothing seemed worse to certain men than to have something masculine about them.

(19) You say these were the disgraceful acts of a few men and what was not done by all could not injure all. Indeed, I have said above quite often that the crime of one man was the destruction of many among the people of God, just as the people was ruined by Achar's theft,[44] just as pestilence arose from Saul's jealousy,[45] just as death came from the counting of the people by the holy David.[46] The Church of God is as the eye. As a speck of dirt, even though small, which falls into the eye blinds the sight completely, in the same way, if some, even though they are a few in the body of the Church, commit filthy acts, they block almost all the light of the splendor of the Church.

Therefore, the Savior Himself called the eye the principal portion of the Church when He said:[47] 'Your eye is the light of your body. If your eye is single, your whole body shall be alight. But if your eye is evil, your whole body is in darkness.' Whence it is that the Apostle said:[48] 'do you not know that a little leaven corrupts the whole mass?' I say that there was not a little but too much of this evil in Carthage, not because many were effeminate, but because the voluptuousness of a few is the ruin of many. Even if they who live indecently are few, there are many tainted by the baseness of the few. For, just as one prostitute makes many fornicators, in the same way the abominable mixture of a few effeminate men infects almost the greatest portion of the population. I do not know

---

44 Jos. 7.1.
45 1 Kings 19.
46 2 Kings 24.2.
47 Matt. 6.22-23.
48 1 Cor. 5.6.

whether the effeminate or the prostitute is the worse in the eyes of God, since they are equally condemned in Sacred Scripture. The Apostle says:[49] 'for neither the effeminate nor men who love men will possess the Kingdom of God.'

It is lamentable and deplorable that such an evil should appear to be the crime even of the whole State and that the universal dignity of the Roman name should be branded with the infamy of an unnatural sin. When men put on women's clothing, they broke their steps more than women do. They fastened on themselves the signs of certain monstrous impurity when they covered their heads with feminine veils. They did this publicly in a Roman city, a city the great and most renowned in that land. What was this but a disgrace to Roman power that the most baneful crime should be openly committed in the bosom of the State? A power, great and most powerful, which can prevent the greatest crime must approve of what is being done, if it knowingly allows it to be done. For he in whose hand it is to prohibit sanctions a person to do an act if he does not prohibit its being done.

(20) Because sorrow once more demands it, I ask those who are angry, among what barbarian peoples were these things done or was it lawful to do them with public impunity? So that there be no further necessity of investigation or debate about this subject, let us compare the destroyers of Africa with the African peoples. Let us see what like evils were done by the Vandals.

Certainly the barbarians, swollen with elation, prideful in their victory, made licentious by the abundance of riches and delicacies, could have been changed by such great good fortune of things that were agreeable to them, even though they had always been most continent and chaste. They had entered,

---
[49] 1 Cor. 6.10.

as it is written in the divine books, 'a rich land abiding in milk and honey,'[50] a land most rich and, as it were, intoxicated with the wealth of all delicacies. In this land it would have been very strange if a barbarian people had not given themselves to luxury where nature itself was, so to say, given to luxury.

Who does not think that the Vandals, when they entered this land, would have plunged into every mire of vices and impurities? To speak most lightly, who does not think they would have done what had been constantly done by the Africans, into whose province they were migrating? Certainly if that were all they did, they, whom good fortune itself had not made corrupt, should be adjudged most continent and restrained. How many are there among the wise whom prosperity does not change, in whom viciousness does not increase with prosperity? Therefore, it is certain the Vandals were most temperate if they, the victors, were like their captive and conquered subjects.

In so great abundance and luxury, none of them became effeminate. Does this seem a small matter? Certainly, the Roman families, even those of noble birth, were in general effeminate. What do I say in addition? None of the Vandals was stained by the incest of the effeminate Romans in that country. Certainly, effeminacy had been long considered a virtue rather than a vice by the Romans. They who subdued men to the worst infamy of feminine use believed they were possessors of great manly strength.

Hence also, boy camp-followers who formerly followed the army were given as the wages of labor for services well done on campaigns. Since they were brave men, they could change men into women! How criminal this was! Yet the Romans did

---
50 Exod. 13.5.

this. I further add, the Romans and not of our time did this! Nevertheless, I do not accuse the men of old. The Romans, but not the Romans of old, were already corrupt, already licentious, already unlike themselves and their people, and more resembling Greeks than Romans. As I have often said already, it would not be very strange if the Roman State did not at some time suffer what it had long since deserved.

(21) This impurity began among the Romans before Christ's Gospel and, what is more serious, it did not cease after the advent of the Gospels. Who, after all this, does not admire the Vandals? They entered the richest towns where all these vices were rampant and took possession of the wealth of corrupt men in such a manner that they repudiated the daily corruption of Roman life and took possession of the use of good things, avoiding the filth of the bad. These facts should be enough for their praise, although I were to add no more. They have abominated the impurities of men. I still add, they have abominated even the impurities of women. They have abstained from houses of ill-repute and brothels. They have abstained from cohabitation and contacts with prostitutes.

Does it seem credible to anyone that the Romans permitted these vices and the barbarians abstained from them? After what I have said, is there anything more to be added? There is still much more. That they avoided foul acts is of lesser value; for, anybody can abhor disgraceful acts, but not remove them. The great and particular merit of the Vandal people is not only that they themselves are not stained by pollution, but that they have made provision that not even others are ever polluted. Indeed, in a manner, he is the guardian of human safety who not only acts so that he himself is good but who strives to bring it about that others may cease to be evil. What I have said is a great objective, great and preeminent.

Who believes that the Vandals did this in Roman cities? The impurity of the flesh has been removed from all these cities. How was it removed? Not as some vices are wont to be removed by the Romans who outlaw theft, yet continue to steal, who outlaw adultery, yet are the first to commit adultery. I can scarcely say they steal; they do not commit theft, but brigandage. A judge punishes a small theft in another when he himself is an embezzler of public money. He punishes rapine when he himself is a plunderer. He punishes an assassin when he himself is a swordsman. He punishes the breaker of doors and bars when he himself is the destroyer of towns. He punishes the burglars of houses when he himself is the ravager of provinces.

Would that this were done only by those placed in high office and on whom the very dignity of the office bestows the right of carrying on their robberies. It is more serious and more unbearable that private citizens do this, that is, the same men who formerly exercised high office. The honor once bestowed on them gives them this much benefit, that they always have the right to rob. Even when they cease to have public administrative power they do not cease to have the private power for robbery. Thus, the power which they had as judges is less than that which they have as private citizens, for, in the former instance, they were often succeeded in office, but never in the latter.

See the value of legal decrees; see what profit accrues from the passage of ordinances for which they who administer them have the utmost scorn. Clearly, the humble and lowly are compelled to obey; the poor are compelled to obey orders and are punished unless they obey. The same method is followed in this as in taxes. The poor alone obey the public orders, just as they alone pay the taxes. Thus, in the laws themselves and in the very justice of the laws the greatest crime of injustice is done, since the poor are compelled to obey them as something divine and the rich constantly tread on them as if they were nothing.

(22) Being driven by indignation, I have exceeded somewhat the intended order of my talk. Let me now return to the topic I was discussing before. I have stated that the cities of Africa were filled with monstrous impurities, especially with the queen and mistress as it were of other vices, but the Vandals were not stained by all this. The barbarians were unlike the Romans about whom I have spoken; the barbarians set themselves to correct the stain of our baseness. They removed from every place in Africa that lowly vice of effeminate men. They even abstained from contacts with prostitutes and, not only have they abstained from or removed prostitution for the time being, but they have made it completely cease to exist.

O holy Lord! O good Saviour! How much the desire for good living accomplishes through You: desire through which the vices of nature can be changed, just as they have been changed by the Vandals! And how were they changed? It is of interest to talk, not only about the effects, but also the causes of the effects. It is difficult to take away impurity by a word or command unless it has been actually removed, and it is difficult to exact purity by a command unless it had been exacted in the past.

The Vandals, knowing this, removed impurity, while they preserved unchaste women. They did not kill these unfortunate women, lest they defile with cruelty their healing of vices and lest, while they sought to take away sin, they themselves sin in lopping off the sinners. They corrected the sinners in this manner so that the accomplishment was curative, not punitive.

They ordered and compelled all prostitutes to enter the married state. They turned harlots into wives, fulfilling that saying and command of the Apostle, that every woman should have her own husband and every man his own wife;[51] that since incontinence cannot be restrained without this yielding to carnal usage, in this way natural desire should receive a legitimate outlet, so that there would not be sin by incontinence.

In this way they not only provided that women who could not live without men should have them, but that these women who did not know how to protect themselves would be safe, as it were, through their domestic guardians. By constantly adhering to the marital course, even if the habit of their previous impurity would entice them to depraved acts, their husband's supervision would nevertheless prevent them from straying.

For the suppression of lust the Vandals also added severe ordinances for chastity. They repressed impurity with the sword of the law, so that the affection of marriage at home and the fear of the law in public preserved the purity of both sexes. Thus, morality rested upon a double defense, since it had love indoors and fear outdoors. The Vandal laws never were in accord with those Roman laws which so removed a portion of the wrong that they could commit the obscene portion, or those Roman laws which forbade adultery with other men's wives, but freely permitted the act with all single women.[52] They thus forbade adultery, but set up brothels. It seems the Romans feared men would be too chaste and pure if they completely prevented them from all impurity.

But not so the Vandals about whom I am speaking, who thus forbade prostitution as well as adultery; who wished

---
51 1 Cor. 7.2.
52 *Cod. Theo.* 9.7,1.

women to be wives to none but their husbands and men to be husbands to none but their wives; who did not permit intercourse to stray outside the legitimate marriage bed. They directed their laws according to the rule of divine Law, so that they believe nothing is lawful in this matter which God does not wish to be lawful. They thought that no man should permit himself anything unless it is permitted to all by God.

(23) I know what I say seems intolerable to some, but I must act according to the reason of things, not to the whims of wishes. Let anyone who is angry at me tell me: Has not Socrates always been considered the wisest of all men and that even by the testimony of the Delphic demon who was, as it were, the prince of philosophers as well as the prince of demons? Let us see what laws Socrates appointed about chastity and what laws the Vandals, about whom I am speaking, decreed. Socrates said:[53] 'Let no man have his own wife, for marriages should be common to all; for thus there will be greater harmony among the cities if all the men cohabit, without discrimination, with all the women: and all the women submit themselves to all the men, without discrimination: if all the men become the husbands of all the women, all the women will become the wives of all the men.'

Have we ever known any madman or one possessed of the devil, or one made raving mad by the various blemishes of insanities, who spoke anything like this? You say, O greatest of philosophers, that by this ordinance all the men are the husbands of all the women, and all the women are the wives of all the men, and the children are the children of all. But I say that, by this ordinance, no man is the husband of any

---

[53] Plato, *Republic* 5, 437.

woman nor is any woman the wife of any man, nor is any offspring the child of any parent, for, where all is promiscuity and confusion, there is nobody who can claim anything as his own.

As some say, it was not sufficient for the wisest of philosophers to teach this unless he practiced it, that is, he gave his wife to another man, just as Cato the Roman who is the other Socrates of Italy.[54] Behold what things are the examples of Roman and Attic wisdom! They made all husbands, inasmuch as was in their power to do so, their wives' pimps. Socrates, however, surpassed the others. He composed books on this subject and bequeathed to posterity these shameful thoughts.[55] He had more whereby he could glorify himself by his teachings. Insofar as it pertains to his teaching, he made a brothel of the world.

He is said to have been unjustly condemned by his judges. This is true, for it would be more proper for the whole human race to condemn him when he was actually teaching these doctrines, just as it has, doubtlessly, condemned him. In this matter, all have repudiated his teaching, all have condemned him not only by the authority of the sentence passed on him at his trial, but what is much greater and more rightly so, by their choice of a way of life.

Let the ordinances he laid down be compared with those decreed by the men whom God ordered to rule Africa. He ordained that no man should completely have his own wife; the Vandals, that every man should have his own. He, that every women subject herself to every man; they, that no woman should know a man other than her husband. He advocated a promiscuous and confused conception of offspring; they, a pure and regulated conception. He wished every

---
54 Cato gave his wife, Marcia, to a friend to breed children.
55 Probable reference to Plato's *Socratic Dialogues*.

house to be a brothel; they, that there be no brothels. He tried to establish brothels in every house; they have removed them even from the cities. He wished to prostitute all virgins; they wished to make prostitutes chaste.

Would that this was the error only of Socrates, and not of very many and of almost all Romans, who follow the teachings of Socrates in this respect, although they do not follow his way of life in other respects. Many men each have several wives, and many wives have several men each. Are not all our cities filled with evil dens and stinking with houses of prostitution? Because I have said all, I mean certainly the noblest and most splendid cities. Such is the dignity and even the prerogative of the highest positions of great cities that, as the cities excel others in size, so are they to the fore in impurity.

I ask: What hope can there be for the Roman State when the barbarians are more chaste and more pure than the Romans? What I say is of little value. I ask: What hope of pardon or of life can there be for us in the sight of God when we see chastity among the barbarians and are, ourselves, unchaste? I say: Let us be ashamed and confused. Among the Goths, the only impure ones are the Romans. There are no impure ones among the Vandals except the Romans. Among them, so much has the eagerness for chastity and the severity of discipline profited them that not only are they themselves chaste, but let me say something novel and unbelievable, something almost even unheard of, they have even made the Romans chaste.

If human weakness allowed it, I would wish to shout beyond my strength, so that I would be echoed over the whole world: You, O Roman people, be ashamed; be ashamed of your lives. Almost no cities are free of evil dens, are altogether free of impurities, except these cities in which the barbarians have begun to live. And we in our misery, who are so impure, wonder if we are conquered by enemy forces, we who are surpassed by them in character. We wonder if they who curse our evils have taken possession of our property. It is not the natural vigor of their bodies that enables them to conquer us, nor is it our natural weakness that has caused our conquest. Let nobody persuade himself otherwise. Let nobody think otherwise. The vices of our bad lives have alone conquered us.

BOOK EIGHT

I AM OF THE OPINION, indeed, I am certain, that the great length of this discourse is tiresome to many, very largely because it castigates the vices of our daily lives. In a way, all wish to be praised. Reproof is pleasing to nobody. What is much worse, no matter how bad, no matter how depraved a man, he prefers to be lauded in a lying manner than reproved in a right manner. He prefers to be deceived by the mockery of false praise, rather than made whole by the most healthful advice.

Since this is the case, what is to be done? Must we be servile to the whim of wicked men? If they wish valueless praise conferred upon them, is it becoming that we, too, heap valueless and laughable praise on them? And this especially since they who wish to be ridiculous should not be laughed at by honorable men, just as they who desire to be decorated even with the label of false praise should not be praised in a lying manner. Our prime consideration should be not so much what they wish to hear as what it is fitting for us to say, especially since the prophet says:[1] 'Woe to them who speak sweet for bitter things and bitter for sweet things.'

Therefore, the truth should be maintained in every way, so that what a thing is in fact, that it is in words; that those things which contain sweetness are called sweet, and those that contain bitterness are called bitter. This is especially true in dealing with sacred things, when many reckon our iniquities as a cause for anger against God. They presume to accuse God so

---
[1] Isa. 5.20.

that they themselves are not made to seem blameworthy. What is it other than to accuse God of slothfulness, abuse, and injustice, when they blaspheme by saying that He is careless and negligent of human affairs, or that He does not govern justly, or even that He does not govern at all?

O blindness of human folly! O madness of raving rashness! O man, you are calling God careless and negligent! If you were to injure any freeborn man with such slander, you would be guilty in the law courts of excessive abuse. Certainly, if you injured a man of the noble and higher class, you would even bear publicly the punishment meted out by law. These reproaches are thrown at boys or generally profligate people. It is the special outcry against evil boys that they be called wasteful, careless, and negligent of their property.

O sacrilegious words! O profane impudence! We call God what is said only of the most profligate of men. And this is not the only abuse hurled at Him. Take note, as I have said before, that the charge of injustice is fastened on Him. If we do not deserve the hardships we are suffering and are unworthy to endure our present miseries, we are calling unjust God, who orders us to endure undeserved evils.

You say He not so much orders as He permits this. Let us suppose that this is so. But, I ask, how far is He from ordering what He permits? For He who knows that we bear these sufferings and can prevent our suffering them proves without a doubt that we should bear and sustain whatever He permits. Hence, we see that this permission belongs to His judgment and that it is according to a heavenly sentence that we are suffering. Since all things belong to God's authority and the nod of God directs all things, whatever evil and punishment we bear daily is the wrath of the divine hand, which we arouse and cause to be kindled constantly by our sins.

We light the fire of heavenly anger and we fan the very flames in which we burn. Indeed, as often as we commit these evils that saying of the Prophet can rightly be applied to us:[2] 'Go into the flame of the fire which you have kindled.' Therefore, according to the Sacred Sentence, each sinner prepares for himself what he suffers.[3] We can impute none of our misfortunes to God; we are the authors of our own misfortunes. God is tender and merciful, and, as it is written, wishes that none perish or grieve.[4] We do everything against ourselves. There is nothing, nothing, more cruel to us than ourselves. We, I repeat, torture ourselves even against the will of God.

Surely, I seem to be contradicting myself. I have previously said that we are punished by God because of our sins, and now I say that we are punished by ourselves. Both are true. We are, indeed, punished by God, but we act so that He has to punish us. Since we ourselves cause our own punishment, who doubts that we punish ourselves for our own crimes? For, whoever gives cause for his punishment punishes himself, according to the saying,[5] 'each one is bound by the rope of his own sins.' Therefore, if evil men are bound by the ropes of their own sins, each and every sinner, doubtless, binds himself when he sins.

(2) Because I have already said much about the impurities of the Africans, let me say a few words about their blasphemies, for in that land very many continue to profess paganism. They harbored within their native walls a native crime. I speak about Celestis,[6] that demon of the Africans, to whom, I believe, the pagans of old gave such a striking

---
2 Isa. 50.11.
3 Ps. 7.9.
4 1 Tim. 2.4.
5 Prov. 5.22.
6 This is the Goddess Tanit. See article, "Tanit," in Pauly-Wissowa, *Real-Encyclopadie der Classischen Altertums-Wissenschaft*.

name that, although she has no divinity, she should at least have a title. Since she did not possess any virtue from her own power, she should at least have dignity from the name bestowed on her.

Who was not initiated in this idol's rites? Who was not initiated in them by his family, perhaps even at birth? I speak about men who are professed and actual pagans and who live as such. Just as these men are lacking in religion because of error, so they cannot be called religious. Paganism is more tolerable and less criminal in men who profess it. Far more injurious and evil is that many of those who avowedly profess Christ serve idols in their hearts.

Which of these who are called Christians did not adore the goddess Celestis after they adored Christ or, what is much worse, before they adored Christ? Who among them do not enter the portal of the Lord's house, filled with the smell of demoniacal sacrifices, and ascend to the altar of Christ, smelling of the foulness of these very demons? It would be less blameworthy not to have come to the Lord's temple at all as to come in this manner, because a Christian who does not come to church is guilty of negligence, but he who comes like this is guilty of sacrilege. It is less difficult to atone for honor that is not shown to God than for injury inflicted on Him.

Therefore, whoever does these things does not honor God. They take honor away from Him. In a way, they have given to an idol the very respect due the Church, because second degree respect is given to the dignity of the one from whom the principal honors are taken away. Take a look at the faith of the Africans, especially of the nobility: behold the quality of their religion and their Christianity! They were called Christians for the insult of Christ. Though the Apostle cried out:[7]

---

[7] 1 Cor. 10.21.

'You cannot drink the chalice of the Lord and the chalice of the demons, you cannot participate at the table of the Lord and at the table of demons,' it was not enough for them to drink the chalice of demons with the chalice of God; they preferred the chalice of demons. Nor was it sufficient for them to pair the table of demons with the Lord's table. Coming to the temple of God after the worship of sacrilegious superstitions, they breathed on the sacrosanct altars of Christ the most unclean breath of the very spirit of the demon.

(3) You say, all do not commit these sacrileges, but only the most powerful and those placed in high office. Let us agree that this is so. Yet, since the richest and certainly the most powerful households constitute the majority of the city, you see that the whole city was corrupted through the sacrilegious superstitions of a few. Nobody doubts that all families are either like or worse than their masters. In fact, they are usually worse. Therefore, when even good masters have slaves who are quite evil, it is easy to understand of what nature all the families in that country were, where the lack of morality in the masters made servile minds, already evil in themselves, still worse.

Grant that what I have said applies to the most powerful and to some who are high in office. Were those vices which are shared by noble and commoner alike less serious? I am speaking of the hatreds and maledictions poured on all holy men, for it is a type of sacrilege to hate the worshippers of God—just as he who strikes our servants strikes us in injuring our servants. If the son of another man is flogged by a stranger, paternal love is tortured by the punishment inflicted on the son. In the same way, when a servant of God is injured by anyone, violence is done to the divine Majesty, as the Lord said to His Apostles:[8] 'He who receives you, receives Me, and he who despises you, despises Me.'

The most loving and tender Lord made honor and reproach common to Himself and His servants, so that, when anybody injures a servant of God, he should not think that he is injuring only a man. Without doubt, injury to God is mingled with injury to the Lord's servants, as God in His most indulgent love testifies to His followers in this fashion:[9] 'for he who touches you, touches, as it were, the pupil of My eye.' In order to express the tenderness of His love, He indicated the most sensitive part of the human body, so that we might understand most clearly that God is injured by so small an insult to His saints as the sharpness of human vision is impaired by the touch of a slight blow. Thus the Africans pursued and hated God's servants and in them God.

(4) Perhaps it is asked in what ways is the existence of this hate proved? In those ways in which even the hatred of the Jews against Christ is proved, when they said to Him:[10] 'You are a Samaritan and you have a demon'; when they ridiculed Him; when they cursed Him; when they breathed into His face and gnashed their teeth over His head. Hence also in the psalms, so said the Saviour Himself:[11] 'all who saw laughed Me to scorn and spoke with their lips and shook their heads.' And elsewhere He said:[12] 'they have tempted Me and derided Me with scorn. They gnashed their teeth against Me.'

In this manner, the Africans manifested their hate against the monks, that is, the saints of God, by ridiculing them, by cursing them, by hounding them, by detesting them, by doing

---

8 Luke 10.16; Matt. 10.40.
9 Zach. 2.8.
10 John 8.48.
11 Ps. 28.8.
12 Ps. 34.16; Jer. 20.7.

almost everything against them which the impiety of the Jews had done against our Saviour before they came to the very shedding of the divine Blood.¹³ But, you say, the Africans did not kill the saints as we read that the Jews did. I do not know whether or not they killed them, neither do I claim they did. However, is it not a great defense for the Africans that the only element lacking in their pagan-like persecution was the objective proper to persecution?

Let us admit that the saints were not killed in that country. Yet, what do we do about the fact that they who hate with the intention of killing are not far removed from killing, especially since the Lord Himself said:¹⁴ 'he who hates his brother without cause, is a murderer.' Not without cause did they persecute the servants of God. For, who can say it was without cause, because they saw men who differed from themselves in all pursuits of life and in every mode of life, and in whom they saw nothing of their own, because everything belonged to God? The greatest cause of disharmony is diversity of objectives, because it cannot altogether or scarcely happen that a man love that same thing in another with which he himself is in disagreement.

Thus, as I have said, not without cause did they hate them in whom they perceived that all things were opposed and inimical to their own tendencies. One lived constantly in wickedness; the other, in innocence. One lived in lust; the other, in chastity. One lived in evil dens; the other, in monasteries. One lived almost constantly with the devil; the other, unceasingly with Christ. Therefore, it was not without cause that within the cities of Africa, and especially within the walls of Carthage, a people as unhappy as they were, lacking in faith,

---

13 A similar situation existed in Rome, according to Saint Jerome; cf. *Nicene and Post-Nicene Fathers* 2.6.48-49, 53.
14 1 John 3.15.

could view without reproach and curses a man cloaked and pallid, the strands of his flowing hair sheared off even to his skin.

And when any servant of God, either from the cenobitic monasteries of Egypt, or the holy places of Jerusalem, or the holy and venerated recesses of the desert, came to Carthage for the performance of God's duties, he received abuse, profanation, and curses at the very moment he appeared to the people. Not only this, he was struck down by the vilest jeering of dissolute men and by the hateful, bull-like whistling of mockers. Truly, if any man who did not know about these things saw them happen, he would not think that somebody was being made sport of, but that some new and unheard of monster was being driven and expelled from the city limits.

(5) Behold the faith of the Africans and especially of the Carthaginians! It was safer for the Apostles in their time to enter pagan cities, and those savage and barbarous gatherings of profane men hated much less their first arrival and appearance than the people of Carthage later hated the monks. The people of Athens, though most superstitious, patiently listened to that holy vessel of election, the Apostle Paul, speaking about the worship and majesty of the one God. The people of Lyconia marveled so much that, when they saw the divine strength that was in the Apostles, they did not believe that they were human. But in Carthage the servants of God were scarcely allowed to appear without insults and curses on the streets and crossroads.

Some think this was not persecution, because they were not killed. Robbers, indeed, are wont to use this proverb, that they whose lives they spare have given them their lives. But in Carthage this favor was owed not so much to men as to laws, for even the laws of the Twelve Tables forbade that any unsentenced man be put to death. From this it can be realized how great was the prerogative of the Lord's religion in that place where His servants could escape being slaughtered at the hands of Christians only because they were protected by pagan law.

And we wonder that they now suffer at the hands of barbarians, when we see that the saints endured barbarous punishment at the hands of the natives. The Lord is just, and just in His judgment.[15] As it is written:[16] 'as they have sowed, so have they reaped,' so that truly the Lord seems to have spoken about the wickedness of this people:[17] 'give unto her according to her work; according to all she had done, do unto her, because she has been raised against the Lord.' Let us not wonder at all nor be angry that they now endure some evil treatment from men. If the dignity of God and their character are juxtaposed, the evil treatment they have given to God before is far greater, and what they suffer is less than they deserve for their deeds.[18]

---
15 Ps. 118.137.
16 Gal. 6.8.
17 Jer. 50.29.
18 Here the text ends abruptly, without a full development of the author's theme. Since the treatise was finished many years before Salvian's death, it is proper to conclude that the text, as we have it, is incomplete.

LETTERS

CONTENTS

		Page
I	To the Monks at Lerins	237
II	To Bishop Eucherius	240
III	To Bishop Agrycius	241
IV	To Hypatius and Quieta	241
V	To Cuttura	251
VI	To Limenius	253
VII	To Aper and Verus	253
VIII	To Bishop Eucherius	255
IX	To Bishop Salonius	256

LETTERS

LETTER ONE

To the Monks at Lerins[1]

LOVE, I know not what to call you, good or evil, sweet or bitter, pleasant or unpleasant, for you art so filled with both qualities that you seem to be both. It is proper to love our friends; it is bitter to offend them. Yet there are times when this comes from the same mind, from the same heart. When there is discord in appearance, there is concord in the soul. For love, indeed, makes us love our friends. Love sometimes compels us to hurt them. These two are one and the same; although one has the good name of love, the other the bad name of hate.

How difficult, I ask, or how bitter it is, my dearest friends, when love is forced to be harsh. I am very much afraid there has happened to me what has often happened to others, namely, that being solicitous for one I may become irksome to many. When I wish to hand over to my inseparable friends the young man I am sending to you, my love for him may be the cause of offense to the others. They who have enough love are not easily offended.

While I am afraid that my recommendation might be less well received by certain people, I think their hesitation is itself not without offense. While desiring greatly to please my beloved ones, I believe my offense annoys them, and, unless

---

[1] Written from Marseilles to his friends, the monks at Lerins, asking assistance for his young noble kinsman, a refugee from Cologne.

I please them adequately, I will bear the penalty of one who displeases.

On this point, although among yourselves who so wholeheartedly received me in your midst there is no place whatever for fear, still, in regard to others, you fear for me. My dearest and most beloved friends, so far am I from being able to displease either your heart or your head that you are afraid, as I am afraid, that I should displease somebody else.

The young man whom I have sent you was, together with his people, captured at Cologne. He at one time had no little fame among his friends. He was well-born and is now well-off. He is one about whom I should perhaps say something more, were it not that he is my kinsman. Thus it happens that I do not say all I could, lest I seem to speak about myself by speaking further about him. The young man to whom I am referring left his mother, an upright and honored widow, behind him at Cologne. She truly is a widow about whom I can speak in a forthright manner. In addition to her other virtues of chastity and wisdom, she is a woman noble in her faith, which is always an additional glory, however honored one is, because without faith there is nothing great enough to ennoble one.

This noble woman, it is rumored, is in such great need and indigence there [at Cologne] that she lacks the means either of staying or departing, because she has not enough either to live on or to flee. She is without the wherewithal requisite for livelihood or flight. The only thing left her is that, seeking food as pay for work, she has hired out her hands to the wives of the barbarians. In this way, although by the mercy of God she has been exempt from the chains of captivity, she is a servant through poverty, but she is not reduced to the condition of slavery.

This lady was not wrong in surmising that I possess the

good will of some holy people here. (Nor do I deny this, lest my denial seem ingratitude. It is clear that, while I do not deny that I possess it, I am quite sure that I do not deserve it, so much so that, although I do possess a measure of their good will, I, nevertheless, am not the cause of it. Whatever good will there is, it has been principally shown me, if I am not mistaken, on account of those who were interested that I should be well received. Consequently, it is perhaps to be feared that, in not acknowledging to them what I have received on their account, I should seem to be denying not so much what is mine but what is theirs.) This lady, thinking that it was in my power or more than in my power to help, sent to me this young man whom I am sending to you, in the hope that through my agency and endeavors the good will of my friends would come to the aid of my relatives.

Thus, I have done what I was asked to do, but I have done it charily and to few people, lest I should be ungracious in using this favor. I have commended this young man to the others, as to you. In the first place, it is not necessary to recommend overmuch a young man who is a relative of mine, no more than it would be necessary to recommend myself. Second, since you reckon me as one of yourselves, you must necessarily consider him who is a part of me somewhat as a part of yourselves. Lastly, my recommendation, being of a different kind, is also of a more excellent character. To others I have commended this young man in body, to you, in spirit; to others for the benefits of the present life, to you for the hope of eternity; to others on account of short-lived and earthly things, to you, for eternal and heavenly things. And rightly so. Because you are less solicitous for goods of the flesh than of the spirit, I have asked you for more of the latter, since you abound more in it.

Therefore, I ask you, receive this young man as my flesh,

and make him, so far as you can, one of your own. Lead and exhort him, teach, train, mold, and regenerate him. May the mercy of Christ our Lord grant that he who is kinsman to me and to the others, because it is more expedient for him, may begin to become kinsman to you, rather than to his own relatives.

I ask you, admit him into those blessed and eternal homes. Receive him into the sacred storehouses. Open to him the treasures of heaven, and so act and proceed that, while you store this young man among your treasures, you make him a part of these very treasures. Powerful is that kindness of the ineffable God that, by adopting him into the fellowship of spiritual goods, you, through him, increase the riches you lavish on him. Indeed, if there is some good natural qualification in him, his hope and salvation should not be of great difficulty to you. Even if he receives no teaching from you, surely the fact that he sees your example is sufficient. Farewell.

LETTER TWO

Salvian to Bishop Eucherius

Your pupil, Ursicinus, recently brought your greetings to me. If he was not ordered to do so, I praise his wisdom, although I do not approve of falsehood. If he was ordered, I wonder why you preferred to entrust a service of love to another rather than to write, that is, why you preferred to send a message through your servant rather than through yourself. Therefore I bring this up and want it corrected, if it is due to negligence and not to pride. Conceit is generally the footmaid of a new honor, although a trace of a vice so universal must not be suspected in you, because your mind and your kindness are almost singular in their kind. Because of this I also now constantly desire a reciprocation of my old regard for you, so that, in case the custom of your duties towards some varies in certain respects, you will not seem to be taking advantage of your new honors.

LETTER THREE

Salvian to Bishop Agrycius

If I wish to excuse my undutifulness toward your holiness, I am more worthy of accusation because either I do not recognize that I am inexcusable through stupidity or I am unwilling to acknowledge it through pride. Therefore, I will not excuse myself, because it increases the crime to make an ostentatious display of innocence when one is at fault. What shall I do, who have no means either of denying or of justifying my crime? I dare not deny things that are evident, and I cannot excuse things that are beyond bounds. Therefore, I must take refuge in the healing of sacred letters, which the greatest crimes. . . .[1]

LETTER FOUR

Salvian, Palladia and Auspiciola, Greetings to Their Parents, Hypatius and Quieta

Although the Apostle Paul, the Master of Speech, Vessel of Election, Master of the Faith, and Receptacle of God, composed all his letters, yet there were some to which he did not affix his own name only. Indeed, to some he affixed the name Silvanus; to some, Timothy; in others, he added his own

---

1 Lacuna in text.

name to that of Silvanus and Timothy. Why did he do this? First, I believe, in order that they who wrote together should be recognized as being together. Next, that they who had been instructed separately by one or the other of them would know that the doctrine of all three was not different. Lastly, that the approbation of all would at length move to conversion those whom the authority of individuals would not change.

In this way we both, little imitators of great examples, write to you whom we have as parents by nature, brethren by faith, and masters by honor. We write, not with the authority of teachers, as the Apostles themselves wrote, but with the humility of servants, so that you who so far have not been moved by our individual letters may now be moved by the supplication of all. To avoid unnecessary fear, know that we, your children, are living together, share the same thoughts, the same fears, and pray in the same manner, not because we know whether you are angry with all, but because we cannot be divided on account of our objectives.

Our fear is the same, even if our offence does not seem the same. Although you are, perhaps, not angry with both of us, surely our mutual love acts in such a way that, when one of us is guilty, the other must feel sorrow at the guilt of his companion. This, indeed, is what makes us withstand anyone and resist together. This, indeed, is why we, both your children, are equally guilty. This, indeed, is why each of us fears more for the other than for himself.

Dearest parents, most respected parents, we request permission to put these questions to you. Can offspring so loving not be loved? Of what great fault are we guilty? Of what kind is the love of a most beloved and most respected master,

---

1 Palladia and Auspiciola were the wife and daughter and Hypatius and Quieta were father-in law and mother-in law of Salvian.

when favor is not shown us as children and offense is not forgiven us as to servants?

It is almost seven years since you have written to us, situated so far from you. Almost on none who sins against God is there imposed such a long time for mourning. . . .[2] The severity of a father should not be an obstacle but a pathway for love, since, whatever the discipline of one has brought to correction, so much should correction return to the love of the other.

Yet, it is more fitting for those parents who have true reasons for being angry with their children about some affairs to act in this manner. But you, who, since you became Christian, have ceased even to have false reasons for being angry, why are you angry? Grant that you, as a former pagan, did not look kindly on my conversion, such as it was. At that time, it had to be borne because of a diversity of interests and even a disharmony of wishes. At that time, though your love was not angry with us, your superstition still opposed us. Though a father should not have hated his daughter, error nevertheless hated truth. Now, the situation is different.

From the fact that you have professed the worship of God, you have given me a favorable verdict. Blame yourself if you continue to prosecute the past causes of anger, namely, that you gave your daughter to a Christian. If that is not the case, why are you angry with me because I now desire to increase the faith in me which you have begun to esteem good in yourself? You who have condemned in yourself what you were, why, I ask, do you not love in me what you yourself are?

I must be somewhat sparing of words, because, to be humble, in a good cause, a son's speech should be humble, when

---
2 Lacuna in text.

at all possible, in the presence of his parents. Forgive me, my dearest loves. The love of God makes me somewhat more unrestrained in His business. If there are other reasons for your anger, I do not deny that I could have sinned against them. But in this respect, whereby you are angry because I seem to love Christ, pardon what I am about to say.

Indeed, I ask pardon because you are angry, but I cannot say that what I have done is bad. I have thus put these pleadings before you in my own name and, as it were, with my own private request. Now you, most beloved and venerable sister,[3] do your share and mine at the same time. You are all the more dear to me than formerly, because it is fitting that love be loved more by one's own in whom Christ caused Himself to be loved. Pray that I may obtain what I ask. Beseech that we both may win our cause. Because you are separated and cannot do so with your lips, kiss at least by supplication the feet of your parents as a handmaid, their hands as a foster child, as a daughter their mouths.

Do not tremble, do not be afraid. We have favorably disposed judges. Love itself pleads on your behalf. Nature itself pleads your cause. You have the votes for the decision to your case in the hearts of your people. They who are overcome by their love assent quickly. Entreat, therefore, and speak as a suppliant: 'What have I deserved? Of what am I guilty? Pardon whatever it is. I seek pardon, though I know not for what transgression.

'As you know, I have never offended you by undutifulness or disobedience. I have never injured you with bitter words. I have never outraged you with an impudent look. By you I was given to a man. By you I was delivered to a husband. Unless I am mistaken, I hold fast to your commands. There

---
3 His wife, Palladia.

clings to my heart the holy mystery of your loving teaching. I believed you ordered me to be obedient to my husband before everything else. I have followed your wishes; I have obeyed your command. In all things I have obeyed him whom you wished me to obey.

'He instructed me in the faith. He introduced me to chastity. Grant me pardon. I believe I resisted what was base. To me this seemed a chaste, modest, and holy act. I confess that when he talked about this business with me I blushed, because I had not begun before this. And then there also came reverence and love for Christ. Whatever I had done for the love of God I believed I was doing because it was right.

'I am casting myself at your feet, dearest parents, I, your Palladia, your jackdaw, your little lady with whom, in so many like words, you once played in your most tender love. I, Palladia, who to you by different names was now mother, now a little bird, now mistress, when there was one word for species, another for childhood, and a third for honor. Behold, I am she through whom the names of parents, and the joys of grandparents especially joined, and, what is above both, the happiness attached to these two conditions, that is, of having children and of enjoying them to the full. It is not that I take any credit to myself for this, yet she through whom God wished you to be happy must not be ungrateful in your presence.

'I ask, therefore, let it not be irksome to you that I wish to give back something to God whom I cannot recompense for everything. You are filled with the most pleasant consolation, surrounded by your dearest offspring, filled with divine blessing. Even outside my own particular case, your affairs prescribe that I return thanks to God. I think I am indebted to Him because He has given you so much.' But enough of this, dearest sister, for we have already beseeched sufficiently through ourselves. The remainder must be done through our daughter.[4]

Let us make use, therefore, (for all things are attempted for reconciling the love of parents), let us make use of the practice and example of those men who, to move judges to mercy in the final stages of lawsuits, produced living examples before the judges who were about to deliver the sentence. They brought forth weeping mothers, or shabbily dressed old men, or bewailing, obtrusive little children. They acted in this way for the purpose of finishing by this spectacle, as a counsel's speech, what their words had already begun.

Accordingly, we, your offspring, offer ourselves to you, dearest parents, with a petition like the above pleaders, yet with a more agreeable petitioner. We present an offspring who is not an unknown, but one of your household, not an outsider, but your own. She is an offspring, not, as those orators presented, strange to themselves and the judges, but one at the same time common to us and to you. We present you an offspring who partakes of your own blood and compels you, not toward the love of persons unknown, but recalls you to love toward your own. Nor does she, as an outsider, commend outsiders to you. She, your own, commends your own children to you. Nor does she pray that you love them whom you have never before seen, but that you should not hate those whom, I think, you have been unable not to love.

Therefore, dearest parents, this business is your affair. Your sympathy and love beg this from you. I ask, be not so angry with us that you do not consult your own interests . . .[5] This offspring at the same time common through us and with us, and who almost sent the first word to you on behalf of our transgression. Truly unhappy is she and miserable her

---
4 Auspiciola.
5 Lacuna in text.

state of mind, who first began to understand her grandparents through the guilty charge laid against her parents.

We ask, have pity on her innocence, have pity on her necessity. In a manner, she who still does not know what it is to offend is compelled to beg on behalf of the transgression of her family. When, at one time, God had been offended by the sins of the Ninevites, He was appeased by the crying and wailing of children. For, though we read that the whole people wept, yet the lot and innocence of the little ones merited the greatest mercy. God said to Jonah:[6] 'You are greatly grieved for the gourd.' And a little later:[7] 'I shall not spare Nineveh, the great city, in which there are more than one hundred twenty thousand persons, who know not their left hand from their right hand.' He thereby declared that, because of the purity of the innocent ones, He was also sparing the faults of the guilty ones.

But why do I speak of the mercy of God who gave not only the things requested, but continues to bestow things which are not even hoped for, and in such a measure that, if it is permissible to speak so, He is greater than men by His kindness and good will by as much as He is greater by His nature and power.

According to Livy,[8] a war was prepared between the Romans and the Sabines. Since the war had begun and since it could be stopped only with difficulty, they had their dear offspring offer up intercessory prayers. While one of those peoples was savage in nature, the other was soured by affiliation, yet the sight of mutual love was of such great worth that neither could the Roman be mindful of the war nor the Sabine of the insult. They who a little while previously were

---
6 Jonas 4.10.
7 Jonas 4.11.
8 Livy 1.13.

untamed semi-barbarians, lusting for each other's blood and each other's lives, began to love each other, because they had already begun to have a mutual offspring and became one and the same people. This was because the love of both was unified.

We do not stand in the battle line. We do not take up arms. We do not use violence. We do not seek recourse to force. We regard as impious those children who take up arms against their parents in order to punish an injustice. Why, I ask, are our children unable to procure for us what the love of the Romans and Sabine children formerly obtained for their people? Are we the most unhappy of almost all beings and do we merit pardon less because we know not how to offer resistance?

We are suffering what you wish us to suffer. If you are angry, we are sorry. If you believe we should be punished, we agree. I ask: What revenge remains after you have done this? Certainly, if parents have just reasons for being angry, there is nothing that can give them greater happiness or fulfillment of their hopes than that their children make satisfaction for their guilt. Thus, it is not considered necessary for the parents to punish them.

But in what respect can we make more satisfaction to you? We are your children who ask you. It is a granddaughter through whom we ask you. Dearest parents, spare and forgive. They on account of whose names you are wont to deny nothing even to strangers are begging on their own behalf. It would be going too far to speak about innumerable examples of love and kindness, and it is absurd to go from greater to lesser examples. Yet, that which I am about to mention is indeed apparently less, but is not less in actuality.

Servius Galba was pleading at one time in the Roman Forum on behalf of his own reputation and life. Because of the difficulty of the situation and the unpopularity of his deed, he placed little hope in his case, and even in his eloquence. He thereupon used skill and tried to move by the love of humanity the minds of the judges whom he could not bend by the solicitation of his prayers. And thus, when all the reserves of his oratorical art and genius had been exhausted and he knew that he had accomplished little, he produced a little boy whom he had with him, as was the custom at that time. This was the son of Gallus, a brilliant and recently dead man. Servius displayed the boy's small talents before the judges' bench in the assembly and in sight of the judges. The minds of all whom he charged in a low voice were touched and favorably disposed when it came time for the judges to deliver sentence. What happened then? The result was that, when the minds of all were favorably inclined, mercy gave to kindness all that justice had denied to entreaty.

O love, how kind you are, how strong which even in judgment could restrict justice. Learn, dearest parents; let this be said of your kindness. Learn, so that you are touched and softened by this example. Certainly, mercy prevailed in that place where mercy had no room. The judges who were about to deliver the sentence, and who had sworn that they would not pronounce a sentence except one based on truth, were unable to exclude mercy even after they had taken an oath. They were so moved by kindness that, while they paid attention to another's affairs, they almost forgot their own.

We beg you for nothing difficult, nothing unusual. Give to your own, for yourselves, what the judges gave to strangers, against their better judgment. Certainly, the cause there was not more just, nor the person more dear, nor the audience more kind, nor the orator more persuasive. There, it was done on behalf of a crime, here for love; there for strangers, here for children; there in the presence of judges sworn to do justice, here before unsworn parents; there through an orator who tried to circumvent, here through a granddaughter who moves you all the more by the very simplicity of her infancy, because she does not yet know how to ask.

What is it that is lacking to the case? What new and unheard of petition must we offer? Must we use the prayers of outsiders to plead with you? There is always caution in love, for there is nobody who loves better than he who greatly fears to offend. Hence, I now ask forgiveness, not because I knew I was offending, but in order to leave no room for reproach. I now ask forgiveness, not in the knowledge of my fault, but by the reason and duty of love, in order that my prayer may merit a greater loving favor in your eyes, and that, being without guilt, the supplication of the innocent may advance the cause of love. Because of your love, you will possess more in your son's prayer for pardon if you have nothing to forgive.

Perhaps we heedlessly flatter ourselves about our innocence, since we do not know what you feel about us. A reason must be had for your feeling towards us more than for our way of thinking. All that remains is that you who deem whatever we have done worthy of offense should not also consider it unworthy of forgiveness. By pardoning the guilt of your children you will make for yourselves an excellent recompense. A forgiving father does not waste revenge on his son, because it is much better and laudable for anyone to forgive his own people, even undeservedly, than to be avenged on them deservedly. Farewell.

LETTER FIVE

Salvian to His Sister Cattura

According to the teaching of the Apostle Paul,[1] 'we do not know what we should pray for as we ought.' Hence it happens that sometimes we do not know for what we should wish or rejoice. According to the love common to the human race (by which we almost all desire lovingly, rather than wisely, that they for whom we care should be with us a very long time), I rejoice that after a long and serious illness you have attained a hope of the present life, a hope which you always have had of the future life.

Blessed be our Lord God, therefore, who was always the guardian of your soul, and now of your body, also. He has remained in you and guarded you. He has stretched forth His hand from your soul even to your body. He has preserved not only the Holy of Holies, but even the entrance and surroundings of His temple. He has spread His protection wider and caused the health of your soul to reach even into the health of your body.

However, I think that this illness of your little earthly vessel which you bore was not even injurious to you, for, ordinarily, as you know, the health of the body is inimical to the soul. Consequently, I think you are now rightly that much stronger in the spirit as you have begun to be weak in the flesh. For the flesh, says the Apostle,[2] 'lusts against the spirit and the spirit against the flesh. For these are opposed, one to the other, so that you do not do the things that you wish.'

Therefore, if we cannot do the things we wish because of

---
1 Rom. 8.26.
2 Gal. 5.17.

the opposition maintained by the body, the flesh must be weakened so that we can do what we wish to do. It is true that the weakness of the flesh sharpens our mental faculties. When muscular strength is weakened, the strength of the body is transferred into invigoration of the soul. Thus, to me it seems a kind of health that man at times should not be healthy. In a way, there is no contest between the soul and the body. There is no contest between an attribute which is divine and an enemy which is of the earth. It is not the heart which burns with unseemly flames, nor hidden incentives that inflame the sickly mind, nor untamed senses that gambol through varied forms of delight. It is the soul alone that exults. It is the soul that rejoices when the body is sick as when an enemy has been overcome.

And so, pupil of Christ, rejoice. Your soul has ever been sincere and calm, but now it is free and purged of its dross. Open the door, as you read, and draw to you the Holy Spirit. Never, as I believe, have you lived more worthily with God as your host. The more weak you are in body, the more pure in soul. O happy one, through the conquest of bodily sickness your soul has conquered, if you always preserve this death of the body for the life of the spirit.

When all incentives to human temptations are dead in you, your flesh, so to speak, also begins to take on the properties of your soul. And so it seems to me that it is by God's great dispensation and by His great gift that you were sickly in times past and are now well. You became ill for the confirmation of the power of the spirit. Now, you are acquiring good health when the flesh is overcome, so that henceforth you may possess a healthy body without any infirmity of the soul. And so, the flesh begins to be well in such wise that temptation no longer arises. Farewell.

LETTER SIX

Salvian to Limenius, Greetings in the Lord

I know that well-meaning hearts are not unmindful of upright love, because good men, zealous for good, so to say, love their own nature. However, since we should increase the love of our friends, to the utmost of our possibilities, I thought you should be reminded of the love formerly begun by me and recently increased by you. When you read my letter, you will kindle a love for me in yourself when you see the increase of your love in me. However, I have no doubt our God will grant that you will become the personification of Christ's love when you are the recipient of Christian love. Farewell in the Lord.

LETTER SEVEN

Salvian to Aper and Verus

Whether it was through a sense of duty or from impudence that I wrote to you before I had received from you any right to ask, I leave to your judgment to decide, rather than to my mere assertion. The reason for this is that, in an affair which is doubtful and obscure, the matter is always better entrusted to good interpreters than to bad defenders. Although this is the case and I consider it to be so, yet, if you think that I should be heard in regard to my understanding of what is true, this is my opinion. Whenever there is a holy contention between inferiors, such as I am, and superiors, such as you are, in regard to a service that is to be rendered, the inferiors do better if they anticipate their superiors by volunteering in writing than if they are anticipated by them.

When there is one and the same eagerness both in writing

and answering, whether for the sake of offering or accepting the position, it is necessarily more humble and condescending to take pains that the service first be offered than to wait until it has to be accepted, because, according to what I have said above, the volunteering of a service may seem to be a running away from honor, and hesitation to accept may seem an ambition for the honor.

Therefore, fittingly and on many counts have I acted reasonably in being first to write. First, because it would be shameful for me, the inferior, to seem to have ambition toward the honor. Second, because the worthiness of your lives so exonerates you from even the shadow of such a reputation that, almost whatever you do, everything is believed to have been done with propriety.

Lastly, because even if you had not written to me with this purpose in mind, so that I, a sinner and a weak man, should offer my service before being invited, I would think that you acted thus out of fatherly concern rather than out of haughtiness. Since you are highly esteemed both by reason of your great humility and very many high offices, no one could believe that you so much wished to deny honor to a friend as that you were unwilling to impose a burden on him.

Though it is proper and the part of religious zeal to anticipate and conquer by humility, yet, when there is a transaction of this nature among people such as we, that is, between the highest and the lowest, the superior does a deed of greater charity if in his office he yields to the inferior. My venerable lords, according to my lowly opinion, I have thought I should write these thoughts to you, not so much from presumption of knowledge as from the reverential honor due you.

If you show that you feel otherwise, I will place my hand on my mouth and, according to the example of holy Job, who, after the Divine Word had spoken, recognized that he was small and weak in comparison with God who was speaking. I will look upon myself and say that I am like sordid earth and dirty ashes. That 'one thing I have spoken'¹ I will not add. Not unreasonably so, for to fall into the error of a wrong belief before you know the truth is the mark of an inexperienced and guileless soul, but to persevere in wrong, after you know the truth, is the mark of a stubborn soul. Farewell.

LETTER EIGHT

Salvian to his Lord and gentle Bishop, Eucherius

I have read the books[1] which you sent me. They are short in composition but abundant in learning, easy to read but perfect for instruction. They are worthy both of your mind and of your piety. Nor do I wonder that you have produced such a useful and beautiful work which is most excellent for the instruction of your holy and blessed children.

After having built in them a choice temple to God, you have bedecked, as it were, the highest point of your building with new and erudite teaching. In order that your holy talents may be illustrated equally by your teaching and life, you have adorned with spiritual education those whom you have formed by moral principles. It remains that our Lord God, to whose gift these most admirable young people are to be likened, may make them equal to your books, that is, that whatever the books contain, wrapped in mystery, both of the students[2] may have in their understanding. And because, by

---

1 Job. 39.35.

1 *Teachings Concerning the More Difficult Questions of the Old and New Testaments,* written by Eucherius.
2 Salonius and Veranus, sons of Eucherius. They later became bishops of Geneva and Vienne respectively. Salvian taught rhetoric to them at Lerins.

divine dispensation and judgment they have already even begun to be teachers of the churches, may the goodness of a most kindly God grant that their learning be fruitful to the churches and to you. By a most surpassing reward may they ornament him by whom they were begotten as well as those whom they have begotten by their own teaching. May the merciful God grant me this, if not while I am here on this earth, then certainly in the next life, that those who were formerly my pupils pray daily for me. Farewell, my lord and dear friend.

LETTER NINE

Salvian to Bishop Salonius,[1] my lord and most blessed pupil, father and son, disciple by instruction, son through love and a father in honor.

You ask me, my dear Salonius, why the name of Timothy was signed to the little treatise *To the Church,* done recently by a certain author of our day. In addition, you add that unless I add a clear reason for using the name, while the surname of Timothy is affixed to the treatise, the books may perhaps be reckoned among the apocrypha.

I am most thankful to you for your judgment of me, by thinking that my faith is so zealous that I would not allow the authorship of a work on the church to be in doubt. Thus, a writing that is most salutary should not be lessened in value because its authorship is uncertain. I have already pointed out that the books deal with issues of today and that they were written by a man of our own day in his zeal and love for things divine. This alone could suffice for removing completely any suspicion of apocryphal composition. Those

---

[1] Son of Eucherius and pupil of Salvian. Salvian dedicated the treatise *On the Governance of God* to him.

treatises which are recognized as not being Timothy's are not suspected as apocryphal.

Perhaps someone is inquiring who is the author, if the Apostle is not the author? They are asking whether he signs his own or a different name to his books. That is true. Indeed, this can be asked, and rightly asked, provided that the inquiry can bring good to anybody. Besides, if the inquiry is useless, why is it necessary that curiosity go to all this trouble, when knowledge will not have any benefit from the curiosity? In every volume, profit is sought more from reading the book than from the name of the author.

Therefore, if there is profit in reading, and each author, no matter who he is, possesses the wherewithal to teach his readers, what matters to him a word which cannot help those who are seeking knowledge? Most worthily the saying of the angel can be answered to this inquisitive person:[2] 'Do you seek the family or the hired servant?' Since there is no profit in a name, he who finds profit in writings unnecessarily seeks the name of the writer. As I have said, this is an adequate statement of the case.

I will tell you the more obvious facts because, my Salonius, my ornament and aid, I cannot refuse you anything. In these books about which I am speaking there are three things which can be asked. Why did the author address his book *To the Church?* Did he use a borrowed name or his own? If not his own, why a borrowed name? If a borrowed name, why in particular did he choose Timothy as the name to be written? Here is the reason for writing the books *To the Church.*

The writer himself, as the very writings themselves testify, is so concerned in his soul for the worship and love of God

---

2 Tob. 5.17.

that he thinks nothing must be put before God, according to that saying of Our Lord:[3] 'He who loves his son or daughter more than Me, is not worthy of Me.' However, the lukewarm and negligent think this saying must be observed only in time of persecution.

As if, indeed, there is any time when anything should be preferred to God, or as though there are men who think that Christ must be considered more precious than all other things in time of persecution, but in all the remaining time He must be considered of less value. If that were the case, we would owe the love of God to persecution and not to faith. Then only will we be good when the evil persecute us. Actually, we owe a greater or certainly not a lesser love to God in times of peace than in adversity.

The very fact that He does not allow us to be afflicted by the evil is all the more reason why we should love Him. He acts toward us with the indulgence of the best and most gentle father, who wishes us, in peace and quiet, to show our faith more by works of religion than to prove our faith in persecution and bodily punishments. Therefore, if nothing is to be preferred to Him at the time when things are going badly with us, should He not also be preferred at the time when He deserves to receive more because of His indulgence? But these arguments are more fitting for another time. Let me now complete what I began.

The writer whom I have mentioned saw the manifold insidious diseases of almost all Christians and realized only that not all things did not stand in second place to God, but that almost all things were preferred to God. The drunken seem to spurn God in their drunkenness, the greedy in their greediness, the unchaste in their lust, the cruel in their cruelty.

---

3 Matt. 10.37.

What is more serious in all these faults is that not only are they committed with criminal violence over a long time, but they are not even corrected afterward by penance. Even in those who are said to be penitents the penance itself is rather a name than a reality, because names of things mean little if they do not possess reality. The name of virtue means nothing if it has no force.

Very many, in fact almost all, who abound in goods and are conscious of their misdeeds and greater crimes do not even deign to redeem them by confession and satisfaction, or, what is easier, by gifts and works of mercy. What is more irreligious, they neglect this not only in time of prosperity, but also in times of adversity, not only when they have security but when they are in poverty. So great is the religious disbelief of men and so grave the sloth of unfaithful souls that, when many leave their greatest wealth to their heirs, sometimes even to strangers, they think their only loss is what they donated for their own hope and salvation. Indeed, though this is serious in almost all, it is especially so in those whom even the profession of sanctity accuses of a like criminal lack of faith. This very malady is great among those who are not laymen, but it is especially so in those who arrogate to themselves the name of religious.

Thus, he who wrote this treatise saw that this evil was general and that this almost universal crime was common, not to worldly men only, but even to penitents and converts, to widows professing chastity, and to young girls consecrated at the holy altars. A sin to be reckoned as monstrous, as I have said, it has reached even to the Levites and priests and, what is much more deadly, even to the bishops. Because of this, many of those I mentioned above, who are without love and without offspring, who have neither families nor children, allot their wealth and goods not to the poor, not to the churches, not even to themselves. What is greater and more outstanding, they do not even allot it to God, but to men of the world, especially to rich men and strangers. Seeing all this, the writer's heart was kindled, during the writing, with a zeal for God like a burning fire.[4]

His marrow glowed with a sacred love, his zeal was unable to do otherwise in such warmth than to burst forth with a voice of sorrow. But nobody was seen more suitable than the Church, of which they who did these things were a part, to whom that voice could be directed. It is superfluous to write for one or for a few, where the case is general. Therefore, this reason convinced and compelled the writer that the books about which I am speaking be sent to the Church.

Now I speak about the second question: why the books are not titled with the author's name. Though there is one special reason for this, I think there could have been many. First, there is that reason which derives from the mandate of God, by whom we are ordered to avoid the vanity of worldly glory in all things, lest, while we seek a little breath of human praise, we lose a heavenly reward. Consequently, God wishes us to offer prayers and gifts to Him in secret. He orders us to commend in secret the fruit of good work, because there is no greater devotion to faith than that which avoids the knowledge of men and is content with God as its witness. Our Saviour says:[5] 'Let not your left hand know what your right hand does, and your Father Who sees in secret will repay you.'

Therefore, this reason alone could satisfy the writer for withholding and concealing his name from the title, that what he had done for the honor of his Lord he would keep for divine knowledge only, and what shunned public acclaim

---
4 Ps. 78.5.
5 Matt. 6.3-4.

would become more commendable to God. The writer must confess that his principal consideration was that he himself is humble in his own eyes and lowly in his own estimation. He thinks he is the least and the last, and, what is more important, he thinks in this manner in pure faith, not by the means of an assumed humility, but by the truth of an honest judgment.

Hence, rightly thinking that others must also evaluate him as he evaluates himself, he rightly inserted a strange name on his books, lest the insignificance of his person detract authority from his salutary statements. In a way, all things said are esteemed as much as is he who says them. Indeed, so weak are the judgments of our day and almost so meaningless that they who read do not consider so much what they read as whom they read, nor so much the force and strength of what is said as the reputation of him who speaks.

For this reason, the writer wished to be completely hidden and to keep out of the way, lest writings which contained much helpfulness should lose their force through the name of the author. This is the reason for anyone who inquires why the author assumed another's name.

There remains an explanation of why the name Timothy was chosen. To answer this question, I am about to return afresh to the author, for he is the cause of all the questions which have been raised. As he excelled in humility when he assumed a strange name, so he excelled in fear and caution when he used the name of Timothy. Indeed, he is fearful and scrupulous, and sometimes he is afraid of 'white lies'; he fears sin so much that sometimes he fears things which should not be feared.

When, therefore, he wished to withhold his own name from the title of the book and to insert another's name, he was afraid of falsehood even in this change of names. He thought that the sin of falsehood should never be committed in the exercise of a holy work. Being thus placed in uncertainty and doubt, he thought it would be best to follow the most holy example of the blessed Evangelist,[6] who, affixing the name Theophilus to both beginnings of his divine works, wrote for the love of God when he was apparently writing to men. He judged it most fitting that he direct his writings to the very love of God by whom he was impelled to write.

Thus this writer about whom I am speaking made use of this argument and counsel. The Evangelist, being conscious that he had done all things in his writings for the honor of God, just as he had done all for the love of God, wrote the name Theophilus. For a like reason did this writer write the name of Timothy. For, as love is expressed by the word Theophilus, so is honor of the divinity expressed by the word Timothy. Thus, when you read that Timothy wrote *To the Church*, you must understand thereby that it was written to the Church[7] for the honor of God, even that the very honor of God directed the writing. Rightly he is said to have written through whom it happened that the book was written.

For this reason, therefore, the name of Timothy is inscribed in the titles of the books. Indeed, the writer thought it fitting that, since he was writing the books for the honor of God, he would consecrate the title to the very honor of the Divinity. You have, my Salonius, my dear one, you have what you demanded. I have fulfilled the work of an ordered task. There remains, since I have discharged my part, that you discharge yours; that is, that you pray our Lord God and, by praying, ask that the books *To the Church*, written only for the honor of Christ, may be as profitable with God to their writer as he desires them to be profitable to all. I think this desire is not

---
6 Luke 1.3; Acts 1.1.
7 One of Salvian's many plays on words.

unjust. It is a desire by which someone asks that they be as profitable for his own salvation as he hopes they will be profitable to all for the love of God. Farewell, my Salonius, my ornament and help.

THE FOUR BOOKS OF TIMOTHY TO THE CHURCH

(*Ad Ecclesiam*)

CONTENTS

Page

Book One 269
    Status of the Church. Prevalence of avarice. Attitude of parents. Two kinds of treasures. God is the possessor of all things created. Avarice is a deadly sin. Leaving possessions to heirs. Alms and expiation of sin. How to give alms. Necessity of giving all possessions.

Book Two 293
    The just should also give alms. Relation of alms to other virtues. The old and new laws. Duties of Christians, widows, virgins, priests and sinners. Advantages of alms. The covetous are their own worst enemies.

Book Three 319
    Disposal of property by those without children. The attitude necessary for salvation. Unequal partition of property between those in religion and those in the world. Consequent injustice of this practice. Parents' motives. Lazarus and the rich man. Necessity of good works for salvation. Attitude of the rich at the hour of death.

Book Four 354
    Good works necessary for saints and sinners. God should be everything to us. Relation of God's favors and alms. Christ as the personification of universal poverty. As we treat God so God will treat us. Not the law but man's morals are culpable.

THE FOUR BOOKS OF TIMOTHY TO THE CHURCH

BOOK I

TIMOTHY, the least of the servants of God, to the Catholic Church spread throughout the world. Grace and peace to you from God, our Father, and from Jesus Christ, our Lord, with the Holy Spirit. Amen.

Of all the other serious and mortal diseases which the old and most foul serpent breathes upon you with the terrible envy of his death-dealing rivalry and the most loathsome breath of his poisonous mouth, I do not know whether any other can undo you with a disease more bitter for faithful souls, and a stigma more loathsome for your children, than avarice. It is slavery to idolatry—a vice which many among you think of little account, when, without the fruit of mercy and kindness, you give yourselves in this life to possessions committed to you by God for a holy deed, and extend your sin even into the future after death.

Perhaps you are looking around attentively, you who are among those whom I am addressing. You do not need a lengthy examination to find out whether you are in that category. I say all, almost all, are in that group about which I am speaking. Indeed, that former surpassing and pre-eminent happiness of the first Christians has departed. It was that happiness according to which all who knew Christ transferred their fleeting store of wordly goods to the eternal wealth of heavenly possessions. They punished themselves with the use of earthly goods for the glorious hope of things to come, buying immortal riches by striving after poverty in this world.

Why? Because today instead of these pristine virtues, avarice, greed, plunder, and whatever is associated with them have replaced them. To these vices are joined, as by sisterly unity, envy, enmity, cruelty, lust, shamelessness, and destruction, because the former vices fight by using the latter. Thus, I do not know why your good fortune militates against its very self. Your vices increase almost as much as the number of Christians increase. Your lack of restraint increases in proportion to your increase in wealth. The investment of your prosperity brings in the interest of great loss.

When the people in the faith are multiplied, their faith is weakened. When the children are growing, their mother sickens. You, the Church, have become weaker as your fertility has progressed. You fall back as you go forward, and, as it were, you are weaker by reason of your strength. Indeed, you have spread throughout the whole world members who bear the name of Christians, but who do not possess the force of religion. Thus, you have begun to be rich in number and poor in faith. The richer you are in multitudes, the more needy you are in devotion. The bigger your body, the more limited your soul. You are, so to speak, both greater in yourself and lesser in yourself. You increase and decrease at the same time by a new and almost unheard of progression and recession.

Where now is your admirable form and perfect bodily beauty? Where is that testimony of the Divine Writings about your living virtues which says:[1] 'And the multitude of believers had one heart and one soul, and nobody said anything of that which he possessed was his own.' O sorrow and grief, whose are you now! You possess the letter only and lack heart.

---
1 Acts 4.32.

In fact, the greater portion of your children now is a dealer in death-dealing concerns. They are like earthly, not to say hellish hucksters and innkeepers, who strive in the market places, ruining others and at the same time suffering a loss themselves. They purchase loss of life with monetary profit in order to obtain things that are not their own. They squander what is their own. They hide baneful treasures in the earth which will bring a brief joy to their heirs and a long lament to their begetters. They deprive others as much as themselves of the use of temporal goods. They stow away infernal wealth in deep cellars, burying their money and their hope at the same time, according to that old saying of our Lord who says:[2] 'Where your treasure is, there will be your heart.'

In this manner they begrudge themselves salvation. They press their own souls, which have a vocation for heaven, into the earth with earthly weights. For the soul of him who piles up treasure follows and is, as it were, changed into the nature of an earthly substance, and that not only now, but even in the future and forever. For since, as it is written, man is confronted equally with life and death[3] and stretches out his hand toward what he wants, it is necessary that whatever a man grasps with his hands in time he must possess forever in eternity, and what here he cleaves to in affection, he must in the future cleave to forever, with his will and mind wholly fixed upon it.

(2) There are some who think they are exempt from this crime because neither their gold nor possessions are dug into the earth, yet, they have them hidden everywhere. Let nobody be deceived by these silly ideas. Those who serve earthly cupidity by increasing their wealth always bury their gold in

---
2 Matt. 6.21.
3 Deut. 30.19.

the earth. This is what the Savior Himself teaches in the Gospel when he says:[4] 'Lay not up to yourselves treasures on earth.' And again:[5] 'But lay up to yourself treasures in Heaven.' These things cannot be heard with carnal hearing. Do all evil men place their bodily treasures in the earth or do the good store them in heaven? By no means is this the case.

Accordingly, the force of the Holy Word expressed the effect and power of spiritual things, because earthly and hellish things are the reward of greed and avarice; heavenly and eternal things are due to alms-giving and generosity. For that reason there is this difference between heavenly and earthly treasure that those who lay up treasures through greed and avarice know they are placing their wealth in hell, while those who lay them up through alms-giving and kindness rejoice because they are preparing heavenly treasures. Scripture named the location of treasures according to the merits of those who lay them up, for treasures are said to be there where they will be who lay them up.

(3) Perhaps the judgment that calls all equally to perfection and binds all by a common law may seem harsh, since there is not a uniform way of life for all. Very rightly it could be said on this point that, since all wish to live forever, all should act so that they could partake of that life. Most ill advisedly and foolishly do some act so that, what they want through love and desire, they seem unwilling to accomplish by deed and act.

However, let us glance at that portion of Christians, that is, especially of your children, who are withheld from perfection by certain impediments of their possessions and, as they think, of unbreakable bonds of family connections. First of

---
4 Matt. 6.19.
5 Matt. 6.20.

all, those in this portion are they who allow themselves to be driven to seek money and acquire tremendous wealth out of preoccupation for their offspring and an all but violent love for their children. This is like saying that there are some fathers who either cannot or should never be parents unless they are rich. They are unable to love their children unless their wealth increases. Their strength and marrow are avarice and greed, because, as they think, just as there cannot be a body without inner nerves, so there cannot be love without greed.

If they are right, all fatherliness is doubtless a cause of evil, nor would the feeling in it be an incentive to virtue but rather to vices. What, then, are we to say of that sacred declaration of divine authority:[6] 'Godliness is profitable to all things.' According to what I have mentioned above, affection is not only harmful to all things but harmful for almost all. If affection is the begetter of greed, it contains within itself much more evil than good; according to Holy Scripture:[7] 'greed is the root of all evil.'

Thus, if greed is the root of all evil and is begotten from affection as its mother and is nourished on its poisonous milk, not only is that greed which is born from affection as a parent to be condemned, but also affection itself, through which such a child is procreated. Whence it happens, if affection is so harmful and evil, it is not expedient either to love or be loved, since neither should parents seek a love harmful to themselves nor should children desire a love harmful to their parents.

Love carries the disease not only to parents but even to children, because it weighs heavily on those who give birth to a baneful heritage, as well as on those who are brought forth

---
6 1 Tim. 4.8.
7 1 Tim. 6.10.

as wicked heirs in the midst of this evil pursuit of gain. Hence, almost all children succeed as much to the vices as to the patrimony of their parents. They take on not only the possessions but also the depravities of their parents, and thus, ever taking up their morals, they begin to be wanton before they possess their inheritance. Children take possession of their parent's goods only when the parents are dead, but, while the parents are living and still in good health, the children assume their morals. Thus, before they begin to have their father's possessions within their own power, they have the image of their fathers in their souls. Before they possess those things which are falsely called goods, they possess those things which are truly proved to be evil.

(4) What therefore? Since this is the case, perhaps I seem to forbid the love of parents for their children. By no means. What is so savage, so inhuman, so inimical to law than if we who profess that enemies should be loved say that children should not be loved? Or do we, who also threaten that love which nature prohibits, prohibit that love which nature allows? Or do we, who strive to implant in the soul that love which it does not possess, wrest from the soul the love which it has?

This is not the case. Not only do we say that children should be loved, but they should be loved in the first place and above all other things; nothing must be preferred to them in any way except God alone. For this is to love in a special manner, to place Him before our children whom it is not proper to place after them in any way. Why do we say children should be loved and in what manner? In what other manner than that ordained by God Himself? For there is no better love of children than that taught by Him who gave us our children.

Neither can offspring be better loved than if they are loved in Him by whom they were given.

In what manner has God ordered that children be loved? This is not for me to say; let the Divine Word itself, speak, which speaks in this fashion to all parents in general. In order that they hand on the commandments of God to their children,[8] 'They should put their hope in God and not be forgetful of the works of their God and they should seek His commandments.' And elsewhere it also says:[9] 'And you, fathers, do not provoke your children to anger, but bring them up in the discipline and correction of the Lord.'

You see what riches God ordered to be furnished by parents to their children. They are not treasures of money nor bags filled with gold, which, indeed, have much weight but still more iniquity. They are not houses, excellent and surpassing, in distinguished towns. They are not steeples raised above the sight of men nor pediments implanted in the clouds for him who dwells in the clouds. Finally, they are not broad lands whose extent exceeds the knowledge of the possessor himself and who deems it unworthy to allow a share to others and thinks that proximity by others is an injury.[10]

God did not order these things, nor did He extend the care of His fatherly affection to slavish services of earthly management. The things which He orders are few but salutary, easy but holy, sparing in precept but great in result, short in writing but eternal in happiness. For the Scripture says: 'Parents, do not provoke your children to anger, but bring them up in the discipline and correction of the Lord,' in order that, as the prophet said, 'they should place their hope in God and

---

8 Ps. 77.7.
9 Eph. 6.4.
10 This is a reference to the Gallo-Roman *potentior*, or holder of large landed properties.

not be forgetful of the works of their God and they should seek His commandments.'

Behold what kind of riches it is that God loves; what wealth He demands should be stored up for the children; what possessions He orders should be prepared. They are faith and fear of God, modesty, holiness, and discipline; not earthly, not base, and not perishable and transitory things. The things He orders are outstanding. Since God is the God of the living and not of the dead, He rightly ordered that those things be prepared for the children by which they would live forever and not those things by which they would be in everlasting death. Nobody doubts that, to almost all evil men and to men who lack the faith, earthly riches are more the cause of death than of life, according to what God says:[11] 'How difficult is it for those who possess money to enter the Kingdom of Heaven.' And again, He says:[12] 'It is easier for a camel to pass through the eye of a needle than for a rich man to enter the Kingdom of Heaven.' This is why He especially orders:[13] 'do not store up treasures for yourself on earth, but lay up treasures for yourself in Heaven.'

In what has been said above and in what is to follow two kinds of treasures are revealed: one by which fathers lay up treasures for their children, and one by which they lay up treasures for themselves. In what manner for their children? By instructing them in their duty and in the fear of God. In what manner for themselves? By laying up treasures for themselves in heaven. Extraordinary indeed, since money which perishes is a training for immortality, and since almost all parents love their children more than themselves, and confer transitory goods on themselves, but eternal goods on their

---
[11] Mark 10.24.
[12] Mark 10.25.
[13] Matt. 6.19-20.

children. In this way they find a place both for their affection and for salvation, since by a two-fold and immortal good and by those things which are eternal, they cause their children to be eternal. For, acquiring their own happiness, they turn by their good works those things which are naturally perishable into eternal worth.

Why are you agitated, fatherly love? Why do you stretch out to acquire wordly and perishable goods? You can do nothing more excellent for your children if it is through you that they can have that good which they will never fully lose. It is not necessary for you to store up earthly treasures for your child. In nothing will you make your offspring richer than if you make your own child the treasure of God.

(5) Although these words are so, and they are true and most salutary for salvation, yet I do not speak in such a manner that I would altogether exclude children from the goods and properties of their parents. I will treat of this later. In the meanwhile, there are some men who do not think they will be guilty if they bequeath their property, not for the honor of the Gospel, not for their own salvation, and not for any service of God. With a pride which is unholy and pagan they transfer for purposes of lust and wantonness their wealth o some heirs who are either without distinction, irreligious, or already rich. Let us see in a few words by whom these possessions were given or why they were given, so that, when we show both the instigator and the cause of the transfer of property, we can more easily establish to whom the property should have been given and to what use it should have been put.

I believe there is no man, who in any way can be represented as belonging to mankind, who doubts that all wordly property is given to all men by a divine gift. Yet there may be some one who has such great wisdom that, though the world itself was given to the human race by God, thinks that whatever is in the world was not given to men by God. Therefore, if God gave to all men all they have, nobody doubts that we must return for the worship of God those things which we receive as a gift from God. We must use those things in His service which we have received from His bounty.

This is to recognize the gift of God and to put His favors to good use, so that in His goods you honor Him from whom you have received the goods themselves. Even the examples of human affairs teach this. If the use of anything is given to any man through the favor and bounty of another, and if he endeavors to take away and alienate from the donor the ownership of the thing given, he is unmindful of the man from whom he received the favor. Will he not be adjudged the most ungrateful and unfaithful of all men, who, forgetful of the man and his most generous favor, wishes to despoil of rightful ownership the man who has enriched him by the possession of usage?

Thus, we receive only the use of those possessions which we hold. We make use of the wealth loaned to us by God. We are, as it were, tenants by *precarium*.[14] When departing from this world, whether we like it or not, we leave everything behind on earth. Since we are usufructory tenants, why do we attempt to take away and alienate from God's ownership what we cannot take with us? Why do we not use in good faith the little things given us by God? We hold property so long as He has allowed, we hold so long as He has permitted, He who has given us all.

What is more right, what is more proper, than when a thing

---

14 The *precarious* holding was revocable at the will of the grantor. The holder had no rights in relation to him who made the grant. The grantor could take back the grant at any time and for any reason. The holder enjoyed the usufruct of the land while he was on it, in return for rent.

is separated from him who has had its use, that its possession revert to him who granted it for usage? Even the very words of God through the tongue of Sacred Scripture order this, saying to one and all of us:[15] 'Honor the Lord from out of your substance.' And elsewhere He says:[16] 'Repay your debt.' How tender and condescending is our Lord God, who invites us to expend the wealth of our earthly substance! He says: 'Honor the Lord from out of your substance.' Though all we have received from God is His own property, He calls it ours so that it is we who may give. Thus, He calls the proprietorship of possession ours so that there may be a greater reward for work, because, wherever effort spent seems to be on what is one's own, the worker necessarily has a greater return.

(6) However, let not the human mind grow haughty because of this, because, when the Lord said that this substance was ours, He added: 'Pay back your debt.' This means that he whom devotion would not entice to be generous, necessity would force to pay his debts, and he whom faith by itself would not attract to a holy work, necessity at least would compel. He says first: 'Honor the Lord from out of your substance,' and then He says: 'Pay back your debts.' This means, if you are Godfearing, give as though it were yours; if you are not, pay back as though it were not yours. And thus He rightly laid down the law that we should be both free to give and bound to pay.

This is to say to every man: 'You are invited by exhortation and bound by compulsion to holy works. Give, if you are willing; pay, if you are unwilling.' The Apostle also ordered this very thing when he advised the rich not to be-

---
15 Prov. 3.9.
16 Eccli. 4.8.

come wise in their pride and place their hope in the uncertainty of riches instead of in the living God who, he says,[17] 'gives us all things for enjoyment in the will to do good works.' In one word he taught two things, that is, who is the giver of wealth and why He gives.

When he said that everything must be hoped for from God who gives everything, he shows that the rich are made by God. He added, however, 'in the will to do good works,' and teaches that that which he said was given by God was given only on account of good works. He says: 'He gives everything in the will to do good works.' This means He made men wealthy in possession so that they be rich in good works, that is, that they turn into something else the riches they receive. Using their wealth for good works, they make eternal by proper use the riches which they hold only for a time in this world, and thus, acknowledging the gifts as from God, they rejoice in a twofold good, namely, they are not only rich in this world, but also deserve to be rich in Heaven.

(7) For this purpose riches must be longed for, sought after, held, and increased. Otherwise, it is an incalculable evil not to use well the goods given by God. Sacred Scripture says:[18] 'There is nothing more reprehensible than a covetous man.' Riches stored to the detriment of one's Lord is the worst and most deadly kind of malady. That is true. What is worse or what is more wretched than for anybody to convert present good into future evil? What is worse than that death and damnation are sought through these very things which were given by God for the purpose of procuring eternal happiness of life from them?

In this matter we must also consider that if the keeping and

---
17 1 Tim. 6.17.
18 Eccli. 10.9.

storing of riches is bad for a man, how much greater is the evil of piling them up. How few there are today among rich men who are of such restraint that they are content to keep their wealth without wanting to pile up more? O wretchedness of our day and of the people of the Church who are reduced to this that they think it a great virtue to add to their wealth, although the Scripture says that even to keep it is a kind of great sin.[19]

And so, as I have said above, how do people think they are not thoroughly guilty, if at the moment of death they fail to consult their salvation by bequeathing their possessions, since they are already guilty by the very fact that they have kept possession of all they have up to the very moment of death. Or, how will they be free from guilt who by infidel vanity have transferred their property indiscriminately to any kind of men, since even they who have not deprived themselves in this life of at least a part of their possessions for the honor of God will be guilty? Our Lord pointed this out through the Apostle, when he says:[20] 'Woe now rich men, weep in the miseries which will come to you. Your riches are corrupted and your garments eaten by moths. Your gold and silver have rusted and their rust shall be in testimony against you and shall eat your flesh like fire. You have laid away treasures against the last days.'

In addition to that severity of the Divine Word which, since it is hidden in mystery, is much greater and more terrible, I think those texts which have been adduced suffice for instilling fear and trembling in all, for He speaks particularly to the rich. He orders them to weep. He announces their evil fate in the next world. He threatens perpetual fire. And these threats are to be feared the more, not on account of murders,

---
19 Matt. 6.19-21.
20 James 5.1-3.

not on account of fornications, not on account of sacrilegious impieties, or lastly, not on account of other vices which strangle souls with a deadly sword and perpetual death. They are to be feared on account of wealth alone, on account of senseless greed, on account of hunger for gold and silver, in order that He might show that these vices suffice for the eternal damnation of men, even if they are not guilty of the others.

What can be said more simply or more clearly? He does not say to the rich man: 'You are to be punished because you are a murderer; you are to be punished because you are a fornicator. But, 'You are to be punished only because you are a rich man, and this because you make evil use of your riches, because you do not understand that riches were given you for holy works.' For, riches in themselves are not harmful, but the minds of those who put them to evil use are sinful. Nor is wealth a cause of punishment to man, but the rich make unto themselves punishment because of their wealth. They are unwilling to use riches properly and they convert these very riches into punishment for themselves.

God says: 'You are laying up treasures against the last days.' Indeed, when He said: 'You are laying up treasure,' He added: 'against the last days,' that is, those who lay up treasures would be still more guilty, since their greed for treasures increases even at the end of life. He says: 'You are laying up treasures against the last days.' Greed is condemned by the word 'treasures' and lack of faith, by the words 'last days.' And this is why there is a twofold sin, both of greed and lack of faith, because to desire wealth at any time is a sin according to the word of our Lord when He says:[21] 'Thou shall not covet,' and it is without doubt a greater sin by reason of the lack of faith involved when one heaps up wealth even at the end of life.

---

21 Exod. 20.17; Rom. 7.7.

(8) Perhaps some have judged that up to this point my manner of speaking has been harsh. And it would be truly harsh if it brought to mind forcibly something which is not based on the authority of Sacred Scriptures. Let it be adjudged harsh if it contains what the Apostle preached on these points, so that I will not add that saying of our Lord in which He pointed out that all who did not renounce all they possessed were completely unworthy of Him.

Since that is the case, I ask: Is it not proper that what I have said is to be considered most lenient and mild, since my point is that I at least am seeking assistance for men whose health is incurable even though I cannot restore them to perfect health, and I am at least attempting to soften death for men whose life I cannot cure. What is perfect health? What is it except to act properly in this life? What is the final cure? What is it except to make provision for the last journey? What is perfect health? What is it except to put to good use the things committed to us by God? What is the last remedy? What is it except to do, at least later on, what you repent of not having done before?

Some think that my statements are harsh. Let them be adjudged harsh, very harsh, except that in comparison with apostolic severity they seem to be lenient and indulgent. The Apostle calls them to contrition; I only to a cure. The Apostle calls wealth a fire; I desire to turn riches into water quenching the fire, according to that saying:[22] 'just as water extinguishes fire, so do alms extinguish sin.'

The Apostle teaches that damnation is the penalty for riches improperly stored away; I hope to obtain eternal life with those things which he says cause eternal death to all. Not, indeed, that I think riches will enable any one bound

---
22 Eccli. 3.33.

up with carnal vices to obtain eternal life if he perseveres in his own sins even up to death, but properly bequeaths all he has at his death, unless he shall have previously renounced his sins and cast away that sordid and dirty garment of his crimes and shall have received the new robe of conversion and holiness from the hand of the preaching Apostle.

Otherwise, a man does not cease to sin, if, when he comes to the end, he gives up his sin, not because he chooses to do so, but because he cannot help it. For he who, only because of death, ceases from evil acts does not forsake his crimes, but is forsaken by them and is, therefore, excluded by necessity from vices. I think he then sins when the sins have ceased, because, insofar as it pertains to his attitude of mind, he who is willing to sin if it is possible to do so has not yet ceased to sin. He does not rely on a good hope who sins in life only that he may redeem the mass of his sins in death. He thinks that he will escape punishment, not because he is good, but because he is rich.

As though God could be seeking not the good life but the money of men, and should be willing to accept money for the crimes of all who act improperly, in the hope that their evils can be thus atoned. They think of God in the manner of a corrupt judge who demands money in order that He may sell sins. This is not the case with God.

It is most certain that generosity is profitable, but not for those who live badly with the ultimate hope of future bounty. Neither is it profitable for those who commit crimes and place their reliance on remedial immunity. It is profitable to those who, being deceived by the temptations of youth, the cloud of error, or the vice of ignorance, or, lastly, by a lapse of human weakness, begin at length to recover as if from all but death, due to a grave infirmity and the distress of a troubled mind. Just as insane men return to their senses after a seizure, so they return to theirs after their errors. Yet they are unlike each other in one thing only: the former rejoice after they have escaped from their illness; the latter repent after they have received back their health. And not unrightful so.

The former are all the more to be congratulated since they feel they have attained health. The latter are that much more embarrassed as they recognize more clearly their faults and errors. Hence it happens that the former must necessarily exult, and the latter mourn. The former, for having been sick, impute their joy to health, but the latter, because they sinned, impute their sorrow to themselves. Thus, the former are glad for a cure; the latter are troubled because of their guilt.

(9) Hence I admonish all, and especially those disturbed by the terror of serious sin and those stirred by the unhappy knowledge and remembrance of their punishable sins, first that, although they have fallen, they should not remain in their sin. Neither should they remain in the wallowpits as is the custom of dirty pigs which, when they grow warm, immerse their bellies in the mud and are never satisfied with their dirty wallowings unless they completely roll their whole body in the mire. They should not follow the natural uncleanliness of these animals, nor should they blandly acquiesce in the evil of their faults. They should not remain in the deep dungeon of their lusts where they bury themselves in their own ruin. Rather, let them rise immediately when they fall and, the moment they fall, let them think to rise. If it is at all possible, let there be quickness of repentance, so that the cure of the penitent will be so swift that there remain hardly a sign that he fell.

In cases of this nature the prime need of healing them is that the sick should have a horror of their ills, the wounded hasten to heal their gashes, and the stricken immediately snatch the arrows from their bodies. The poultice or *fibula* is properly placed on wounds still fresh and wounded flesh which is not long allowed to lie open is joined together more quickly. An open sore on the body, if it becomes infected, is enlarged, and, if a cancer follows the wounds, death necessarily follows the cancer.

Therefore, sinners must flee from evil, nor must room be given to the devil, lest he hurl those who waver into ruin and cast those who are fallen into death. If the power of the disease is so great or neglect of the sick so great that they cause health to decline even to the point of death, I do not know what to say and most certainly do not know what to promise. It would be harsh and unholy to restrain those so endangered from seeking the last cure, but it is rash to promise anything in such a late treatment.

Doubtless, it is better that hands withered by a chronic paralysis be raised to heaven by some exertion than that they be destroyed forever by fatal hopelessness. It is better to leave nothing untried than not to prescribe medicine for a man who is dying, especially since, whether or not there is any healing in trying something at the moment of death, I certainly know that to try nothing is ruin. And one thing I know. For him who has reached such a state of wretchedness at the very end of a protracted disease, it is impossible to say how much lamentation he who has never realized that he made an error owes for his errors.

(10) What will be done in situations like these? When will a man weep who can no longer weep? When will a man make amends who has no time for amendments? I suppose he will take refuge in long fasts. This is indeed something,

if it is combined with almsgiving, according to that saying,[23] 'fasting, with alms, is good.' But how long will a long delayed confession profit him who is about to die? He will punish his flesh with a coarse hair shirt; he will cover himself with cinders and ashes in order that the harshness of his present austerities will make compensation for the wantonness of his past pleasures; and he will make reparation for the guilt of prolonged indulgence by bringing self inflictions to his rescue. But when will he who is already cut off by his approaching death, even from intercessory agents, perform such heroic acts?

Severity, the judge of faith, will subject a man who is guilty in his body to the cross of various tribulations, in order that he may deserve the leniency of eternal forgiveness by striving after pain in this world. But, when the body is already falling apart, where will the soul be rigorous enough to exercise the duty of severity? The judge cannot impose a severe verdict when the guilty one will not endure being judged.

There is, therefore, one counsel which could aid the tottering and destitute man when all help and resources are lost. He should take refuge in that holy and helpful counsel of the most blessed Daniel, who wished to cure the King of Babylon of the sores contracted through sin by prescribing a poultice fashioned out of the King's works of mercy:[24] 'Wherefore, O King, let my counsel please you and redeem your sins with alms and your injustices with works of mercy to the poor. Perhaps the Lord will be patient with your sins.'

Let a man who is at the point of death do as the prophet said. Let him use for his own wounds a medicament prescribed for another. Let him fear the example of the stubbornness of the disobedient man. Let him think what he himself will suffer

---
23 Tob. 12.8.
24 Dan. 4.24.

in death when he sees what the King of Assyria bore in life. The warning is clear about pride and rebellion. Let him consider whether he, if he does not heed, will escape when dead, when he sees that the king who did not heed was lost while living. Therefore, when dying, let him offer at least his goods to save his soul from eternal punishment, because then he cannot do anything more. However, let him offer them with compunction and with tears. Let him offer them with sorrow and grief.

For, offered otherwise, they are of no value, because they please not when offered as a purchase price, but only in love. This soul of the giver is not measured by the value of the gifts, but the gifts by the soul. Money does not make faith acceptable, but faith money. Therefore, let him who wishes that the gifts he offers God be profitable to himself offer them in the manner I have said. Neither does a man confer a favor on God by the things he gives, but God confers a favor on man by the things He accepts, because even what man possesses is the gift of his God and Lord. Thus, in those gifts which are offered by man, man does not surrender his property; God receives back His own.

Accordingly, when someone offers his property to God, let him offer it not as with the boldness of one who gives a gift, but with the humility of one who pays his debts. Let him not believe that he is absolving himself from his sins, but that he is mitigating them. Let him not offer them with the confidence of buying redemption, but with the duty of supplication. Let him not offer them as paying the whole debt, but as wishing to pay a little part of a big debt, because, even if he gives the full measure of his possessions, he does not pay back what he owes on account of the enormity of his sins. Therefore, although he makes an offering, let him pray God that his offering be acceptable. Let him lament because his offer is given late. Let him sorrow and repent that it was not offered earlier. Thus, perhaps, according to the Prophet, God will be appeased for your transgressions.

(11) Somebody asks if he should offer all that he has to God? Let him not offer all he has if he does not think that he owes all he has. I do not ask whose it is that is offered or from whom it was received before it was paid back. I only say this: Let him not offer all for his indebtedness if he does not think he owes all for his sins. A man, though a sinner, asks should he give all? Let him give nothing, if not with faith; nothing, if not with entreaty; nothing, if not with prayer; nothing, if not with intention of reckoning that what he has in mind to pay back are God's gifts. Let him think that there is more profit for himself in those things he leaves to God than in those possessed in this life, because what he held from man is transient, but what is bequeathed to God is eternal.

Does anyone say that he must offer all his property? I say this all is very little. Why? Does anyone know that his offerings compensate for the full measure of his sins? Does anyone know if the effort he makes to appease God is commensurate with the gravity of his sin? If any sinful man thinks he knows at what price he can redeem his sins, let him use that knowledge for their redemption. But, if he does not know, why does he not offer as much as he can? If he cannot make recompense for his sins because of the greatness of the price, at least let him do this with devotion of mind. A man exhibits the perfect fruit of conscience who leaves no sin on his conscience.

Doubtless some may say this is harsh and immoderate, especially since the prophet about whom I spoke seems to have admonished the King of Babylon on this point only, that he should give much, not that he should throw away everything. For the time being, I do not offer the testimony of the

Gospel, nor do I take refuge in the word of God. I do not say one thing is commanded by the Old and another by the New Law. Hence, the Apostle says:[25] 'Behold, the Old has passed. All things are made anew, but all things are from God.' By these words he teaches not that the old should be done according to the letter, but the new according to God.

For the moment, I am content solely with what the prophet Daniel said. For he had speech with the king, and not with a king of one city, but, as it then seemed, with the king of the whole world who was unable to hand over to the needy, by his will, the peoples whom he ruled. Nor was he able to give the barbarian nations as money to those in want. Nor was he able to convert his kingdom, diffused far and wide, into a gift for the poor. Therefore, the prophet said: 'redeem your sins in alms,' that is, give gold to the needy, because you cannot give them your kingdom. Distribute your wealth, because you cannot share your power. In this way he seems to have ordered him to give all, since the only thing he did not order him to distribute was what he could not give away.

(12) Perhaps I am exaggerating my point in what I say and putting it on too high a level. Let me see if that is so. God says: 'redeem your sins by alms.' What is it to redeem something? I think it is to pay the price for the things that are redeemed. I am not asking what were the sins of that king. Let him who committed the sins know how much he owed for redemption. I tell you, for whose sake I am speaking, I call on you whose verdict is in question. This should be done as the prophet said: 'redeem your sins in alms.' Do not bequeath to God what you have, if you do not think all you have is necessary for your sins.

Think most diligently of all the faults you have committed.

---

25 2 Cor. 5.17-18.

Think of the different kinds of sins. See what you owe for lies; what for cursing; what for perjury; what for carelessness in thoughts; what for foulness of speech; finally, what for every desire and evil wish. Take into account, also, whether there are on your conscience any of those sins about which the Apostle spoke:[26] adultery, fornication, impurities, drunkenness, uncleanliness, hateful to God, avarice, the servant of idolatry, and after these sins perhaps others contracted by the shedding of human blood.

When you shall have computed the number of all, weigh the price of each one. After this I do not ask that you give all you have to God for your sins. Give only what you owe. I add, however, after all these sins, that when you have investigated and appraised your sins you will owe that much more for your sins as you adjudged your sins the more vile, because, says the Apostle,[27] 'He who thinks he is something when he is nothing, deceives himself.' I should not have to order you as that king, perhaps young and who had life ahead of him, was ordered that he should hasten to redeem his sins. You are all the more indebted on your behalf, because you do these things when you are dying or on the very point of death.

In the next world great will be the generosity and love which can recompense you for paying back these things at last to your Lord when you yourself cannot have them. This is all the more so when there is added to all this what the prophet who called the king to redeem his sins said: The king should do certain things, not as security for pardon, but as the means of acquiring salvation. When he says: 'redeem your sins in alms and perhaps the Lord will be appeased for your sins,' the very saying in which he says 'perhaps' indicates hope, but does not promise surety.

---

26 Gal. 5.19-21.
27 Gal. 6.3.

From this it can be understood how difficult it is for sinners at the last moment of life to receive perfect leniency by any kind of liberality on their part, when the prophet, who urges that God's appeasement must be sought, did not dare to promise that God's appeasement would be deserved. He gives advice about the act, yet doubts about the effect. He made himself the exhortor of what should be done, not the author of procuring it. Why was this? Because all sinners must attempt everything for themselves at the last moment, although they cannot presume anything. If the prophet did not promise full clemency to the king through liberality of good works, the sinner can understand that, when penance for sins is not done, there is need for great and copious liberality at the hour of death. This is the sinner who wishes to obtain from God by late devotion what he cannot appropriate through the Law.

BOOK TWO

I HAVE talked about the remedies for sins, or rather about the hopes and consolations of remedies. The first step for acquiring salvation is that the sinner should repent of his sins. Then, according to the Sacred Word, he should redeem his sins by alms-giving. Lastly, if he has not already done so, at least he should leave nothing untried when dying, and should come to the aid of his soul by offering his substance at the last moment. Perhaps somebody will object that, if sinners are necessarily bound to redeem their sins, without doubt, the holy who are devoid of sins are not bound. Therefore, there is no reason for those to make gifts of their substance who have no sins to redeem by alms. Very well. But we will see what kind of an argument that is.

In the meantime, even if there are no past sins which a holy man must redeem with all his possessions, there are everlasting goods which he must buy at a high price. But I will treat of this more fully later on. Now, I say this, and say it without reservation, and assert it firmly that there is not one of the professed religious who is not a debtor to God for many things, and, therefore, whatsoever he has given to his Lord he is not so much making a gift as paying back a debt.

First of all, let me mention benefits in general. Each one of you, either of the religious or of the rich, was born, raised, and educated through the kindness and gift of God. You are strengthened by the things necessary for life. You are enriched also with the non-necessities of life. Your Lord gave you more for usage than the measure of usage demanded. Finally,

He extended His gifts beyond your hopes, and, what is greatest and most singular, even your prayers obtained His gifts.

I add that, after all these benefits, the same Lord who first of all begot you by His gift later saved you by His Passion. On account of you, O man, earth and clay, (and in fact only a tiny bit of earth and clay), the Lord of the universe descended on earth, proceeding from a human body and living in His own flesh. He was humiliated even to the shame of a human birth, to uncleanliness of clothes and the lowliness of a stable. He tolerated in Himself the unworthy frailties of this life, such as eating, drinking, the troubled interchanges of sleep and wakefulness, and the humiliating necessities of this brief period on earth. He tolerated the disgusting association with men who lived around Him. He tolerated people befouled with the mire of sordid sins. He tolerated men always guilty of crime in their evil minds, who breathed the vapor of acts base in themselves and, therefore, incapable of heavenly commands. They could not endure the radiance of holy light, because the brilliance of the divine light blinded their eyes made dim by sin.

Not only this, but, after all these indignities, add the impudent objections of a prideful people. Add the reviling. Add the curses, the unholy insults, the false testimony, the cruel condemnation and mockings of the people, the spitting and flogging, indeed, the harshest punishments. Add the indignities more harsh than pain: the crown of thorns, the draught of wine mixed with gall. Add the Lord of the universe condemned by men, hanging on a cross for the salvation of the human race, a God dying by a law made by men.

(2) Since this is the case, whoever you are, whether you are just or believe you are just, tell me, I ask you, if retribution can be made for these indignities alone, even if there were

none other? No matter what man endures for God, what God suffered for man cannot in any way be repaid. Even if their suffering did not differ in the mode of punishment, there is necessarily a wide difference in the persons of the sufferers. Perhaps you object that according to what I have said the debt of all men is universal, and thus the race of human beings is, without exception, liable. I agree.

But why should anyone owe less if another owes the same? If the bonds of one hundred men are written as one hundred *sestertii* apiece, should the debt of one be lessened on the basis that all are debtors within the same group? 'For each one,' says the Apostle, 'will bear his own burden and each one will give an accounting for himself.'[1] Therefore, the burden of one should never be mitigated so that it will weigh on another, nor should the guilty one be absolved by the partnership of the many. Condemnation of one man for a fault is not less terrible for being common to many accomplices.

As I have said above, although the debt is universal, there is no doubt, however, that it is individual. Although it is common to all, it is, however, the particular debt of individuals. Thus it comes to all equally that nothing is taken from the sum of each. Christ suffered for all and each, and spent Himself equally for each and all, and gave Himself wholly for all and wholly for each. Therefore, because the Saviour gave all by His Passion, both all and each owe all to Him, or rather each owes more than all, because each has received as much as all. There is greater envy where one receives what all receive, even if the measure is alike. Accordingly, although one receives the same, he seems to owe more because he becomes more liable when he seems to be compared to all. I have been insisting on these matters because some of the holy ones

---

1 Gal. 6.4-5.

think that they are not indebted to God since they cannot estimate the amount owed.

(3) Perhaps someone objects, not indeed that those in religion are not debtors, but that the debts of people in the world, whose sins are greater, are much greater. This is like someone saying: 'I am not guilty, therefore, since someone else is more guilty; I am just, therefore, because the other is unjust; I am especially good, therefore, because the other is particularly bad.' In the first place, it is unbecoming to a holy mind to think that his goods increase with others' ills, and to think he is better by comparing himself with those who are worse. It is a most unfortunate kind of consolation to take comfort from the misfortunes of sinful men, since the Apostle orders us to rejoice with those who rejoice and weep with those who weep.[2] He orders each of us to think not of those things which are our own, but of those which belong to others.

Grant that a comparison of this kind seems just and right. Can it also be considered as trustworthy? Who is absolutely certain about the great and terrible future judgment of God? Or who can say: 'I owe less and he owes more.' Lastly, who can presume about himself or despair about another? 'For we all,' says the Apostle, 'will stand before the tribunal of Christ' and 'each one will bear his own burden.'[3]

Someone asks: 'Is there, therefore, no difference between saints and sinners?' Certainly, there is a great and almost immeasurable difference. Scripture says:[4] 'Blessed is the man who is always fearful.' The mind of a wise man is ever uneasy about his own salvation. Although there is a great difference between saints and sinners, still I ask all those who profess a religion: Who, according to his own conscience, is sufficiently

---

2 Rom. 12.15.
3 Rom. 14.10, 12; Gal. 6.4.
4 Prov. 28.14.

holy; who does not tremble about the fearful severity of a future judgment; who is untroubled about his eternal salvation? If this is not the case, just as it should not be, I beg, let any man tell me why he does not strive with all the power of his goods to redeem, by a holy death, whatever sins he may have committed by transgression during his lifetime. Though I say these things, I wish all men who read to know that I am speaking not about all the holy ones but only about those who, although they profess religion, do not put aside their riches.

About those who are disengaged from all burdens and follow the paths of the Savior and purchase the Lord Jesus Christ, not in holiness only but in poverty, there is nothing that can be said, except what the Prophet said:[5] 'but to me, O God, your friends are exceedingly honorable.' I honor all these not otherwise than as imitators of Christ. I revere them not otherwise than as images of Christ. I look up to them not otherwise than as members of Christ. For this only am I mindful of them, that I may become worthy of their remembrance.

(4) Perhaps what I have said above may seem injurious to the religious profession. Someone will object: 'What about the rich widow who preserves her widowhood in the midst of her possessions? What about the virgin who has professed virginity and has kept the holiness of her body intact? What about an unconsummated marriage in which the parties deny themselves, behaving as though they were not married? What about a monk who fights for God from the moment of his birth? What about a cleric who fulfills by faithful service the offices of the holy ministry? Are they in danger of losing the fruit of eternal salvation, if, while living, they possess their

---
5 Ps. 138.17.

wealth intact or, when dying, they do not leave it to the needy?'

My speech and authority are small for putting forth an opinion about a question of this nature. Therefore, let us see what the language of the Holy Books and the words of the heavenly precepts pronounce about these questions. Then, most rightly, will I direct the rule of my opinion according to the norm given by God. First of all, no one should think he has a right to seek solace in the old examples by saying there were some saints in the Law or before the Law who were rich.

Indeed, that time has gone and the general character of things has changed, for, before the Law, the choice was free to all either to possess or strive after wealth, because wealth was not chastised with the rod of heavenly prohibitions. The Apostle says:[6] 'for where there is no Law there is no transgression.' The Law, therefore, makes a thing unlawful. The Apostle says:[7] 'I did not know concupiscence if the Law did not say, "Thou shalt not covet." '

Man possessed without restriction the wealth which God had not condemned before the Law. Nevertheless, according to the Law, the Law gave the same right to all, because the Law did not completely forbid man, as long as he did it in a just way, to possess what he wished. Thus, at that time all holy men used all their wealth according to the prescribed limits of the Law. We read:[8] 'They walked in all commandments and justifications of God, without blame.'

So also walked these people about whom these words are mentioned. The prophetess Anna lived in fastings and prayer. So also Nathaniel, who, we read, was exalted and praised as a true Israelite and was admirable according to the testimony

---

6 Rom. 4.15.
7 Rom. 7.7.
8 Luke 1.6.

of the Lord God Himself. So also Tobias, who exceeded the precepts of the Law by the greatness of his devotion, served by burying the dead even at the danger of death, and consoled the needy even to bringing want on himself. So great was his love for liberality that he allotted to his hired servants a portion of all his goods. What is more strange, he was rich. What is more singular, from a poor man he had become a rich man. After one has been in want, wealth almost excites a greater greed for riches.

(5) Such, therefore, were the holy men of that time. They possessed all things according to the Law and left all things behind according to the Law. Every man who obeyed the Law was perfect, and he who then did less under the Law was as devout as he who now does more under the Gospel, for at that time the Law was, as it were, the Gospel. Accordingly, he who represented himself as then obeying the Law fulfilled, so to say, the Gospel. Therefore, let no one think he must now take refuge in the Law. As the Apostle has said:[9] 'The old have passed away, and all things are made anew.'

At that time there was more indulgence and more was allowed. At that time the eating of meat was taught; now abstinence is taught. At that time there were few fast days in all one's lifetime; now all one's life is like one fast. At that time vengeance was at hand for injury; now there is patience. At that time the Law was the accomplice of those in anger; now it is their opponent. At that time the Law stretched forth the sword to the plaintiff; now it extends love. At that time the Law was lenient toward carnal pleasures; now the Gospel is against indulgence to the eyes. At that time bodily pleasures had a certain permission; now the eyes are ordered to keep restraint. At that time the Law was extended so that the bed

---

9 2 Cor. 5.17.

of one man could receive many wives; now the Law restrains by the devotion of chaste love, even to excluding one wife.

'It remains,' says the Apostle, 'that they also who have wives be as if they have none, and they that weep as though they weep not, and those that rejoice as though they do not rejoice, and those who buy as though they do not possess, and they who use this world, as if they do not use it, for the fashion of this world passes away.'[10] See how concisely a teacher sent by God has brought all things to the right measure and how he enclosed all things within one perfection, by prohibiting not only unlawful things. but even by restraining licit things. He restricted the usage of marriage, the pagan flow of tears, the intemperance of joys, the lust for possessing, and the greed for purchasing, that short and elusive pleasure of this world.

And why all these things? Why except, as the Apostle said, the fashion of the world is passing away? How far removed are they from the commandment of God who, when God orders them to renounce their wealth while they live, seek to keep it in the possession of their relatives, when dead? Or, how far removed from holiness are they who, in order that they may disinherit themselves on God's account, are unwilling to disinherit strangers for their own good? To these, willingly and in all freedom, I would say: What madness, O most miserable people! To have any kind of people at all heirs, you are willing to disinherit yourselves; to leave others rich for a short time, you condemn yourselves to eternal beggary.

(6) Someone will possibly ask: how is it that God demands more now from Christians through the Gospel than He demanded formerly from the Jews through the Law. The

---
10 1 Cor. 7.29,31.

reason is clear. We now pay more to our Lord because we owe more. The Jews had a certain semblance of things; we have the reality. The Jews were servants; we are adopted sons. The Jews received the yoke of bondage; we receive liberty. The Jews received curses; we receive grace. The Jews received the letter that kills; we receive the spirit which gives life. A servant was sent as master to the Jews, but to us a Son was sent. The Jews passed over the sea into the desert; we enter into the Kingdom through Baptism. The Jews ate manna; we enjoy Christ. The Jews ate the flesh of birds; we enjoy the Body of God. The Jews ate the hoar frost of Heaven; we enjoy the God of Heaven. As the Apostle says:[11] 'He who when He was in the form of God, humbled Himself even unto death, even to the death on the cross.' He was not content to undergo an ordinary death for us. He went beyond the very undertaking of a voluntary death by suffering the greatest torments.

For this alone what can man, for whom Christ spent Himself through the greatest and most harsh punishments, repay? Or what worthy recompense will man, who owes God Himself by Whom he was redeemed, make on his own behalf to the Lord? This, then, is the reason for which the Lord wishes us to be more devoted to Himself; He bought our devotion at such a great price. The most blessed Paul says:[12] 'Who therefore will separate us from the love of Christ? Shall tribulation, or distress or persecution, or famine, or nakedness, or danger or the sword?' The Apostle did not say that either money alone or riches were owed by us to God, but he did say tribulation, want, hunger, the sword, suffering, shedding of blood, the breathing out of the soul, and death itself from every kind of punishment were owed. Hence, let all religious

---

11 Phil. 2.8.
12 Rom 8.35.

men understand that they are paying God back insufficiently even if they give all their possessions, because, though they give away all their goods, they still owe themselves.

Therefore, as I began to say above, if there is a widow, let her never think that the name of widowhood suffices for eternal salvation. Let her see to it that she is a widow such as God orders through the Apostle when he said:[13] 'She who is indeed a widow and desolate, let her hope in God and continue in supplication night and day. For she that lives in pleasure is dead while she is living.' By one and the same injunction the Apostle indicated two kinds of widowhood: the one of life, the other of death. The one of death he finds in pleasure. Without doubt, he does not wish her to be rich whom he does not allow to be pleasure-loving, because all the fruit of riches is found in the enjoyment of delights, for, when, the enjoyment of delights is taken away, there are no other reasons left for wealth.

(7) Since the Apostle who does not wish that anything be reserved for the usage of death said that in delights there was death for the widow, it is clear that he wishes everything to be scattered for the reaping of eternal life. He says: 'She who is indeed a widow and desolate, hopes in the Lord,' teaching that it is of little value if the widow is neither pleasure-loving nor rich, unless she is a widow devoted to God, unless she is given to prayer, unless she is free from all the snares of the world. Through all these things she is indeed a widow.

If this is the case, let any widow at all, who wishes to belong to life and not death, know that she is never sufficient unto herself merely because she has given up pleasures and riches on account of God, unless she has merited it by prayer and labor, in order that she may seem to be indeed a widow

---

13 1 Tim. 5.5-6.

of God. There is no doubt that in what manner one is devoted to Christ in this world, in that manner will he live in the body of Christ, according to that saying:[14] 'My soul seeks after you, your right hand has received me.' This passage declares that the right hand of God will receive in the next world only that soul which clings to God in this. This, therefore, is the criterion of widowhood.

As regards married people who make profession of continence and are filled with the spirit of God, can we doubt that they, who have cut themselves off from the world, are willing to bestow their wealth on human heirs? How do they deny themselves to each other who bequeath to others the goods which belong to themselves? Endowed with such a rare virtue, treading underfoot, in the austerity of an admirable continence, permissible pleasures, and, what is still more, pleasures whose sweetness they have tasted, how do they who have caused God Himself to live within them not vow any of their wealth to God? It can be said most rightfully, in my poor opinion, about such a marriage:[15] 'Rejoice, you barren, because you have not produced, break forth and shout because you have not given birth, because the children of a deserted woman are many, more than of her who has a husband.'

She is a sterile thing because she has not produced, and deserted because she has separated from all wordly pleasures, and without a husband because, without the use of a husband, she has a husband in such a way that she seems not to have one. Who doubts that such married people, not only while they live, live to God both in their possessions and in their persons and, likewise, when they depart from life, who doubts but that they pass with their possessions to God, for whom they lived? If any of them bequeath his property to those

---
14 Ps. 62.9.
15 Isa. 54.1; Gal. 4.27.

dedicated to the world and to the world itself, in vain has he ascribed to himself the name of religion. He seems ever to have lived for those whom he enriched when he died. This is enough about married people.

(8) Let me turn now to holy virgins. To these the Saviour Himself prescribed the law of love by the examples of the ten virgins,[16] of whom He says that only that number of the foolish virgins who will be deficient in works of mercy should be given over to eternal punishments. By this statement He most clearly taught the great value of abundant alms, without which, He said, chastity itself would not profit a virgin.

Perhaps some virgins flatter themselves and think that it is sufficient for them to give little when they possess wealth. Nor do I deny that they should believe this way, if there is a reason. Let little be given if to give little is sufficient. I am not sure that a little is enough. In fact, I am quite sure that a little is not enough. If these virgins know otherwise, let them think that way. I myself know one thing, that God said the lamps of the foolish virgins were extinguished because they did not have the oil of goods works.

But you, whoever you are, do you think you have oil in abundance? Indeed, those foolish virgins about whom I have spoken thought in this manner. If they did not believe they had sufficient, they would have taken care to get it. The Lord says they wished to borrow and sought it with all zeal and exertion. Without doubt they would have asked beforehand, were it not that the confidence of getting it had deceived them. And you, then, virgin— whoever you are—see to it that you are not in this way without it, even though you believe you have got it.

You are of the same name as they; you are of the same

---

16 Matt. 25.1-13.

profession. You are a virgin and they were virgins. You presume you are wise and they did not think they were foolish. You think you have your light, your lamp. Indeed, they lost their light because they presumed they would find a light. Therefore, it is written that they trimmed their lamps, because they believed the lamps were to be lighted. What more need I to add? I also think that a weak bit of light still remained in the lamps.

When they, as we read, stood with their mouths open before their lamps which were about to be extinguished, they indeed possessed something whose extinction they feared. Their fear was not without foundation. Indeed, the lamps were extinguished and gave no further light. Even though there seemed to be a little flickering of virginity, this was no proof of their integrity, since there was no substance of oil to feed the light. From this we understand that what is little is as nothing, because it is no use lighting a light that is to go out at once, nor can a sun that sets as soon as it rises help to give any illumination; neither does it help to give only the beginning of life for the sole purpose of having the beginning of death. Thus, there is need of a lamp that is full if the light is to last.

If in lamps which men use for a short time the light grows dim and fails, unless oil is poured in copiously, what an abundance of oil you need—whoever you are—if your light is to shine forever. If anybody thinks he has what he has not, he does not have a sufficiency for eternal life. Foolish presumptions are the causes of damnation, not of salvation. The Apostle says:[17] 'for he who thinks he is something when he is nothing, deceives himself.'

Perhaps it may be, whoever you are, that the measure of

---
17 Gal. 6.3.

liberality has been revealed to you by God and that you know the limit of what must be given as prescribed by the Holy Spirit. It may be that you think it is a crime to overstep these boundaries and you judge that it is a kind of transgression if you are more holy than you are ordered by God to be. If this is so, I do not forbid that you use the knowledge given by God. But, if this notion is as false as it is ridiculous, what madness is it that you do not do as much as you can, with careful and fearful foresight, since you are completely ignorant of what is appropriate for your salvation?

(9) It now remains to say a few words about clerics and priests, although it may be superfluous to say some of these things. Whatever is said about all the others, without doubt, pertains more to them who, by example, should be above all and whom it behooves to be as much above others in devoutness as they are in dignity. What is it to be above others without deserving it, except the mere title of honor without reality? What is a dignity in one who does not deserve it other then a jewel in the mud? Therefore, it behooves all who are raised above others on the holy altar to excel as much in merit as in rank.

If God gave such and so perfect a rule of life to men living among the people and to women who are more weak by their very sex, how much more does He order those by whom all are to be taught to seek perfection, in order that their pupils may be perfect? God wished them to be of so great an example to all that He bound them to a singular rule of life, not only by the severity of the New, but also by that of the Old Law. Although the Old Law granted to all copious means of obtaining wealth, nevertheless it bound all Levites and priests to a certain property limit and it did not permit them to possess either corn, or wine, or even any land for tillage.

From this it can be understood whether God wishes His clergy who now live in the Gospel to bequeath wealth, which He was unwilling that those placed in the Law should even possess, to wordly heirs after their own death. Hence, in the Gospel, the Savior Himself pointed out to the clergy, not a voluntary duty of perfection as to others, but a commanded one. What do we read that He said to the young layman? 'If you wish to be perfect, sell what you have and give to the poor.'[18] What did He say to His clergy? He says:[19] 'Do not possess gold, or silver, or money in your purses, nor a wallet for your journey, nor two coats, nor shoes, nor a stick.'

See how great is the difference in both these salutary warnings of God. To the layman He says: 'If you wish, sell what you possess,' but to the cleric: 'I do not wish you to possess.' He judged that it was of little value for the one to put away from him the possession of a more ample substance, unless He took away from the Apostle who was about to undertake a long journey even the wallet itself and punished him by allowing him only one coat. What more besides this? This was not enough. He also especially orders His servants to go around the whole world in their bare feet. He took away the shoes from feet stiffened with the cold.

What more could he add? He snatched the shepherd's crook from the hand of the Apostle. To His ministers, wandering throughout the whole world, He did not leave the use of one little stick. After all these things it is very little for those of their successors, that is, the Levites and priests administering great and divine things who alone happen to be opulent, unless they also cast aside their rich heirs. I say, let us blush at

---
18 Matt. 19.21.
19 Matt. 10.9-10.

this lack of faith. Let it be sufficient for us that we seem to scorn God even to the end of life. Why do we so act that we also extend contempt of Him into the next world?

I have spoken about persons and the duty of individuals, and all this because, as I have said above, some who profess religion either think they, like other worldly people, do not owe their substance to the Lord or certainly think they owe less. Indeed, they owe more, because the servant who knows the will of his master and does not do it will receive many strokes, but he who does not know will receive few strokes.[20]

Religion is the knowledge of God. Therefore every religious, by the very fact that he follows the religious profession, testifies that he knows the will of God. Accordingly, the profession of religion does not take away but increases the debt, because the assumption of the religious name is the pledge of devotion. Therefore, each one owes as much by his actions as he promised by profession, according to that saying:[21] 'It is better not to vow than after a vow not to perform the things promised.'

(10) Perhaps someone will say: 'If this is the way things are, lack of religion, therefore, is more safe than religion.' By no means. The religious man is the debtor through the fact that he professes to be religious, but the irreligious man because he has neglected religion. Therefore, both are debtors, but according to the difference of way of life. The religious man owes whatever he professed that he knew, but the irreligious man owes because he does not deign to know, according to that saying which the Divine Word says particularly about him:[22] 'He did not wish to understand that he might do well.' Because I seem to have burdened religious people with this fact, that is, that I have said the profession of religion

---

20 Luke 12.47-48.
21 Eccli. 5.4.
22 Ps. 35.4.

is the pledge of religion, let us remove this burden; let us think that what I have said is not so. Let us consider not what we ought to do because we are professed, but what we should do because it is right. Let us consider not what we ought to do because we have taken a vow, but what we ought to do because it is salutary.

Tell me, I beg you, all religious men, is there any man who has not his own salvation or at least some good in view when he does something? No one, I suppose. All are led to doing and desiring what is useful by the warning and instinct of their very nature. Therefore, soldiers seek their glory, businessmen their profit, and farmers what will increase their crops. Need I add more? Even thieves and robbers, poisoners and assassins, and every kind of criminal think that what they do is proper for them, not because base things are agreeable to anyone, but because he who uses base things believe that what is base is suitable to himself

Therefore also, I think, we have sought a philosophy of religion for no other reason than that we thought it was suitable to us. We are thinking of the brevity of present things and the eternity of future things; how small one is, how great the other. We think also of the future judge and the serious outcome of this tremendous judgment. We think of a vale of perpetual tears burning in the midst of people who stand around. To enter and suffer in this valley is an evil so great as to be unthinkable; even for it to be seen and feared is a part of this greatest evil.

Think also of the excellent and most felicitous things in the midst of these fearful and most penal things. We think of new skies and a new earth, a more beautiful appearance on all things. We think of the eternal abode of justice, the recent building by creatures, the golden houses of all the saints above the ill-made skies, the courts polished with glittering jewels, made precious by the glow of immortal metals, the light there sevenfold more bright, radiating in an ever purple glow. We think of the happiness rich in ineffable goods, everlastingness glad with its inhabitants, the fellowship of the patriarchs, the association with the prophets, the brotherhood of the Apostles, the honor of the martyrs, the likeness of angels in all the saints, the fullness of heavenly riches, the abundance of immortal pleasures, the life in common with God.

Thinking of these things, contemplating these thoughts, we take refuge in the worship and service of holy religion. We have taken on the intercessor and advocate of most efficient intercession, to obtain these good things for us. We have betaken on ourselves with ambitious humility its protection and patronage.

(11) Hence, since we have thought of and likewise sought these great benefits, let us consider now and weigh most diligently whether we can purchase these great favors from God either by our acts or by our wealth. But if we cannot, why, I ask, does not each one of us offer on his own behalf all he has, because he cannot offer all he owes? Especially so, since our God and Saviour Himself said that nothing was safer and more salutary for anybody than to allocate his property and wealth for the use of alms. He commanded this in both the Old and the New Law, when He said that they who divide their goods are become richer and that alms free us from death.

Elsewhere He said about the holy men:[23] 'He scattered his goods, he gave to the poor, and his justice lives on forever.' And also in the Gospel He says:[24] 'Do not lay up for yourselves treasures on earth.' And again:[25] 'You cannot serve God

---
23 Ps. 111.9.
24 Matt. 6.19.
25 Matt. 6.24; Luke 16.13.

and Mammon.' and again:[26] 'Woe to you, O rich men, who have your consolations.' To those guilty of avarice as well as of the crime of unkindliness He says:[27] 'Depart into eternal fire which My Father prepared for the devil and his angels.'

It is easily understood what will be the eternal punishment of these whose lot is shared with the devil. The greatest and most dreadful crimes of fornication, or murder, or sacrilege are not punished with the greatest torments. Only avarice and inhumanity, the disclaimers of mercy, are so punished.

Hence, it behooves us to understand what sufferings they will endure who join avarice to their other sins. Though devoid of all other sins, they whom the crime of avarice alone has condemned to death are to be afflicted with the greatest punishment. If we believe all these things about the future, we must doubtless avoid them. If we do not avoid them, then we do not believe. If we do not believe them, by no means are we Christians. We can never call anyone a Christian who does not think that Christ must be believed.

(12) Grant that, being guilty, we have no fear of the punishment I have just mentioned. Can we, who do not deserve it, also hope for reward? If we do not give our wealth for the redemption of sins, let us give it, at least, for the purchase of beatitude. If we do not give lest we be condemned, let us give, at least, in order that we may be rewarded, because, even if there are not past sins which the holy ones must redeem, there are, however, everlasting goods which they must purchase at a great price. Even if we do not fear punishment, we are, however, seeking a kingdom. Therefore, even if the holy have nothing to redeem, there are things they must purchase. It may be that some fear they will suffer a loss by

---

26 Luke 6.24.
27 Matt. 25.41.

purchasing, that is, they fear they will furnish more than they receive. They fear that big returns will not be made to those who lend little. They fear that the return will not recompense for the expenditure. They fear that, once the great price is paid, the money of the purchaser will be endangered. They fear that, if they furnish something great to the Lord on the earth, perhaps Christ will not have in heaven the wherewithal to repay them.

Surely, if there is this doubt, I urge that nothing be done, because nothing is profitable to him who doubts. Doing is useless, if there is not assured confidence; in vain does he lend who despairs of a return. Christ, as we believe, compensates for all that is done. If you think a man is poor because unable to pay, or that he is untrustworthy because unwilling, how can you expect compensation from God whom you condemn as being both unable and untrustworthy?

But, if it is not so and you doubt that He will do what He said, how foolish and erroneous not to give Him as much as you can, since you do not doubt that you will receive much more than you gave? How badly off you are when you prefer to receive nothing from those riches which you bequeath, when you can fully possess all that you think you can? But, alas! I suppose God is not trusted. And I think what I say. Would to Heaven this were only a doubt and not a certainty! Perhaps I should labor to overcome my ideas and compel my mind not to believe doubtful things so that I might apply my mind to better things.

What am I doing? I am convinced by things which are not in doubt and compelled by facts that are self-evident. Who believes in the Lord with his mind and does not trust Him with his wealth? Who hands his soul over to God and denies Him money? Who accommodates his faith to God's promise and yet does not act so that he can participate in those promises? Therefore, when I see men not doing these things, I am forced to recognize openly and publicly there are men who do not believe. It is not lawful for me to think those men show their faith in God, when by their deeds they proclaim their denial.

In this respect it is necessary to lament and bewail the lack of faith shown by almost all. O misery, O perversity! Man trusts man and he does not trust God. Hope is bestowed on human promises and is denied to God. In human affairs, all is done with hope in the future. Is not this temporary life itself also nourished and sustained by hope?

We believe in corn from the soil so that we receive credits from those who will use it. The greatest labor is done in the vineyards, because the hope of a vintage comforts men. Businessmen empty their purses in order to buy because they hope to fill them again by what they sell. Sailors entrust their life to the winds and tempests in order to enjoy the things hoped and prayed for. And what more is there to add? Peace between wild and barbarian nations also rests on hope and is made firm by mutual trust. Even robbers and assassins do not deny faith in each other. What they mutually promised they hope will be kept. Finally, as I have said, everything is done by hope between men. It is God alone of whom we despair. Though our Lord made the elements themselves and the nature of the world trustworthy, He alone who caused that all things should be trusted is the only one who is distrusted by almost all.

(13) Perhaps it can be said at this point that sometimes it is not because of lack of faith, but because of necessity, that men use their wealth in this manner. Perhaps it can also be said that the religious do not trust in God, but that they retain things necessary for use in life. Perhaps it can also

be said that many people are sometimes prevented from the highest perfection of giving their wealth in alms, either by their sex, their age, or by the very weakness of their ailing body.

Grant that this can be borne. Yet, even if it is borne, it must be borne in such a manner that, according to what is needful in particular cases, what is sufficient should be retained, what is excessive should be curtailed. The Apostle says:[28] 'For having food and clothing, with these let us be content. For they who wish to become rich fall into temptation and into the snare of the devil.' We see, therefore, that salvation consists in having only necessary things; snares, in having superfluous things. The grace of God consists in moderation; the chain of the devil, in riches. What did the Apostle add immediately? He speaks of riches 'which drown man into destruction and perdition.'[29]

If riches contain destruction within themselves, let us avoid opulence, lest we fall into destruction. Full and abundant means are said to bring perdition. Full possession must be avoided, lest deep perdition follow. Therefore, whether sex, or age, or infirmities require necessities, they should be so content with what is sufficient that whatever is beyond their present need should be devoted to religious purposes.

And for the rest, if you, whoever you are, in the holy profession, if you are overeager about preserving wealth and piling up possessions, in vain are you making a pretext of your infirmities. Can the weaker sex not conduct its life otherwise than by distending its spiritual cares by having to administer a huge patrimony? Can the consecrated girl or the widow vowed to chastity not preserve intact their perseverance in the holy profession, unless they are encumbered with the

---
28 1 Tim. 6.8-9.
29 1 Tim. 6.9.

weight of gold and silver and with the certain knowledge that they possess more wealth than is required for their own usage?

Or, when sex and decorum make quiet an urgent necessity for them, is there one who imagines that she can find absolute quiet in the midst of managing her household, if the clattering of her servants beats upon her ears and she is made deaf by the tumultuous noise of the crowd around her? Indeed, to a holy soul desirous for true peace it is an exceedingly great disquiet to bear these crowds; in a certain manner, even to see them is a part of it. Though someone would want to subject these crowds to discipline and silence, it is not possible to. control their unruliness and keep her own calm. Therefore, the very correction of disquiet from outside causes is a disturbance of our quiet.

The statements I have just made about the female sex pertain to all and apply equally to every age, sex, and infirmity. Let no one think that riches advance and do not hinder piety. They are hindrances, not aids; burdens, not assistance. Piety is not sustained by the possession and use of wealth, but it is overthrown by it acccording to what our Lord Himself said:[30] 'and the care of this world and the deceitfulness of riches choke the word of God and is become without fruit.' Rightly and with perfect taste did He say that riches were deceptive. Riches are regarded and called good, and, therefore, since they are the causes of eternal evils, men are deceived by the name of good bestowed on them in this world.

(14) Although what I have been saying is as God Himself taught, let us consider the miseries and weakness of some who think they cannot carry on life without very great

---
30 Matt. 13.22.

wealth. Grant that you, whoever you are in the holy name and holy profession, grant that you have riches; grant that you have wealth up to the end of this life, provided you at length confer them on yourself at the last. Grant that you wish to use your property and possessions in this life, provided you do not forget yourself when you are dying. Remember that your wealth must be given back for the worship and honor of Him from whom you know you accepted it as a gift.

What is sought from all you, O rich of this world, is what is pleasant and pleasurable. If it cannot be obtained from one of you that he wish to be poor in this world, let him at least make provision for himself, lest he be a beggar for all eternity. You who flee poverty only in this world, why do you not fear for eternity? Avoid, you who are careful in shortlived things, a long and unending calamity. Why do you abhor poverty so greatly in this life; why are you terrified? It is less than much that you are afraid of in this world.

If you consider temporary poverty serious, what kind, I ask, will that be which never ceases? What I am pleading for is a matter both of your soul and of your vow. If you do wish to do without the use of your property completely, act so that you will not do without it sometime. I am asking you for what is pleasing and pleasurable to you. You who do not agree to live completely without riches, act so that you may always be rich, according to that saying:[31] 'If, therefore, you delight in thrones and sceptres, kings of the people, love wisdom that you may reign forever.'

Otherwise, what error or what madness to think that there can be any man who, after a life spent in ample wealth even up to the very last (and this alone suffices for his guilt), is not even fully and helpfully mindful of himself at the

---
31 Wisd. 6.22.

moment of death that he does not make provision for himself out of his own goods in his last weak moment? This is especially so in the case of riches which of themselves accuse their possessors, according to that saying: 'Woe unto you, O rich!' For, to the possessor of wealth those other kinds of sin are never lacking, which, as it were, spring from the fecund womb of wealth as from a natural source. Not even in his last days does such a man act, labor, and propitiate with every bit of his wealth, lest he depart guilty; lest he go out guilty. He does not act, lest his soul, which is to be punished even for the present, abandon his body to be punished later on.

Who is then so unbelieving or so mad? Who does not think of these things? Who does not fear them? Who takes care of others more than of himself from his own wealth? Who, being completely destitute of all hope of this life and of all aid, loses the one sole plank to which, as a shipwrecked man in the midst of the sea,[32] he could cling, and not only loses it, but throws it away and casts is from himself completely? Who labors in every way, lest he cause something, by which he may escape as he is about to perish, be left for himself?

(15) Since this is the case, I ask you, all you who love Christ: Can any men be as savage and cruel against their enemies as the rich are against themselves? Indeed, there are no individuals so fierce and so inhuman that they do not cease to pursue their adversaries when they are desperate and dying. Even in death these people persecute themselves.

Can there be a greater persecution than that a man be disinherited by himself, to become banished from all his goods, to be sent into exile by himself? And this not in a common

---

32 Cf. Saint Jerome, 'Wedlock is like a plank offered to a shipwrecked man' (*Nicene and Post-Nicene Fathers* 2.6.216).

and wonted custom, but by a novel and most cruel one, where the soul itself is sent into exile, where the soul is disinherited of its wealth. O how much more lenient are strangers and enemies in the flesh! They are enemies only of the body; you are enemies of your souls.

Their hatred is light in comparison with your crimes. It is light when something is injurious in this world, but that is serious and evil which will kill for eternity. The Saviour Himself said:[33] 'Do not fear those who can kill the body, but cannot kill the soul.' The hatred is light which injures the body and does not injure the soul, because, when the body is injured, the soul is beyond damage and the happiness of souls is not corrupted by the sufferings of the flesh. Therefore, that sin is without expiation (it cannot be judged at all), which will condemn, without end, the whole man. Therefore, your enemies are less formidable to you than yourselves. Indeed, every other kind of enmity is dissolved by death; you act against yourselves in such a way that you do not escape your own enmity even after death.

---

33 Matt. 10.28.

BOOK THREE

MY MISTRESS, the Church of God, I have spoken in the two foregoing books as if separately to your two kinds of children, that is, to the one who is the lover of the world, to the other who bears the stamp of true religion. But in this book, God willing, I desire to speak to both as the nature of the case may demand, now addressing one or the other separately, now both alike. It remains for me, after having recognized in the course of reading what pertains to them in particular, to desire that both receive with the love of God what I have written for the love of God.

I have recently said that mercy and almsgiving are the virtues proper to all Christians. I have established, it seems to me, by numerous and conclusive proofs that herein are found the chief merits of the saints and the most effective remedies for sinners, and I believe no more should be expected. If anyone desires further proofs, let him consult the Books of God, so full of information that the attestation of all the Sacred Letters is almost uniform on this point.

It remains for me to say a few words in answer to those infidel objections which certain people sometimes offer by way of sinful self-excuse. The Saviour, speaking in the Gospel, says that money and wealth are loaned to men by God in order that the loans may be returned with multiple interest, when He says to the very avaricious debtor:[1] 'wicked and slothful servant, you knew that I reap where I do not sow, and I gather where I have not scattered. Therefore you ought

---
[1] Matt. 25.26.

to have given My money to the bankers, and at My coming I would have received what is Mine with usury. Therefore take the talent from him and give it to him who has ten talents.' And a little afterwards He said:[2] 'Cast the wicked servant into exterior darkness. There will be weeping and gnashing of teeth.'

Although these words can refer to another subject, they can be fittingly applied to our present discussion. Since the bankers mentioned by the Saviour are lightly understood to be the poor and needy, because money, which is distributed to such people, is increased, doubtless whatever is distributed to the poor is returned by God with interest. Hence, the Lord Himself elsewhere more openly orders the rich to distribute the riches of the world and to make to themselves little sacks which do not grow old.[3] But His Vase of Election points out that riches are given to the wealthy by the Lord, in order that they may grow rich by good works.[4]

Therefore, I, also, the least and most unworthy of the servants of God, say that it is the first and the most salutary duty of religion for the rich Christian, while he is in this life, to expend the riches of this world for the name and honor of God. Secondly, if the ensnared one has not done this either through fear, or weakness, or any other necessity, let him at least distribute all his wealth when he is dying.

(2) Perhaps the rich Christian says: 'I have children.' In regard to this, the very first pages of this book brought to mind many appropriate replies and the word of the Lord suffices in plenty to answer them when He says:[5] 'He who loves his sons or daughter more than Me is not worthy of Me.' I can

---
2 Matt. 25.30.
3 Luke 12.33.
4 1 Tim. 6.7-19.
5 Matt. 10.37.

also add that prophetic saying which says that neither fathers must be judged for their children nor children for their fathers, but each one among men must either be saved by his own justification or he will perish by his own iniquity.[6] Therefore, whatsoever riches a man accumulates for his children, the fact that he leaves a rich heir will profit him nothing before the judgment seat.

Grant that it can be overlooked in parents, if they leave a portion of their hereditary wealth to their children, provided those to whom it is left are good and holy. Grant, also, that they can be pardoned, if they leave something to the evil and corrupt. They seem to have some kind of excuse when they say: 'Parental love overcame us; the ties of blood compelled us; nature itself, as by the hand of love, submitted us to its authority. We know what the justice of God asks, what sacred truth demands, but, we confess, we were brought under the yoke of blood relationship and we surrendered ourselves as captives to the bonds of charity. Faith gave way to blood and the obligations of relationship overcame our duty to religion.'

Something can be said for this argument, but not by a man who wants to be saved. Their argument is the shadow of the shadow of an excuse and does not excuse. It gives to the guilty one the merest semblance of an excuse, but no real freedom from his guilt. I never tell anybody who loves something more than God that he can possess steadfast assistance from any of his wealth according to that saying which is written, that the future judgment will consist in this, that the light came into this world and men loved the darkness more than the light.[7] Nobody doubts that all whatsoever a man preferred to divine love will become for him darkness. These things, then, are true.

---
6 Ezech. 18.20-30.
7 John 3.19.

Grant, as I have said, that allowances can be made for parents who make allowances for nature without thinking of their salvation. Yet, some who do not have children turn themselves away completely from having regard for their own salvation and from the remedy for their sins. Although they are without children of their own, they seek out others to whom they bequeath the substance of their own wealth. They ascribe to them some faint title to blood relationship. The nominal parents make them as their adopted sons, so that the offspring of perjury takes the place of those offspring who are non-existent.

In this way some very wretched and most unholy people, who are not bound by the bonds of children, nevertheless provide for themselves chains with which to bind the unfortunate necks of their own souls. When there is no crisis at all within the home, they summon one outside the home. Although the causes of dangers are lacking, they rush headlong, as if into a voluntary death. In regard to these people, some cannot make up their minds whether to regard their unhappy errors with feelings of anger or of sorrow, for error is worthy of sorrow and lack of parental feeling is worthy of execration. We are brought to tears by misfortune, to anger by lack of faith. On the one side, we bemoan the folly of men, and on the other are moved by the love of God, whenever we remember that it is possible to find a man at the very end of this brief life, and at the point of death, and about to go before the judgment seat of God, thinking of something else but his end, of something other than his death and the danger before him, and neglecting all hope for his soul— which he ought to be helping in his last moments with all zeal and effort and all his possessions. What is he doing instead but turning over this single thought: how sumptuously his heir is going to devour his substance.

(3) O most wretched of all men, for what are you apprehensive, for what are you excited, for what do you make yourself the begetter of things that will perish? Do you fear, perhaps, lest heirs will be lacking who, when you are dead, will greedily swallow what you leave? I do not want you to fear; I do not want you to be apprehensive. Would that you were to be saved as easily as all your goods will go to ruin! O lack of faith! O peversity! It is also commonly said that all want to be better disposed toward themselves than toward one another. This is a new kind of monster, that anyone should want to consult only the interests of another and not of himself.

Behold, you are about to depart, O most unhappy of all men, to the holy examination, to that fearful and formidable judgment seat where there cannot be any solace whatsoever for the erring and troubled soul, except only a good conscience, a guiltless life, or, what approaches a good life, almsgiving. At that judgment seat there is no help for the guilty man except only a generous soul, fruitful penance, and alms abundant given with willing hands. At that judgment seat you will get, according to the diversity of your merits, either the greatest good or the greatest evil, either an immortal reward or punishment without end.

And you go on thinking only of enriching some heir or other. You go on sighing about the wealth of a blood relative and kinsman, whom you are making very rich by your patrimony. To him you are assigning the ornaments of changeable household utensils. You fill his warehouses with your goods. To him you leave the greater number of your slaves. O most unhappy man of all, you are thinking of how well others will live after you. You are not thinking how badly you yourself will die.

Answer me, I ask, O man, wretched and lacking in faith. When you divide your patrimony among many, when you enrich many with your wealth, are you so badly deserving of yourself alone that you do not leave the place of the heir for yourself even among strangers? Behold, the sacred judgment seat is awaiting you who are about to depart from this life. The terrible angels and ministers of everlasting torments await you, and you go on turning in your mind the future pleasures that the heirs on earth are going to have when you are dead. You go meditating on others' pleasures, namely, how well your heir will breakfast on what is yours after you are gone; how full he will feed himself; how he will stuff his glutted belly even to recurring nausea.

O most unhappy of all men, what are you doing with all these trifles, with all these absurdities, with this foolish error, with this destructive vanity? Can this bring you aid in the midst of the greatest suffering, if he who lavishly consumes your wealth belches after he has wined and dined well?

(4) If the subject and occasion still demand after what I have just said, I will append some remarks on those about whom I am now speaking. In the meanwhile, I say in a special way and emphasize with a particular reminder that nobody in any way should prefer his offspring, even the most beloved, to his soul. Neither is it wrong for a Christian man to provide less well for his legitimate heirs in this world, provided that he make provision for himself, in as many ways as possible, for eternity. It is easier for the children to lack something here on earth than for the parents to be lacking in the next world. Poverty in the present life is much lighter to bear than eternal poverty, because in the next life not only poverty but even death and punishment are to be feared. Thus, it is easier for the heirs to lack some of the patrimony here on earth than that in the other world something be lacking for the salvation of those who made the will. And they to

whom the heritage is left and remain behind in this world, if only they have some affection in them, should especially wish that they who bequeathed the heritage should not perish. If they do not feel like this, they are unworthy of being bequeathed anything, because a wise testator does not with justice leave what an unfeeling heir does not deserve.

Therefore, it is best for each one to consult his own interests and leave all things for the good of his soul and for his salvation, although there may be sometimes not only children to whom, according to nature, more seems to be owed, but also other offspring who, because of their merit or way of life, have a claim either by justice or by reason of religion to a share in the beneficence. To bequeath them something is an act of piety; to bequeath them nothing is an act of impiety. Such cases include relatives who have met with reverses or brothers who are loyal or spouses who are faithful, or, that I may extend further the function of goodness, kinsmen who are destitute, or their relatives by marriage who are in want, or, finally, those who share any relationship at all, or certainly, what is above all else, those who are dedicated to God. The chief and outstanding factor is that what one does as a service of love, one should do out of love for God.

Blessed is he who loves his own people in the spirit of divine love and whose love is the worship of Christ. Blessed is he who, in the bond of nature, envisages God as the Father of natures, and, by converting the functions of love into sacrifices, procures for himself a great amount of immortal profit and blessed rewards. Blessed is he who, by giving to his offspring, gains interest for his Lord. By the very fact that he gave temporal grants to his own people he begot for himself an everlasting reward.

Indeed, today most differently and unholily, those to whom the least is left by his parents are the very people to whom most is owed out of respect for God. The persons whom paternal love regards the least are the very ones most recommended by religion. In short, if some children are offered to God by their parents, those so offered are placed after all the other children. They are judged unworthy of a heritage, because they were worthy of consecration to God, and, therefore, by this one fact alone they are become valueless in the eyes of their parents, because they have begun to be of great value to God. From this it can be understood that hardly anybody is held to be more cheap among men than God, in contempt of whom parents scorn those children who have begun to belong to God.

(5) Indeed, they who do these things give an excellently calculated reason to justify their conduct when they say: 'What need is there for leaving an equal portion of the heritage to children who are already in religion?' Therefore, there is nothing just, nothing more fitting than that they beg, because they have begun to be in religion. Not, indeed, that this poverty is going to overwhelm them by pauperism, since they have voluntarily renounced their wordly possessions and possess heaven in hope and soon will possess it in reality. This is brought about by the rule and protection of God who rewards them with the immortal hope of eternal things, together with a sufficiency of temporal things. Yet they are in need, if we look only to the inhuman conduct of their parents, since they were so abandoned that they are in need. Although they are not completely banished from the home, and the house is not completely forbidden them as if by water and by fire, they are left on a much lower social scale than their brothers, so that, even though they are not needy to the point of indigence, they are at least indigent in comparison with their brothers.

You ask: What need do religious have of a rightful portion of the patrimony? I answer: that they may perform the obligation of religion, in order that religion may be enriched by the things of men in religion. I answer: that they may be able to give generously, so that all those who do not have may receive from those who do have; finally, if their faith and perfection are so great by reason of this, that they are to renounce forthwith what they get, they are all the more blessed in this, that they are soon not to have what they have.

I ask, O most inhuman parents, why do you impose on them the necessity of the most unbefitting poverty? Leave this decision to that religion to which you have handed over your children. More meritoriously are they made poor by themselves. If you only wish them to be in need, leave that to their choice. Let them be allowed, I ask, to wish to become poor. Let them be allowed to choose poverty, not to be forced into it. Lastly, even if they are to bear poverty, let them bear it with love, but not suffer it to their own damnation.

Why do you expel them, so to say, from nature, and disinherit them as from the right of blood? I wish them to be poor, yet I wish poverty itself to have its own reward. I wish that by an honorable exchange they may choose want from plenty, that from their choice of poverty they may attain plenty. Why do I try to drag you to kindness and goodness by using holy reasoning as a motive, since this is a special obstacle and the thing which should make parents good makes them bad?

While you should leave more of your patrimony to your children in religion, so that through them at least some of your wealth would return to God, you thereby do not bequeath property to your children, lest they have in God what they left. Indeed, with excellent reasoning and caution you are content not to acknowledge your children, lest they acknowledge that they are children of God. They are making recompense for God's sublime exchange of favors, while you attend to it most zealously that the dignity of God will have nothing through your children, when you have everything through the gift of God. Why, I ask, do you act so without faith, so without reverence?

I do not demand that you bestow your wealth on the Lord; give something of His own to God. Why do you act so covetously, why so disrespectfully? What you are denying God is not your own. Do you judge it unjust that you make your children in religion equal in wealth to your children in the world? You make those whom religion has made lowly among you to repent of having begun their religious life. It is the just and good Lord who preserves in them their religious purpose. Besides, you act, insofar as it depends on you, so that you make them worshippers of the world by preferring your children who have remained in the world before them. To hold one in contempt on account of religion, what else is it but to prohibit the religious profession?

(6) Perhaps I may seem unjust by uniformly accusing all parents in this matter, since, indeed, all do not act with like injustice towards their children. There are, some say, many parents who make equal portions for their children except that they distinguish between them with this stipulation only: in those very portions which seem to be bequeathed to those in religion, the parents order its use for those in religion, its ownership for other children.

Indeed, this is much worse and more unjust. It is more excusable if a father leaves little, with the rights of ownership, to his children than for him to take away from them completely the rights of ownership of property. To a certain extent this conditional clause can be borne, if, following this same procedure, a portion is left with the same restriction to friends, to relatives by marriage, or to kinsmen. Indeed, he who does not give the ownership of property to his children leaves them nothing. But the most unholy lack of faith among parents has found out how it can completely exclude God from their patrimony by taking away rights of ownership of property from their children in religion. The parents give the use so that the children may live from it, but they take away ownership so that they may have nothing to leave to God.

O new cleverness of the mind lacking in faith! It has found a way by which it seems to provide for the needs of its children by a greater irreverence towards God. It has caused that saintly offspring which has the use of property, but does not have the rights to property, to live seemingly in riches, but to die in poverty. Thus, the most unbelieving testator can depart from this life with unconcern, because he knows that none of his property will reach God. Yet, by the very fact, as I have presented above, that children in religion possess some semblance of wealth through the use of property, actually they do not possess. Though use gives the appearance of possession, they know in their hearts that they have nothing. He who has nothing of his own cannot believe he is a rich man, even for a short time.

(7) What are you doing, O most wretched unbelief and, as I might say, O error of pagan impiety? Do you hate God so much that you can not even love your children for the sole reason that they belong to God? Some leave their freedmen in better circumstances than you leave your children. Indeed, it is daily practice that some slaves, though not in the best and certainly not in bad servitude, are endowed by

their masters with Roman freedom,[8] according to which they take possession of the ownership of private property and obtain the right of making a will, so that while living they give their property to whom they wish and when dying transfer it in gift. Not only this, but they are not forbidden to take from the home of their masters those things which they acquired while in slavery. Sometimes the favor of a generous patron bestowed so much on them that the patron even took away from his own jurisdiction what he bestowed to the proprietorship of the freedmen.

O father, most lacking in faith, whoever you are, how much better do these masters act towards their freedmen than you towards your children! What they give, they give with a perpetual right attached; you give with a temporary right. They give their freedmen the choice of making a will; you take it away from freemen. Lastly, they give their slaves to liberty; you, as it were, sentence your sons to slavery. What else is it than to sentence to slavery those whom, as freeborn, you do not wish to possess anything.

You make use of the custom of those who sentence to the yoke of Latin liberty[9] their slaves who are undeserving, because they judge them unworthy of Roman citizenship. These are the slaves whom their masters order to act under the title of freedmen while they live, but whom their masters do not wish to possess anything when they are dying. Since the choice of a last will is denied them, their successors also, when dying, cannot donate those things which they possess.

---

8 A grant of Roman freedom to a slave gave the recipient full citizen rights.
9 The recipients of Latin liberty had not received *manumissio legitima* and were not full Roman citizens. They could engage in trade, but could not vote or fill public office or make wills. This social status was abolished by Justinian, 'for there are now no others, there being no more *Latini*' (*Institutes* 3.4).

In this way, therefore, you order your children in religion to live like Latin freedmen, so that they live as freeborn and die as slaves. They are bound by the jurisdiction of their brothers as by the chain of Latin freedom. Even if they seem to have free choice while they are alive, they die, however, placed, as it were, under the authority of their brothers. I ask: Why do you think there is so much crime in the title of religion? Because your children in religion have begun to be children of God, why do you not believe that they are your children? You, O man of good will, of what crime have they become guilty, so that on that account you think they must be considered worse because they hope to be better.

(8) But you say these are not your intentions. That is the same as if someone says he performs evil acts with a good intention, or that he commits the outrage of irreverence with a holy frame of mind. O most inhuman parents, what does it profit you to declare that you dishonor your children in religion with a good intention? The actuality of the situation rejects this; the deed shows that you are speaking falsely. It is of little value that your assertions are unsupported, since by your acts you bear witness against yourselves. Do you think it unbecoming that your offspring, holy and pleasing to God, are to be compared with your children who are the slaves of the world? It is true and your judgment is correct if you use this judgment justly and contrary to what you do. That is, that you do not think the evil and sinful are to be compared with the good and holy children, and that those who, in the sight of God, excel in their lives and merits, may, in the same way, excel in your sight, in favor and honor.

What is more fitting, what is more just, than that they who are better should at the same time be more honored. They who are successful in a lawsuit should likewise win the reward.

They who are distinguished in the Holy Gospel should likewise be placed first in the wills of human beings, and in this affair, at least, the good will of parents should be in accord with the will of Christ. Parents should give preference by honor to those whom God, by selection, chose before others. Not only is this not done, but all things are done contrariwise. The defiled are preferred before the stainless; the unholy, before the holy. Darkness is preferred to light; the earth, to heaven; the world, to God. Parents of this kind who unworthily trample underfoot the worship of God and the grandeur of His judgment think that in this they will escape the judgment of God.

(9) Indeed, parents say they do these things not in contempt of God but in accordance with justice and reason. They say: To whom will religious who do not have children leave their property? I will say to whom. I will not name those whom I have called above the poor of God, nor outsiders, nor people far away, lest perhaps that seem harsh and inhuman. I will designate for you men who are dear to you, and inseparable from you, and whom fittingly, even you who have many offspring prefer over your children. O most unworthy parents, I call them wicked. I repeat, I call them wicked![10] Can anything be found that is nearer and dearer to anyone whatsoever than oneself? To each one of you I commit the care of your soul, of your own salvation, of your own hope.

Do you call yourself affectionate because you love your children? Indeed, nothing more harsh, nothing more inhuman, nothing more savage, nothing more unholy, can be said of you, since you cannot really be made to love yourselves. The devil said in Holy Scripture:[11] 'skin for skin and all that a

---
10 Text is corrupt and I have given the more probable translation in accordance with the context.
11 Job. 2.4.

man has he will give for his soul.' Even the devil did not deny that a man's own soul was most dear to man. The devil, who tries to turn aside completely all men from the love of their own souls, confesses, however, that their souls should be most cherished by all men. What madness is it that your souls are considered worthless by you, the souls which even the devil thinks are most valued? What madness is it that your souls are considered valueless by you, the souls which he, who tries to make them valueless, says should be dear to you? Therefore, they who neglect their souls love themselves even below the evaluation put on them by the devil. Since this is the case, look at yourselves, you who pretend that persons in religion do not have those to whom they bequeath their own wealth. See, according to the opinion of the devil, see if they who have themselves have not got something.

(10) I think that these statements which I have already made suffice for that portion of the matter about which I am now treating. But perhaps you desire that I demonstrate my statements, not only by the force of facts, but also by the authority of examples. Let me say that the greater commandments of God exist in all examples. Whether men fulfill them or not is of no consequence for increasing the authority of the divine words, because it is certain that their force is derived from the person of the Lord and not from the obedience of His servants. We cannot add or take away from things whose honor is always constant because God is their author.

If human weakness wishes to rely on human examples to accomplish more easily what it knows others did formerly, I have pointed out in the preceding book[12] that the things

---

12 297.

which not a few imitators of Christ practice today were practiced, not in part but in full, not by a very few but by the people at large. They were practiced not by persons of a past age but by men of most recent times. What is that new thing which is portrayed before our very eyes in the Acts of the Apostles? 'All those who believed had all things in common together.'[13] And again:[14] 'Great grace was also in them all, for neither was there anyone needy among them. For whoever were owners of lands or houses, selling them, they brought the prices of the things sold and placed them before the feet of the Apostles.' Elsewhere, also:[15] 'and nobody among them said that what he possessed was his own.'

And it is not of a small number of believers of which Scripture speaks, lest the authority of the holy words lose some of their force if some were to think that only a few gave such laudable examples. It can be known what was then the numerical strength of the first Church from this fact alone, that in these first foundations, at least in the period of two days, 8,000 men [16] are reported to have come into the Church. It is clear to him who thinks how the multitude of every kind of members increased in the other days, when only two days begot such a great abundance of men, without taking the women and children into account.

Since the crowd was then so innumerable and so perfect, I ask all of you parents to whom I am speaking, in these so many and so great thousands of believers living then in such a great perfection of faith, did all have children or did all not have children? Neither, I think. There is no church congregation which is not a mixture of both. Therefore, those

---

13 Acts 2.44.
14 Acts 4.33-35.
15 Acts 4.32.
16 Acts 2.41; 4.4.

Christians who do not have children can understand to whom they should leave their wealth, when they see to whom they who did not have children at the time of the Apostles left their property. If they have children, let them learn what they also must do, when they see that the parents at that time preferred the love of God over their own children.

Every age, every station in life, has here a model to follow. Whosoever is a partner of the faith, let him make himself a partner of a holy example. If the faithful then gave their goods for God and disinherited themselves, learn, I beg you, to make yourselves heirs to your own wealth at the hour of death. Believe me, you must not forget your salvation and your souls in the midst of care for children. Your children are related and very close to you, but, believe me, nobody is more related than you, nobody more close to you, than you yourselves. Thus, love your children. I do not object. Love your children, but in a degree second to yourselves. Love them in such a way that you do not seem to have hated yourself. A love mindful of another and unmindful of itself is ill-advised and foolish. Holy Scripture says:[17] 'The son shall not bear the iniquity of the father and the father shall not bear the iniquity of the son.' And the Apostle says:[18] 'Each and everyone shall carry his own burden.'

(11) Thus, riches left to children do not free parents from poverty. Indeed, the wealth of parents left, with too great abundance, to their children is eternal poverty. Therefore, there are none more injurious to parents than children who are loved to excess. While the children abound in the riches of their parents, the parents are tormented for eternity. Even if there is a son so affectionate that he wishes later

---
17 Ezech. 18.20.
18 Gal. 6.5.

on to share the wealth he has inherited with his father, in the hope of mitigating his father's punishments, his efforts will be of no avail. Indeed, the love of a son will be unable to give after death to a father what the father's want of religion and lack of faith have denied to himself.

Therefore, according to the Apostle, let each and everyone think of his own load, because each and every man will bear his own burdens. The flames of the unhappy dead are not cooled by the riches of heirs. That rich man in the Gospel[19] who was clothed in purple and soft silk, who doubtlessly was rich in this world, also enriched his heirs by his death. It was of no profit to him that his rich brothers got their hands on his wealth and gold, while he could not obtain a drop of cold water. They lived in plenty, he in want; they lived in joy, he in sorrow; they lived in riches, he in torments; they lived, perhaps, constantly in luxury, he always in flames.

O unhappy and miserable way of life! He by his wealth made preparations for the happiness of others and prepared torments for himself. He who prepared joys for others prepared tears for himself. He who prepared a short-lived pleasure for others prepared perpetual fire for himself. Where, then, were relatives by marriage and other relatives? Where were his children if he had any? Where were the brothers of whom he was mindful and whom he certainly loved with such a great love that not even in punishment does he forget them? What did they profit him; what help did they bring him?

The unhappy man was being tortured, and, from those who devoured his wealth, he who was on fire sought and could not obtain a drop of cold water. Thus, if anything more could be added to the punishment, he demanded that it be given by him whom, at one time, he had held in contempt;

---

[19] Luke 16.19.

by him who had rotted in pus and disease; by him from whose stench and filth he had long since fled; by him who had terrified the dogs by the ulcers of his limbs; by him on whom swarming throngs of worms crawled even within the hidden parts of his wasted body.

O how exceedingly serious and doleful was his lot! The poor man bought happiness by his poverty; the rich man bought punishment by his wealth. The poor man, when he had absolutely nothing, purchased eternal wealth by his neediness. O how much more easily could the rich man, with so much possessions, have obtained these riches. He burned in the midst of torments and in the midst of sufferings he cried out:[20] 'Father Abraham, have mercy on me and send Lazarus that he may dip the tip of his finger in the water to cool my tongue, because I am tormented in this fire.' The rich man did not then shudder at the hand of the formerly poor Lazarus, nor did he disdain his aid. He asked that Lazarus' fingers be inserted in his mouth, and that the insupportable fire in his throat be lessened by the service of his hand which in former times was stinking and dirty. O what a great change there has been! He desired then to be touched by him whom he previously disdained to look upon.

(12) Let the rich who are unwilling to make amends with their wealth think of these punishments, lest they suffer them. He was the rich man about whom I now speak, and they the rich men to whom I am now speaking. Their designation is the same. Let them beware, lest their destination also be the same. For, rich children will not liberate guilty parents, nor will the heir, rich in abundant pleasures, quench the fires of the wretched testator.

It is hard when anybody bequeaths little to his children

---
20 Luke 16.24.

and relatives. It is much harder to be tormented for eternity. I think the rich man, in the midst of his tortures, was less pleased by the wealth of his heir than he was pained by the sufferings of his body. I think he was less pleased at seeing his heir feasting well than he was pained by seeing himself in terrible torments. I think he was less pleased at seeing his heir rich in the choice of delicacies than he was pained by himself sunken into unbearable fires. I think he was less pleased at seeing his heir feasting hangers-on and gluttons with the riches he bequeathed to him than he was pained because he was feasting on flames, even to the marrow of his bones.

I think that if anybody had then given him the choice, whether he would prefer his heirs to be rich or himself not to be in wretchedness and suffering, he would certainly have wished that they be disinherited of all wealth, provided he could be free from all his torments. He would have wished to offer all he possessed, provided he could escape from his sufferings. He would have wished to give, on his own behalf, all the wealth which he possessed and also his transitory treasures of silver and gold, in order that the perpetual cross of everlasting torments and everlasting fire be cast aside. If at all possible, he would quench with the mass of his wealth, stop the overflowing balls of fire with the opposed immensity of his huge wealth.

Why do I say he would wish to stop this unending torment at the price of his wealth? I will say more. He would have wished to give all his substance, so that, having been placed in the fire, he could procure for himself at least one hour's respite. If he desires, for alleviating the flames in his throat, the finger of a poor man dipped in water, in what way and at how great a price does he who demanded a small drop of cold water with so great an effort not desire to purchase a respite?

What did it profit or in what did it help the wretched one who was most unwilling to do so before, that he wished to offer everything on his own behalf? What then did it profit him who gave nothing for himself at the time when he had everything, that he wished to give everything which he had already lost? As the Holy Spirit says in Scripture, late indeed is the penance of the dead. How? The Divine Word says to God the Father:[21] 'for there is no one in death who is mindful of you. And who shall confess to you in hell?'

The prophet declares publicly that the dead sinner is completely excluded from the confession of his sin. Nor can anyone who was forgetful of himself in this life be mindful of God in the next. All hope is completely taken away and all access to eternal life is closed, so that, since the only way of salvation for the guilty one is to pour out his prayers to God and to beseech the heavenly mercy unceasingly, by such punishment of deadly oblivion is the sinner punished that there is not even left to him a remembrance of God by whom he should hope.

Therefore, let them who, while they desire to have rich children after their death and are not mindful of future punishment at the moment of death, think of these things. And let them think who, in order that in this short and passing life they may have rich heirs, condemn themselves with eternal death. Indeed, they do not so much love their children as they hate themselves, because that love is not as benefical which consults its interest in short-lived things, as that hate is harmful which will punish in eternity. Therefore our God, as I said a short while ago in the first book,[22] orders

---
21 Ps. 6.6.
22 274-277.

parents to lay up treasures of good training and not of money for their children. He orders them to bestow everlasting gifts, not gifts that will perish. Property and holy work of this nature profit children and parents alike; to the children through teaching of discipline, to the parents through bountiful alms. Thus, discipline is excellent for the children, that they may gain eternal salvation. Alms are good for the parents, that they may escape from eternal death.

(13) To whom am I saying these things, and why am I saying them? Where can I find ears that are open and eyes that see? We read about the ungodly:[23] 'Almost all have turned aside, they have become unprofitable together; there is none who does good, there is hardly even one.' A new madness has befallen men who live in the world, as well as on some who profess religion. Indeed, as I began to say a little while back, they bequeath their own wealth and goods, that is, the price of their own redemption, not only to their children and grandchildren who are born in the course of nature, but even to kinsmen and blood-relatives, both those who come in a direct line and those in collateral and distantly removed lines, even preferring distant and false genealogy.

It hardly matters whose interests they consult among men, provided they do not fully consult their own. If any of those about whom I am speaking do not have children when death is near, they seek out, most unbelievingly, those whom they call relatives or blood-relatives. If, perchance, they do not do that, they seek some fictitious pretext of new relationship. As I have said, it does not matter to them whom they remember, provided they forget themselves. It does not matter whom they say they love, provided they hate their own

---

23 Ps. 13.3.

souls. It does not matter whom they make rich, provided they destroy themselves with everlasting poverty.

(14) O unhappiness. O madness! I only ask why the most wretched of all deserve so badly of themselves. While they cater to the pleasures of others, they unceasingly take revenge on themselves. See how new and noble relatives are searched out by some with most unbecoming vanity. See the scandalous claims of unknown relatives and the laughable fabrications of new and powerful marriage relatives, when someone speaks about some adopted and sudden relative. They say: 'I appoint such a one my heir because he or she is my relative.' Some widow or girl professed in holy religion will say: 'I constitute such and such my heir because he or she is my neighbor.' Thus, suddenly at the moment of death, some consider as relatives those whom they regarded all their life as strangers[24] and foreigners, and those who were always outsiders begin to be the close relatives of the dead.

They hastily bring into their will those whom they never brought into their affection, and, as I have said, these are especially either the rich, or the noble, or the honored, who, were they not powerful, would perhaps never have been relatives. The intentions of the wretched will-maker are laughable. He gives the wealth of his own resources to buy a false relationship. He purchases the name of an heir with the price of his heritage, and he is lavish of the resources of his patrimony, lest he who is appointed heir disavow the fictitious relationship. The result is that the most unhappy testator—when the heir has been ennobled by a vanity that is most foolish and pitiable—who seemed lowly during his lifetime takes on a certain distinction at the moment of his death.

---

24 This is the *heres extraneus* of Roman law, according to which one 'may become heir by a mere intention or by doing an act as heir' (*Institutes* 2.19.7).

O blindness. O madness! With what great zeal, O most unhappy human beings, do you act to make yourselves wretched in eternity. With how much less care, with how much less ambition could you do good to yourselves, so that you could be happy forever! I cannot find another reason for this attitude except unbelief or the lack of faith, that is, that either men do not think that they are ·to be judged by God or that they do not believe they will arise from the dead. There is no one who is certain that he will arise from the dead and be judged by God for his good and evil works who does not strive to fulfill his hope and happiness by meriting eternal wealth by his good works, or who is not in fear and uncertainty of suffering eternal evil for his bad works.

(15) They who bear the Christian name seem to shudder that anyone would say they do not believe in the future. What kind of a reason is there when one believes what God said, but does not fear what God threatens? If a Christian does not believe in the words which God said, does he believe in the rewards which God promised? He who does not act in such a way that he can attain the rewards promised by God does not prove his belief in God's promises.

Indeed, in man's everyday life, if anybody knew that he was to be judged by human authority and that he was to be dragged before an earthly tribunal, he would seek out lawyers, procure patrons, and purchase the good will and favor of officials. He does all these things in the fear of a judgment he is about to undergo when he cannot buy the outcome of the judgment. Thus, although he cannot buy a favorable verdict itself, he buys the hope of a favorable verdict at a great price.

Tell me, whoever you are, you who say that you believe in the judgment of God, if you believe that you are to be judged by God according to the example of the men named above, whether you will buy your hope and salvation at any price? Indeed, you do not so believe, you do not believe and, although you wish to prove your belief by words, you do not believe. For, says the Apostle, you confess with words, but deny with deeds.[25]

Finally, that from your very self I may prove to you your lack of faith, tell me, I beg, whoever you are—you who leave your substance to any relative whatsoever, or to a rich man or to a relative by marriage, or, if perchance they are lacking, even to a stranger—why did you not give away your substance when you were in good health? Why, when you were happy and sprightly, did you not give it outright to your heirs? You are most prudently cautious in your will and you write carefully and attentively. 'When I shall have departed from human affairs, then you, my most dear one, are to be my heir.'

Tell me, I ask, why do you contribute nothing that is yours, why do you give nothing that is yours to the one you call your most dear and devoted heir as long as you think you will live, but only at the moment when you see you are going to die? Why do I say: 'When you see you are going to die?' You provide most cautiously that your heir will have nothing of yours either while you are breathing or while you are dying, but only when life is utterly finished and you are dead. It is a wonder that you permit even this that he will possess your goods when you are in your grave and not merely when you are being carried out and entombed. You even say: 'when I shall have departed from human affairs.' You seem to have provided for that. To depart completely from human affairs means that the whole and complete man with his body has ceased to have an existence in the midst of human affairs.

---

25 Titus 1.16.

Tell me why you provided so carefully for this in your will, why you put in this clause with such care and prudence? Without doubt it is that, while you are alive you judge a thing your own because it is necessary for you. You do not wish to alienate yourself from your resources. You think that it is most wicked that, while you are alive and well, another should become rich from your property and you should be reduced to poverty. You are right. I do not deny that it is an irrational precaution, and I approve of what you say on this question. But on one point, however, I desire that you do me satisfaction.

Why is it that you, who think the use of your wealth so necessary to you, do not think that the enjoyment and returns from your wealth are necessary to you after your death? You doubtless, say: 'A dead man requires nothing, nor must anything be reserved for me against that time, because, since I am dead and have no feelings, neither can I be delighted with the possession of my wealth, nor can I be tormented by its loss.'

The reasoning is clear. Therefore, on that account you allot your substance to another, because you yourself cannot reap the fruit of it after death. But the Apostle Paul, the most select vessel of God, testifies and cries out and gives a reason, because[26] 'Whatsoever a man sows in this life, he reaps after death and he who sows sparingly, reaps sparingly and he who sows in blessing, reaps from the blessing.' From this he clearly wished it understood that they who sow benediction parsimoniously cannot reap in abundance. For when he says, 'he who sows sparingly, reaps sparingly and he who sows in blessing reaps from the blessing,' he clearly makes 'benediction' depend on generosity. He showed that

---

26 Gal. 6.8.

the stingy would reap poverty and generous sowers would reap benediction.

(16) Perhaps, to any of you who lack faith, these statements seems to be either without validity or clarity. The Lord Himself most clearly teaches in the Gospel that a Christian loses nothing from his good works, when He said:[27] 'Whosoever shall give to drink to one of these least ones a cup of cold water only, in the name of a disciple, Amen I say to you, he shall not lose his reward.' What could be said more clearly? He said that one would receive a reward in the next world for a thing that was valueless in the present world. He attached so much honor to worshipping God that faith will give merit in heaven to that which is worthless in this life.

Lest anyone delude himself by the false hope that those who have much can buy much for little, He implied that the reward for even a cup of cold water would not be lost. He showed clearly thereby not that much will be received for having given little, but only that any work done with faith would not go unrecompensed.

You have the undoubted surety of future recompense. You have a most suitable guarantee that good works are acceptable to Him. You have Him whose assurance, mercy, and goodness are so great that He not only pays what He promised as a debt, but even points out something by which He makes Himself indebted to you. He who said that He would give Himself as a reward for a cup of cold water not only wishes to pay for what He had received, but also points out the reward which He is paying. Tender and full of mercy and desirous of rewarding not only the liberality of the rich, but even the tiny kindnesses of the poor, He points out also how we can

---

27 Matt. 10.42.

lend at interest and make God indebted to us, even though we have nothing whatsoever.

(17) To any of you who are rich, perhaps this charity seems unworthy of your wealth, and you wish to hear some pledge of the Holy Promise particularly pertinent to you. In the first place, you have that saying which God spoke to that rich man in the Gospel: [28] 'Go, sell all your goods, and you will have treasure in Heaven.' Next, that saying wherein He orders with a general prohibitory command: [29] 'Do not lay up for yourselves treasures on earth, but lay up for yourselves treasures in Heaven.'

Lastly, He spoke these words with which He invited all possessors of wordly goods to the duty of abundant alms with the hope of eternal reward, because every man who for the honor and love of God put aside either his house, or field, or any other wealth whatsoever as alms would receive a hundredfold in the next world: 'But moreover,' He says, 'he will possess eternal life.'[30] What better answer could He, who promised that He would pay back a hundredfold interest to those who loaned Him wealth, give to them who believe in Him?

Not only this, but He said: 'he will possess life eternal.' This is much more than the actual hundredfold return, because what anybody receives a hundredfold he will possess forever. Eternal life will not be a perishable and transitory possession, nor will it be like earthly riches of passing semblance, or perishable in the manner of vanishing dreams. Whatsoever will be given by God will be immortal and whatever has been received will remain without end. And therefore, as I said, he who so receives, receives more than a hundredfold,

---
28 Matt. 19.21.
29 Matt. 6.19.
30 Matt. 19.29.

because he wins the prize of the hundredfold and that is an everlasting hundredfold.

(18) Since this is the case, and since he who believes in God will doubtless receive great rewards in return, how can you think that riches given by you to God will not profit you after death? God has promised you these riches—not only their use, but also the fullest measure of return from them. Or, perhaps you do not wish to receive these great returns? But it does not stand to reason that you do not wish to receive them.

There is no one among men who chooses to be sad when he can be happy; there is nobody alive who, when he can have the delights of the greatest good, wishes to suffer the punishment of the greatest evil. There is no one at all—not even you. Unless, perhaps, your nature is abnormal and you differ from the human race in that you alone do not wish yourself well, you alone flee from happiness, you alone delight in punishment.

If this is not your nature, when you are dying and have arrived at the last moments of life, why do you not render the obligation of the highest sacrifice with the whole of your wealth, so that, if you can deserve it from God, you may be eternally rich and happy? If, on the contrary, you cannot do this, act so that you may merit not to be truly wretched, that you may not burn, that you may not suffer, that you may not be destroyed in the exterior darkness, and that you may not burn in everlasting flames.

As I have said, what reason is there that you do not do these things? What reason is there that you do not purchase eternal goods? What reason is there that you do not fear do not think you are to be judged by God or you do not fully eternal evils? What indeed, except, as I have said before, you believe that you will arise from the dead? If you did believe, would you not flee from that immeasurable evil of the future judgment and avoid the torments of eternal punishments?

You do not believe; you do not believe; though you assert otherwise by word and profession, still you do not believe. Your speech and profession make a display of your faith, but your life and death make public your lack of faith. Convince me otherwise. I want to be convinced. I do not ask that you prove to me your belief by acts of your past life. I am content with the one proof furnished by your last moments.

Behold, behold, you are on the point of death. You are about to depart from the home of your body, not knowing where you will go, where you are to be taken. You do not know to what punishment, to what foulness, you are being dragged. You, to whom only one thing remains in the midst of your last moments, to you there is given one slight hope as an asylum for fleeing eternal fire. Offer at least on your own behalf what you have of your substance, because you do not have anything else you can offer to God. You are unmindful of yourself, forgetful of your own salvation. You are thinking about new legatees, you are longing to enrich your heir.

When you act as you do, do you say that you believe in the judgment of God? You who are being judged, do you consult your own little interests in the midst of your last moments? Do you say that you believe that you are occupied with the salvation of your soul, you to whom nothing is more base than your own soul, you, to whom it almost does not matter whom you favor provided you injure yourself? Do you say that you believe in the future judgment, you with whom there is nobody less and more despised than the Judge Himself? You scorn Him so much, you despise Him so much, that you do not consult your own interest with Him as long as you regard His commands with contempt.

If I am lying, refute or convince me. Behold, your Judge, who is about to judge you, cries out to you, who are dying, that you are not to love anyone more than yourself when you are handing out your property and resources; that you, when you are dying, are not to consult the interest of your substance more than of yourself; that you are not to think someone more dear and more closely related to you than your own soul. The Saviour says:[31] 'What shall it profit a man if he gain the whole world and suffer the loss of his soul? Or what will a man give in exchange for his soul?'

This means: what will it profit you, O most unhappy man, if you possess the whole world or leave it to your near relatives, if you suffer the loss of your salvation and soul? Damnation of the soul takes everything completely with it. Neither can a man possess anything whatsoever, who loses himself with the loss of his soul. The Saviour says: 'Or what shall a man give in exchange for his soul?' This means: O man, do not look to money or possessions and do not hesitate, when you are dying, to offer as much as you can of your property and wealth in exchange for your hope. Whatsoever you give on your own behalf is too little to offer. Whatsoever you offer on your own behalf is a small price, because, in comparison, your soul is more valuable than all riches. Therefore, have no hesitation in giving on your own behalf, because, if you lose yourself, you lose everything in yourself. But if you gain yourself, you shall possess all things with and in yourself.

(19) Though your Lord proclaims these facts to you who are already dying, O man, whosoever you are, you close your mind and ears and assert your faith with words alone. You think words suffice for you, instead of deeds. You think you have a sufficient strong basis in faith, if you seem to

---
[31] Matt. 16.26.

honor with lying words the God whom you despise in deeds and works. The Holy Scripture says:[32] 'My son, if you have anything, do good to yourself and offer worthy offerings to God.' And elsewhere it says:[33] 'have pity on your own soul.' See how merciful is the Lord, our God, who asks us to have mercy on ourselves. He says: 'have pity on your own soul.'

This means: have mercy also on that for whose compassion you see Me broken: have mercy on that of whom I am always compassionate; have mercy on your own soul at least when you see Me merciful to another soul. And after these facts, why do you not agree, O most wretched man, when God acts thus towards you? He asks you to have pity on yourself and do you not wish to do so? He pleads your own case before you and cannot He win the decision from you?

How, O most wretched man, whoever you are, how will He listen to you afterwards, beseeching Him before His judgment seat, when you are unwilling to listen to Him begging you on your own behalf in this world? Indeed, the reason for which you cannot listen to God is great. Your relatives and family stand around you when you are sick. The rich matrons of the family stand by. The distinguished men of the family stand close to you. A crowded multitude clothed in silken and ornamented garments lay siege to the bed of your sickness. O what great reward of eternity it is to bequeath your goods to such poor people! Indeed, there is a just and worthy reason why you should take wealth from your own soul and leave it to the needy ones, such as these!

Without doubt, you are crushed by pity and you are overcome by the tenderness of your weeping relatives. That is certainly a reason. Indeed, you see men most rich and splendidly dressed weeping for you. You see people wearing a

---
[32] Eccli. 14.11.
[33] Eccli. 30.24.

made-up sad appearance, but festive in dress, making a display of sorrow for you. They are buying your legacy with a feigned anxiety. Who is not moved by such great tenderness? Who is not moved by such great sorrow? Why, when you see all these people, should you not be forgetful of yourself? You see the tears that are rooted forth, the simulated sighs, the feigned anxiety which hopes that you will not recover and is waiting for you to die. You see the faces of all fastened on you, as if they were blaming the slowness of your death.

O you, most unhappy and most wretched man, whose last breath is longed for by such a great crowd of relatives! I know and am very certain that the prayers of such people are of no avail whatsoever with God. I may perhaps wonder that you are alive, you whom so many wish to die. On account of these, whosoever you are, on account of such as these are you forsaking your own soul and saying you believe in the judgment of God, though you scorn His commandments for the sole purpose of leaving your patrimony to people such as these?

The prophet said of him who believed in God:[34] 'He has distributed, he has given to the poor, his justice will remain forever.' But the Saviour Himself said to all rich men:[35] 'Sell what you possess and give alms.' And elsewhere:[36] 'Sell what you have and give to the poor.' Did He say: Give to your close relatives, to your relatives by marriage? No, indeed—but to the poor and needy. Did He say: to a rich relative, or to any powerful man? No indeed,—but to the indigent and poverty-stricken.

When you give your substance to your rich relatives, does your justice remain forever? When you increase their riches

---
34 Ps. 111.9.
35 Luke 12.33.
36 Matt. 19.21.

with your riches, will you have treasure in heaven? The prophet says, 'woe' to those 'who call the sweet bitter and the bitter sweet.'[37] God also forbids that you praise people like these; do you not fear to enrich them? He does not wish that laudatory words be given them; do you bestow your gold on them? He forbids that their life be honored with fictitious words; do you further add to their treasures and riches?

Perhaps you fear the looks of your relatives sitting around, and are afraid to offend them as they press and crowd around your bed. The Lord says through the prophet:[38] 'Fear not their words, nor be dismayed at their looks for they are a provoking house.' Be you also unafraid and constant, therefore; do not fear their faces, nor be broken by their display.

Scorn them who are lusting after your heritage and already dividing your substance among themselves. They love your patrimony, but not you. They curse you in greed for your possessions. While they impatiently thirst after your wealth, they hate you and regard your presence as a rival and adversary to themselves. They think the fact that you are alive is a barrier and obstacle to their greed.

Scorn people such as these and esteem them of no value. Let not their flattery move you, for their flattery is poisonous. Do not notice their fawnings. They are swords to cut your throat and are indeed more deadly than the iron swords of the enemy. All men see the latter; those lacking in caution do not see the former. The latter, which rage in the open, can be avoided. The former, which lie in ambush, kill, and are thereby more dangerous and more terrible in this new form of injury. For there is no one who really wishes to be injured by iron swords, but many are willing to be killed by the swords of flattery. This is a new and deadly allurement, incalculably

---
37 Isa. 5.20.
38 Ezech. 2.6.

evil. Whoever is struck by iron swords is tormented equally by pain and sorrow, whereas whoever is killed by flattery is full of joy.

Therefore, flee from this evil; flee from adulation waiting in ambush for you; flee from obsequiousness injurious to you; flee those who surround you and who are there to deceive you. Flatteries are services which cut your throat; they are services which drag you to death. Flee from the blandishments of people such as these! Flee from their assiduity. They are your hangmen and tormentors who truly surround you in the present life, but kill you in the next world. With joined hands and a partnership mutually sworn, as it were, they try to force and throw you into the eternal fires of Hell. Do not fear them, therefore; do not be terrified of them. Raise up your mind and take on the strength of holy power. For, if they strive so hard in order that you may perish, why do you not strive harder so that you may live? Be comforted and consult your own interests with an unchangeable mind. He is most lacking in faith and most foolish who prefers to benefit others that he may be wretched, rather than benefit himself in order to be happy himself. That he may make others affluent in transient pleasures, he hands himself over to be burned in eternal fires.

BOOK FOUR

IT DOES NOT escape my knowledge, O my mistress the Church, the nourisher of blessed hope, that those statements I have made in the preceding books are displeasing to many of your children who love Christ little. I do not put great weight on what they wish, because it is not strange that words spoken about God should not please them whom perhaps God Himself does not please. Nor must I expect they they who do not love salvation itself and their souls shoul like a discussion which treats of souls and their salvation. Just as on other topics, so also on this topic, my convictions and the judgments of the saints are sufficient for me. As regards those among us who think the same as I, we are indeed certain that God Himself also thinks as we think, because, since the spirit of God remains in His saints, God is doubtless where that portion is from which the spirit of God has not departed.

Therefore, the opinions of impious men, that is, of pagans or men devoted to the world, are either to be judged as of little or of no value at all. The Apostle says:[1] 'If I wished to please men, I would not be a servant of Christ.' It is harder to bear, I think, that some of your children, who live under the title of religion, belie the profession of religion and forsake the world in their dress rather than in their hearts. Unless I am mistaken, these people think and assert that every Christian, when dying, should take his relatives rather than Christ into consideration.

---
[1] Gal. 1.10.

Because this attitude of mind is in itself wholly profane and execrable, they strive, as I think, to cover up this most pagan assertion with a kind of veiled excuse, and say that only all those in perfect health who believe in God should be devoted to Christ. In addition, they say those who are departing from the world should remember their relatives rather than divine obligations. Just as though some Christians should be healthy and others dying, and all should present themselves to Christ—some when they are healthy, some when they are dying, some early in life, some late in life.

If this is true, each will have one Christ as a young man and another Christ as an old man; men must be changed as often in faith as they are in age. If one will be vigorous in the worship of God, the other will be weak; one healthy, the other sickly. Thus, as the condition of the human body is variable, so will God Himself be changeable to man, and, as often as there will be bad health in a man, so often will there be a difference in his religion. Just as though they who are in health should belong to Christ, those who are dying should not belong to Christ.

What about this saying:[2] 'He who shall have persevered to the end, shall be saved,' or that oracle of the Divine Word in the sacred proverbs:[3] 'Wisdom is proclaimed at the moment of departure.' These sayings show that, though wisdom is helpful in every age, all men should be particularly wise when they are leaving this world, because the wisdom of past years will not fully deserve praise if it does not terminate in a good end. Wisdom is proclaimed at the moment of departure.

Why did the Sacred Scriptures say that wisdom was pro-

---

2 Matt. 10.22.
3 Prov. 1.20. Here Salvian is playing with the words, *exitus,* a street, and *exitus,* the moment of departure from life. The Scriptural text is: 'Wisdom cries aloud in the streets.'

claimed not in boyhood, not in young manhood, not when possessions are unimpaired, not when we are prosperous in goods? Indeed, because whatever is praised in all these is transient. For, as long as one undergoes change, he cannot be praised without reservation, and therefore, as Scripture says: 'Wisdom is proclaimed at the moment of departure.' He who is departing from uncertainties and dangers will merit a sure judgment when he has escaped the changeableness of all these things, because praise is then steadfast and lasting when the merit of him who is praised cannot perish. Scripture says: 'Wisdom is proclaimed at the moment of departure.'

What is the wisdom of the Christian, I ask? What is it but fear and love of Christ? Scripture says:[4] 'The fear of the Lord is the beginning of wisdom,' and elsewhere:[5] 'Perfect love casts out fear.' Therefore, as we see, the beginning of wisdom is in the fear of Christ; perfection, in the love of Christ. Thus, if the wisdom of the Christian is in fear and love of the Lord, in this way we are at length truly wise if we love God always and above all other things, and this at all times, especially at the moment of departure from life, because wisdom is proclaimed at the moment of our departure.

(2) If wisdom is proclaimed at the moment of departure from life and if God is to be loved above all things, what madness for anyone to say that they who are in health must prefer Christ over their blood relatives, but that He must not be preferred by those who are dying? Why should they who are in health give Him preference if the dying are not obliged to? Or if anyone at the moment of death piously

---
4 Ps. 110.10.
5 1 John 4.18.

can give preference to his relatives by blood and marriage over Christ, why does he not also give Christ preference before death? Or, if there is any hour at the end of life in which one should love others more than he loves either himself or God, why does he not love them more in the course of life?

Thus it happens that all things are changed, pass away, and perish. No one considers anyone more base than himself, nor more lowly than God. If there is a time at which anyone can legally place God second to his blood and marriage relatives, there is no time in which God must lawfully be placed ahead of them. But if, because it is true, there is no time whatsoever in which He should not be given preference, there is no time when He can lawfully be placed second to them. Indeed, there is no time, not even at the point of death, because the prophet says that even the just man will perish on the day he errs.[6]

If every transgression is punished with the destruction of him who has erred and the life of men is endangered by these errors by which usually and commonly human innocence is defiled, what do we think will happen when we sin against God Himself with a hateful lack of faith? The Apostle says:[7] 'For if every disobedience receive a just recompense of reward, how shall we escape if we neglect so great a salvation?' There is no one who neglects true salvation more than he who puts something ahead of God. Since our salvation is the gift and alms of God, what chance has he for securing salvation who scorns the very God in whose mercy our salvation consists?

Since God is the judge of all the living and the dead, what hope can there be for him in the judgment of God, who, even while he is dying, despises God by his own judgment, and

---
6 Ezech. 3.20.
7 Heb. 2.2-3.

yet, the moment he is dead, is to be judged by God? Therefore, as Divine Scripture says:[8] 'for with what judgment he judges, in that will he be judged by God.' This means: according to the judgment he judges about God, in that will he himself be judged by God. Nor can he who placed God after all others in this world think it wrong if the Lord places him after all others in the next world. Nor can he complain if God judges him more worthy of condemnation than all others, since he himself considered God of less worth than all others.

(3) Someone will say that he does not do these things with the intention of having contempt for God or thinking Him worthless, but one with which he loves or honors those whom he constitutes his heirs. Let us grant that this is so. This kind of excuse stands well for all, for almost all others are guilty of the most infamous and reproachful crimes. Because they are overcome with the heat and weakness of their bodies, it would thus be lawful for fornicators to say that they do not commit fornication with the intention of spurning God. Murderers can say they are not acting in contempt of God when they shed human blood. They can say they excel in crime only because of hate or greed. What profit is this excuse to the wicked, since it does not at all matter for what reason anyone says he sins, because every sin is an injury to God? I grant, as I have said above, that some give wealth to another rather than to God, without the intention of contempt for God. They are constrained to do this for the honor of their heirs, or are compelled by love for them. What can we do, since this very act proves a greater neglect and contempt of God? Whoever you are, by the fact that you leave your property to your heirs or to anyone whatsoever, you show that you

---
8 Matt. 7.2.

honor and love them, and when you do not leave things to God, you show that you neither honor nor love Him. Therefore, whatever you say on your own behalf is against yourself and the love and honoring of others amounts to contempt and insult of God.

For, if the reason why you leave your goods to others is to honor them, then, when you do not leave something to God, it is because you do not honor Him. Therefore, when you leave much to others because you love them, when you leave nothing to God it is because you do not love Him. Man and God stand alike to you when you are dying and making your will. The act is clear and unobscured; you give preference to him whom you choose. If honor is given to one alone, you must have contempt for the other. If a man who is given preference rejoices because he is loved by you, God must necessarily sorrow because He is not loved. He is passed over.

You think that God does not need the generosity of man. Therefore, what is the necessity, you say, for man to give something to God, when God Himself gave to all all they have? We shall see whether the Lord needs or does not need our generosity, or how He needs or does not need it. Meanwhile, for you have not dared to deny that all that men have has been given to them by Him, He is more worthy, without doubt, of our generosity because He is generous to us. We should try to be that much more justly responsive in our duties to Him, as we become unequal to Him because of His favors.

Both nature and the common custom of men bind all by this general law that, when we accept a gift from someone, we owe thanks to them for it. Generosity received compels us to make an acknowledgment for the thing given. All are free before the use and generosity of another's bounty; one is not weighed down with the interest on the capital of favors. All are forced by their conscience to make reciprocal recompense after they have begun to be debtors.

In this way, therefore, we owe more to God by the fact that we received all things from Him. We are that much less capable of matching His favors that, even if we desire to pay back what we owe Him, we are, however, paying Him back from out of His own goods. For this reason, we should not be complacent about our generosity. Just as nothing that a man receives from our Lord is his own, in the same way, nothing that he pays back is his own. Therefore, he who denies to God the things given by God should be punished for dishonesty. He who returns what he has received cannot impute this to his own generosity.

(4) But, you say, God is not in need of being paid back. There is nothing less true than that He does not need it. He does not need it if we consider His power, but He does need it for the fulfilling of His precept! He does not need it if we consider His majesty, but He does need it according to His law. Indeed, He does not need it for Himself, but He does need it for the many. He does not seek liberality for Himself, but He seeks it for His people; therefore, He does not need it if we consider His omnipotence, but He does need it by reason of His mercy. He does not need Godhead on account of Himself, but He needs our devotion on account of us.

What does God say to the holy and generous givers? 'Come, you blessed, possess the kingdom of My Father, which was prepared for you from the beginning of the world; for I was hungry and you gave Me to eat, I was thirsty and you gave Me to drink.'[9] and other words in this fashion. And, lest this perhaps seem little for the subject about which I am speaking,

---

9 Matt. 25.34-35.

He added the contrary. He said to the covetous and those lacking in faith:[10] 'Depart, you cursed, into everlasting fire, which My Father prepared for the Devil and his angels: for I was hungry and you did not give Me to eat; I was thirsty and you did not give me to drink.'

Who are they who say that the Lord Jesus Christ does not need the service of our gifts? Behold, He declares that He is hungry, thirsty, and cold. Let anyone of them answer, does He not need, He who complains that He is hungry? Does He not need, He who says that He thirsts? I add something further. Christ not only needs in company with others, but He needs much more than others need. In every group of poor men the poverty of all is not alike.

There are some who, though they need clothing, do not need food. There are many who are wanting in lodging, but are not wanting in clothes. There are many lacking in homes, but not in wealth. Finally, there are many who are lacking in many things, but not in all things. Christ is the only one to whom, on the human level, there is nothing that is not lacking. None of His servants is exiled, none is tormented by cold and want of clothing, with whom He is not suffering. Christ alone feels hunger with the hungry, and He alone feels thirst with the thirsty. And therefore, insofar as it pertains to His compassion, He is in need more than others. For every needy person is in need only for himself and in himself, but Christ alone begs in the universality of all poor men.

Since these things are so, what do you say, O man? You who say you are a Christian, when you see that Christ is in need, do you leave your wealth to those who are not in need? Christ is poor, and do you further increase the wealth of the rich? Christ is hungry, and do you prepare delicacies for those

---
10 Matt. 25.41-42.

who are surfeited? Christ complains that He even lacks water, and do you fill the storehouses of the drunken with wine? Christ is weakened by the want of everything, and do you gather an abundance for those who are in luxury? Christ promised you eternal rewards for the gifts given by you, and do you bestow everything on those who will give nothing? Christ declared everlasting goods for you and for the good, and eternal evils for the evil. Are not you persuaded by heavenly goods nor moved by eternal evils? And you say you believe in your Lord, whose recompense you do not desire and of whose anger you are not afraid?

(5) As I have said in the preceding book, you do not believe and, although you pretend religion by your clothes, although you proclaim faith by your cincture, although you feign holiness by your cloak, you do not fully believe; you do not believe. I say this not only to men in religion but to women. They do not believe. Let any woman at all clothe herself with dress of the holy name and proclaim for herself the title of holy religion, if out of her wealth she consults the interest of others more than her own, she most certainly does not believe.

Nobody is a believer who prefers his wealth to be more profitable to others than to himself. Nobody is a believer who is happy to buy happiness for others at the cost of misery to himself. Nobody is a believer who, in order that he may procure transitory pleasures for others, desires to undergo eternal poverty. Therefore, he who consults by his patrimony the interests of others more than his own interests does not believe that the things he gave to God will be of any profit to himself. Let some of these people tell me why they leave their wealth to others? Is it not because they do not doubt this wealth will profit him to whom they left them? This is doubtless so.

Therefore, whoever you are, you leave your riches to others because you are certain they will profit him to whom you left them. Indeed, if you believed that those goods which you put aside for religious purposes would be profitable to you, you would put them aside, especially for yourself, because, as you love yourself more than you love them to whom you leave your wealth, so would you leave them to yourself if you judged by a slight margin of opinion that they would be profitable to yourself.

You do not hate yourself so that you do not want to consult your own good, but you do not think that the wealth you would leave to the poor would be of advantage to yourself. Hence, you consult the good of others rather than your own good, because you do not believe that a godly work will be profitable to you. Therefore, as you believe, so do you receive. You consider the Savior as of little value, and the Savior considers you as nothing. You place Christ after others and Christ places you after all others. To you, the Lord is unworthy in comparison even with all other men who are past recovery, and you will be placed in the midst of the very last of the damned.

(6) As I have already said, perhaps you are flattered by your view of the religious calling. You are a greater debtor, because by your declaration you promised greater holiness, and you will suffer more punishment because you will have paid back less for your pledge. Outwardly, you promised great things; actually, you have given back nothing. You are guilty of the crime of forgery; you are lying to God in all things. Not unrightly does the Sacred Word testify that judg-

ment must be begun from the temple of God, when it says:[11] 'judgment should begin at the house of God.' And elsewhere it says:[12] 'and begin at the sanctuary.' But let us return to our preceding topic.

God said to the covetous and to those lacking in faith:[13] 'Depart into eternal fire which My Father prepared for the Devil and his angels.' Perhaps you think you are to be freed from this evil by certain corporal works. Indeed, you boast that you have loved chastity. But take note that the Saviour did not mention unchastity in those whom, in the Gospel, He handed over to eternal punishment. Are you mindful that your sobriety pleased you? Nor are they, about whom the Scriptures speak, punished for the crime of drunkenness. Do you say you have fasted? Neither did eating make them guilty.

Surely, the reason by which you please yourself with fasting and abstinence is great. You have fasted for this end, you have lived frugally and meagerly, not to feed the poor with your wealth after your death, but, perhaps, to increase the money to each of your heirs. Surely, you wish for great rewards for your abstinence, for you have eaten less bread in order that another would have more gold. Your stomach grew less through frugality, in order that, perhaps, the treasure of some wicked man would increase.

Therefore, when you shall come to the tribunal of God, you can lawfully count on your fasting when you say: 'O Lord, I have fasted and I have abstained, and that for a long time. I have restrained myself from partaking of delicacies. And the actuality proves this. For behold, my heirs now abound because of my wealth; they are overflowing in the abundance of immense riches.'

---

11 1 Peter 4.17.
12 Ezech. 9.6.
13 Matt. 25.41.

And in order that you may take to yourself something from the reading of the Gospel, what the Saviour said about the rich man you also can say about your heirs. They are dressed in purple and silk and they feast richly. They get their hands on gold hidden in the earth by me. They chew on pressed cakes of gold and silver. For them I have also procured the wherewithal for all pleasures. They are distended by delicacies left by me. Therefore, I have long abstained in order that they may now become drunk.

Their excessive drinking is due to my frugality. The floors where they recline at table are swimming in wine. They make mud of the noble wine of Falernus.[14] Their tables and embossed furniture are constantly wet with unmixed wine. They themselves are always soaked in wine. They satisfy their lust behind the curtains which I made. They commit fornication in the silks which I left them. And when you have said all these things on your own behalf, how can you not merit the remuneration made by Christ, for whom you have prepared an abundance of so many delicacies in such holy people?

(7) O how much better, whosoever you are, how much better and salutary that you were poor and needy rather than rich. Poverty could recommend you favorably to God; riches have made you guilty. It were more fitting that you should be saved through want than to have weighed down yourself and others with your riches: yourself, by ill-advisedly putting the possessions you left to a most inhuman use, and, on their demise, ill-advisedly passing them on to others.

If you wish, whoever you are, if you wish to consult your own interests, if you wish to possess eternal life and desire to see happy days, leave your wealth to the saints who are

---

14 In Campania at the foot of Mount Massicus; famed for its wines.

in want; leave it to the maimed; leave it to the blind; leave it to the weak. Let your wealth be the nourishment of the wretched. Let your abundance be the life of the poor, in order that their comfort may be your reward and their nourishment be your heavenly food. If they eat of your goods, you will have your fill. If they drink of what is yours, you will quench the heat and burning of your thirst. Their clothing will clothe you; their sunshine will delight you.

Do not think it is worthless and worthy of contempt to leave your substance to the wretched and needy. You will make Christ your heir in them. And what shall I say about the name of Christ? Indeed, if you may make Christ your heir, you will receive the full returns of the heritage. Whatsoever you leave to Christ you will possess through Christ.

I suppose you adjudge all I have said as foolish and despise it as dreams and ravings, for you do not believe that Christ spoke truly. Your actions prove that you never believed in Him. You, who do not follow His commands at the last moment of life, either think that they are as nothing or condemn them as false. In this respect it is good for all holy men to weep and cry, because you and others like you believe in any one rather than in Christ.

If somebody promised you something from the shops, you would not refuse trust to him who make the promise. If a huckster or a dealer in pickles asked for a loan from you, you would not fear that he would not give back what you gave. Finally, belief is even placed in liars and sometimes in perjurers when their bond is taken and security given.

Christ gave you the most trustworthy bond and the best security. His bond is the Gospel. His security is the Apostles. If that is not enough, the patriarchs, prophets, martyrs, and finally the whole series of divine letters. And do you not believe in Him and accord Him trust? I ask: Whom can you find so base and so wretched among men to whom you would deny your confidence with so much security? Therefore, give your possessions to the rich, and deny them to the poor. Give them to the wanton, and deny them to the holy. Give them to anybody who is, perhaps, beyond being saved, and deny them to Christ. According as you have judged, so will you be judged. As you have chosen, so will you receive. You will not have a portion with Christ whom you have despised. You will have a portion with them to whom you have given preference.

(8) Perhaps someone from the number of those lacking in faith says that this is not a reason worthy of moving God or of dragging human beings into eternal danger. I know, indeed, that all guilty men always think their crimes are pardonable. Thefts are light faults to thieves and drunkenness seems harmless to drunkards. With the unchaste, fornication is not a sin, because no crime committed is so great that it is not excused by its performer.

If he who wishes to know from sinners how gravely great sins are to be estimated by God, let him learn how the saints punish even light sins in themselves. They are conscious of the future judgment from the words of God Himself, and through the words of the Lord Himself they search out judgments, and are, therefore, always engaged in the work of God, always in repentance, always in mortification. Blessed are they who, although they have mercy on all, never fully pardon themselves. They spare themselves in nothing, but expend themselves fully to the limit with God. Therefore, they are worthy of reward in the future judgment, because in this world, in their own eyes, they are constantly blameworthy.

What shall I say about their alms and generosity? This virtue is, in their eyes as it were, the beginning of all virtues. Very many of them regard their wealth as the birth and cradle of their way of life, so that before crossing the threshold of the holy profession they leave nothing to themselves of their wealth, according to that saying of our Lord in which He says:[15] 'Sell all your goods and give them to the poor, and come, follow Me.'

They who are about to follow God who calls them sell everything before they follow. Considering riches in the category of burdens and excess baggage, they do not think they are equipped for following, unless they have first thrown away all hindrances of wordly loads. And at the same time, as is the custom of migrators, they transfer their possessions to the place of their destination before they move themselves. When they have transported everything that belongs to them, then, when their wealth and possessions have been sent on ahead, they move into the house filled and crowded with imperishable goods. They are confident, without doubt, that nothing will be lacking to them afterwards. The saints, as they are about to depart from a base, contemptible, and crumbling dwelling, leave absolutely none of their perishable possessions in their former place of habitation.

This is their hope, this is their confidence. Thus, they exercise foresight for themselves with a splendid exchange of possessions, so that they enjoy the eternal bounty of everlasting wealth. You, whosoever man or woman you are, who, forgetful of your soul and salvation, despoil yourself of your trifling possessions, how in the next world will you find, as if stored up and prepared, those things which you left either to the wealthy or, at any rate, to those who were not poor? Why do you believe that God will give back to you the things you did not give Him? In short, how do you expect to have returned what you do not want to commit to others? No-

---

15 Matt. 19.21.

body ever asks that someone pay him for what he has never loaned him. No one is so unreasonable as to hope that that which he never put out to interest be given back to him.

Therefore, you can never hope that anything must, so to say, be returned by God, which you yourself, not entrusting to God, did not want God to return to you. Hence that Divine Word is fulfilled in you: because you have left your wealth to others or to strangers, your sepulcher will be your home forever.[16] And that word which the Savior spoke was spoken to one like you:[17] 'because you are lukewarm, and neither hot nor cold, I will begin to vomit you out of my mouth.' Do you say: 'I am rich and I have my riches and I do not need anybody.' and do you not know that you are wretched and poor and blind and naked?

Let nobody who prefers man to God in his will flatter himself about the prerogative of his life and profession. A dangerous security carries penalties for man; presumptuous hopes are burdens of sin; arrogated forgiveness prepares the way for damnation. Whoever excuses himself to himself, accuses himself before God, according to that saying:[18] 'for he who thinks he is something when he is nothing, deceives himself.' Therefore, to nobody let his own case be easy; nobody escapes with more difficulty than he who presumes he will escape.

(9) Perhaps these statements seem harsh and severe. Why not? The Divine Word says:[19] 'all chastisement is not joyful but sorrowful.' These words are harsh and severe. But what are we to do? It is not possible to change the nature of things, and truth cannot be proclaimed otherwise than as the very

---
16 Ps. 48.12.
17 Apoc. 3.16.
18 Gal. 6.3.
19 Heb. 12.11.

essence of truth demands. Some think these words are harsh. I know and I agree. But what are we to do? We reach the kingdom only by hardship. The Lord says:[20] 'narrow and straight is the way which leads to life.' And the Apostle says:[21] 'I think that the sufferings of this time are not to be compared to the future glory which will be revealed in us.'

He calls every human work too small a price to pay for the gaining of future glory. And, therefore, nothing should seem harsh and austere to Christians, because, no matter how much they offer to Christ for the purchase of their future happiness, what is given is worthless where what is received is so great. Nothing great on earth is paid back to God by man, since the greatest reward is acquired in heaven. It is hard on the covetous to give away their goods. What is strange in this? Whatever the unwilling are ordered to do is difficult for them to perform.

Almost every Divine Word has its opponents. There are as many forms of opposition as there are forms of commands. If the Lord orders generosity in men, the covetous man is angry. If He demands frugality, the spendthrift curses. The evil-doer considers the Sacred Words his own particular enemies. Robbers shudder at whatever is ordained as to justice. The proud shudder at whatever is ordered as to humility. The drunken resist where sobriety is proclaimed publicly. The unchaste foully call God to witness where chastity is ordered. Either nothing must be said or whatever is said will displease someone of the above-named men. Each evil-doer prefers to curse the law rather than to correct his own opinion. He prefers to hate God's commandments rather than his own vices.

In the midst of these things what do they do, to whom the

---
20 Matt. 7.14.
21 Rom. 8.18.

duty of speaking is ordered by Christ? They displease God if they are silent; they displease men if they speak. But, as the Apostle answered the Jews, it is more expedient to obey God rather than men.[22] I offer this advice to all to whom the law of God is heavy and burdensome, when they refuse to accept what God commands—which otherwise might be pleasing to them. For, all who hate the holy commands possess within their very selves the reason for the hate. To everyone, aversion to the law is not in the precepts, but in one's morals. The law is, indeed, good, but the morals are bad. For this reason, let men change their intentions and viewpoints. If they will make their morals commendable, nothing that a good law has ordered will displease them. When anyone has begun to be good, he is unable not to love the law of God, because the holy law of God has that within itself which holy men have in their morals. May the grace of our Lord Jesus Christ be with your spirit. Amen.

---

22 Acts 5.29.

INDEX

INDEX

Aaron, and the golden calf, 49; —punished, 52

Abel's offering acceptable, 39

Abimelech, 42, 195

Abiron, 52-53

Abiu, 50

Abraham, his life a proof of God's governance, 42; tribulations of, 42; 43

Absolom, 63, 64

Achar, theft of, 151

Actions and professions, 86

Adam's transgression, 38; God's judgment on, 38

Ad Ecclesiam, mental attitude of its author, 258-259; purpose of, 259-260ff; why written anonymously and Timothy chosen as author, 260-261f; zeal of author, 261; written for honor of God, 262

Adultery, 81;—and homicide, 105

Adversity, leaves Christians uncorrected, 172

Africa, cities of, 98; material prosperity of, 205;—the distress of the human race, 206; vice and sacrileges in, 206-207;—an Aetna of unchaste flames, 207; unnatural vice in, 211-214;—suffering a just punishment, 232

Africans, enormity of sins of, 204;—compared with barbarians, 207; impurity synonymous with, 208; churchgoers in Africa generally unchaste, 211; distorted mentality of, 211;—surpass Romans in impurity, 211;—abuse the saints of God, 229-230;—ridicule the saints of God, 230; reasons why—hate saints of God, 230-231

Agrycius, bishop, 241

Alani, 115, 207

Alaric, 172 n.32

Alemanni, 115

Alms, and generosity, 272; necessary for the hour of death, 293; almsgiving most salutary, 310; almsgiving frees from death, 310; universal lack of, 312-313; impediment to, 313-314;—devoted to religious purposes, 314;—by rich at hour of death, 316-317;—the beginning of virtues, 367-368

Alpine crags, 149

Alps, 154

Ambrose, St., 13

Ammon, 63, 64

Amorreans, 103

Amphitheaters, 156

Ananias, 152

Anger, 79;—and hatred, 72

Animals cured by surgery, 185-186

Anna, prophetess, 298

Anointment of kings with oil, 70

Aper, 253

Apocalypse, 123

Apocrypha, 256

Apostles, reception of—by pagans, 231

Apostolic precepts, 73-74

Aquitaine, description of, 186; special gifts from God to, 188;—first in riches, first in vice, 188-189; position of mothers in households in, 190-191; corrupt masters in, 191f.;—cleansed by barbarians, 193

Aquitainians, 187; not repentant after punishment, 189; vices of, 189-190; female slaves of, 191;—poor but corrupt, 192; —delivered to barbarians by God, 192;—continue impurities among barbarians, 192

Arguments of the ungodly refuted, 33;—based on sacred materials, 67

Arles, transference of Roman government to, 4

Assyria, king of, 288

Assyrians, 195, 203

Athletes, 156

Athens, 231

Auguries, 155

Augustine, St., 13, 14; *City of God*, 14

Auspiciola, 4; daughter of Salvian, 241; request of—to grandparents, 247

Avarice, 150;—of the religious, 259-260;—in slavery to idolatry, 269;—most mortal of diseases, 269;—of Christians, 271;—and inhumanity receive eternal punishment, 311; its punishment, 311

Babylon, king of, 287, 289
Bagaudae, 136 n.14, oppression and revolt of, 136-137;—and liberty, 137
Barbarian auxiliaries, and Roman Empire 203; pagans and heretics, 112, 128-129; vices of, 114;—and Christian swearing compared, 118; see actual conduct of Christians, 120-121; — dependent upon their teachers, 130;—belief and God's judgment, 130-131; charity of, 132-133; dignity of, 135;—and Roman compared, 149;—and Christian in eyes of the Law, 154;—nations overrun Gaul, 172;—and Roman trust in God compared, 197-198;—races raised up by God to destroy Rome, 201; invasions of—do not amend Romans, 202;—pass from Gaul into Spain, 202; pass from Spain into Africa, 202; 203;—more chaste than Romans, 222
Belgians, 202
Belief in God with faith, 70
Benedad, king of Syria, 195
Blasphemies of Africans, 226
Blasphemy, enormity of sin of, 122; a hideous crime, 122-123;—peculiar to Christians, 123
Blood and marriage relatives not to be preferred to Christ, 356-357
Boniface, 200 n.22
Book, subject of—is more important than name of its author, 257
Brigands, 84

Cain and Abel, proofs of God's judgment, 39; Cain murders Abel, 39
Cancerous wounds, 286
Capharnaum, 103
Capital punishment, 98
Capitatio and *jugatio,* 8-9
Carmel, 60
Carthage, capture of, 173; officials in, 208; description of, 208-209;—an example of African prosperity and sin, 209; proscription of orphans, widows, and the poor in, 209-210; poor in—pray for coming of barbarians, 209-210; vice in- is likened to ambushing brigands, 210; temple in —only place free from vice, 210-211; monks abused in, 231
Castinus, 200 n.22

Catholic, law, 113
Catholics, 130
Cattura, 251
Cautery and medication, 180-181
Celestis, 226; rites of—in Africa, 227
Charity, chief of all virtues, 133;—of first Christians, 270;—in the early Church, 334
Charybdis, 149
Chastity, 81
Children, not to be excluded from properties of parents, 277;—to be loved in a second degree, 335; consequence of —loved to excess, 335-336; speech humble in presence of parents, 243-244
Cicero, 28; *De Natura Deorum*, 27 n.1
Cincinnati, 31
Circe's cup, 144
Circumcision 125
Circuses and theaters, impurities of, 156
Cirta, 173
Cities too poor to undertake games, 165
Christ, swearing by the name of, 116-117; birth and sufferings of, 159-160; His sufferings cannot be repaid, 295;—purchased man's devotion, 301; His admonition to clerics and laymen, 307;—the compensator of all, 312;—as heir, 366; His bond is His gospel, 366
Christian, lukewarm, 13-14, 124; his disregard of Christ's precepts, 65-66; his attitude towards adversities, 69-70; his faithfulness, 70; his disregard for the Law, 71-72;—princes, 75; his disregard of charity, 76; his disregard of commandments, 79; his disregard for God, 82; scorn of God for —, 83; morality, low degree of, 84; depravity of, 89; faith of, 90; philosophy of, 112; pagan beliefs of, 121; his conduct scandalizes pagans, 121; his guilt greater than pagan guilt, 126; toward God, 171; his provisions for legitimate heirs, 317; his wisdom, 356
Christians, cannot deny God's rule, 58;—anointed in baptism, 70;—granted goods by God, 70;—must follow in Christ's footsteps, 73; as a reproach to Christ, 119; they act as God's superiors, 132;—sin with knowledge, 146-147;—reject goodness for folly, 153;—prefer levity to wisdom,

153-154;—attending circuses and games seen by God, 158; they irritate God by impurities, 159;—recompense God by attending circuses and theaters, 159;—turn laughter into crime, 161;—prefer plays to churches, 163;—prefer games to ecclesiastical feasts, 163-164;—leave churches to attend games, 163-164; games a sacrilege for, 171;—forget God in prosperity, 171;—turn times of peace into times of crime, 171-172;—turn good into evil, 172;—not excused by ignorance, 183;—likened to hucksters and innkeepers, 271;—pile up treasures on earth, 271;—considered relatives more than Christ, 354

Christianity among African nobility, 227-228

Church, lack of parity of good and evil in, 152

Churches, irreverent attitude toward, 84

Circus abhorred by God, 158

Clemency and chastisement of God, 93

Clerics and priests to excel in merit, 306; dignity of, 306

Clergy, and sin, 147;—not all "converted," 147; treatment of—in Africa, 228-229; holy ministry of, 297; perfection in the, 306;—and rich heirs, 307

Cologne, Salvian's friends in, 4; games not now at, 164; 237 n.1; condition of Roman inhabitants in, 238

Coloni, 9; 142 n.16; 143; loss of citizenship, 144; social status of, 144

Colonus adscriptus, 143 n.17

Coloni inquilini, 144 n.18

Complaints, 80

Conceit and new honors, 240

Concubinage not rife among slaves, 100

Concubines, 99

Conscience, examination of, 290-291

Constancy on deathbed, 353

Continence, and bequeathing of property, 303; and marriage, 303

Constantius, 178 n.44

Consuls, 155

Consular year, 155

Conversion, of one and the many, 87; continuation in sin after, 148-149;—and the way of life, 183

Converts and crime, 147-148

Core, 52-53

Corruption in the hearts of men, 168
Crimes, of men, 84;—customary of the day, 105;—of one injure all, 151
Crime and punishment, 226
Criminality among the rich, 96
Cupidity of Christians, 271-272
Curiales, restricted avocation of, 8 n.19;—and injustice, 85; methods of, 134;—demand taxes from the clergy, 134;—and brigandage, 134
Cursing, 79, 80

Daniel, 88, 287, 290
Dathan, 52-53
David, insulted by Nabal, 60;—avenged by God, 60-61; favored by God, 61;—causes death of Urias, 62;—punishment proves God's judgment, 62;—punished by God, 63; his tribulations and misfortunes, 63-65; repentance of, 63, 122; example of, 122; census by, 151; God increased daily, 201
Death excludes man from vice, 284
Debt is universal and individual, 295-296
Delphic demon, 220
Denunciation of self, 150

Depravity general in Roman world, 210
Detraction, 80, 82
Devil, the, delights in theaters and circuses, 158;—acknowledges dearness of man's soul, 333
Devils, the, tremble before God, 93;—at sites of games, 171
Dignity, of man respected by God, 58;—of the person and guilt, 168
Diocletian, 134 n.9
Discipline by and indulgence of God, 180
Disinheritance, an act of contempt, 359
Disobedience to God, 78-79
Divine love and care of human affairs, 38
Divine Word, on love of children, 275;—speaks to the rich, 281-282
Divine wrath kindled by one bad man, 152
Drunkards, 84
Duty of man to love God, 109

Egypt, proof of God's judgment, moderation, patience in, 45; 203
Envy, 80

Epicurean, philosophic absurdities, 29;—essence of truth, 369-370
Eucherius, 5 n.12; letters to, 240, 255; writings of, 255 n.1
Evangelical councils, 71
Eviction of neighbors, 149
Evildoers, desire to continue in evil, 153; strive to excel in wrong doing, 153
Exile of the soul, 318
Extraneous heirs, 341

Fabii, 31
Fabricii, 31
Faith, defined, 70; attested by good works, 92; without good works, 92; lack of sin against God, 357
Falernus, wine of, 365
Fasting and almsgiving, 286-287
Fault, slight, great injury to God, 169
Fervor of spirit, 124
Fibula, 286
Fire consumes 14,700 men, 53
Flattery at deathbed, 352
Flesh to take on properties of the soul, 252
Flood, 42
Forgery and perjury, 105

Fornication, 111; unlawful among the Goths, 193
Franks, 115, 120; ignorant of injustice, 141; 207
Freeborn become slaves, 144
Friedländer, Ludwig, 154 n.11

Gaius, 208
Galla, wife of Eucherius, 5
Gallus, 249
Games, expenditure for, 12;—and spectacles, 12; all crimes and vices found at, 154; bestiality at, 154; care taken to provide for, 154;—and mental guilt, 155; their evil effect on the mind, 156-157; they are an occasion of sin, 156-157;—are sinful for performer and spectator, 157; they are an apostacy from the Faith, 161;—are renunciation of baptismal vows, 161; they are the work of the devil, 13, 161-162; they are a forsaking of Christ, 162;—are not pleasure but death, 162;—are not among barbarians, 162-163;—cease when cities captured by barbarians, 164;—performed now because of depravity, 165; not now because of necessity, 166-167;—are suicide to man and injury to

God, 170;—attended by Carthaginians during the capture of the city, 173

Gaul, cities of, 96;—and Spain, 162;—made worse by misfortunes, 174; degeneracy in, 176-177;—demand circuses from Emperor, 178; description of after capture of, 178; gradual destruction of, 202

Gauls, 136

Generosity, and forgiveness of sin, 284-285;—and love, reward for, 291

Genesis of man, 38

Geneva, 255 n.2

Gennadius, 5-6

Genseric, 173 n.35

Gepidae, 115, 120

Germany, 201

German tribes and Roman Empire, 7

Gideon, 195; his army and the Lord, 195-196

God, regarded by pagan philosophers, 27; He rules in accordance with reason, 35;—and worship, 36-37;—implanted principles of conduct in man, 38; 'repented'—41; blasphemy, toward 50;—punishes misdirected carelessness, 51;—does not watch over in order to neglect man, 57;—with man all days, 59;— is eternal and just, 65; recompense to, 108-109; He abhors circuses and theaters, 158; He heeds merit, not strength, 195; —not careless and negligent, 225;—a gentle father 258; —demands repayment of debt, 279;—an uncorrupt judge, 284;—needs generosity of men, 359

God's, care proved by Holy Scripture, 29;—future judgment and the apparent unbeliever, 32; care of all forms of life, 35-36;—will is highest justice, 40;—resolve to punish man, 41;—judgment of the blasphemer, 50;—judgment inexorable, 52;—severity and mercy, 53-54;—presence, governance and judgment to be proved by reason, example and authority, 55;—presence taught by human nature, 60; —verdict immutable, 65;—love for His creatures, 106-107;—paternity, 107;—justice, patience, and chastisement, 132;—punishment for oppression of the poor, 141; —judgment for mistreatment of the poor, 145;—demands on Man, 188;—demands not a burden but an ornament, 188; — blessings, 196-197; command on treasures for children, 339-340

Good, happiness of the, 30

Goods, everlasting, 293

Gospel, rich man in, 336

Goths, 132, 134, 141, 193, 197, 207; charity among, 149;—call prosperity a gift of God, 197;—demand God's help, 197;—trained by evil teachers, 197

Government, and taxes, 8, officials and slander, 85

Governance of God, 65. 103; theme of, 6; probable date of composition of, 7; Goverance of God is His judgment, 35;—proved by reason, example and authority, 35;—and creation, 106; examples of—from daily life, 106

Greed, root of all evil, 273

Greek philosophers, and the State, 32;—and virtue, 32

Guarantee of future recompense, 345

Guilt, of the baptised greater than that of pagans, 163;—of keeping possessions to the moment of death, 281

Gymnasia, 170

Haemmerle, Alois, 164 n.21

Hate, and love are the same, 237

Health of the body and of the soul, 251

Heaven, joy of, 309-310

Hebrew, people grumble, 52;—leaders revolt, 53;—leaders punished, 53;—tribes, two holy names of, 91

Hebrews, desert wanderings of, 45-46;—long for flesh meat, 169;—punished by God, 169-170

Hell, relatives unable to help rich man in, 336; torture of rich man in, 336-337

Herba Sardonica, 186 n.2

Heres extraneus, 341 n.24

Heretics, unwittingly, 130; they have tradition rather than Scripture, 130; — adjudge Christians heretics, 130;—sin through ignorance, 131; from Roman teachers, 132—excel Catholics, 132

Holy men, and the practice of poverty, 30; mental outlook of, 30-31;—purchase everlasting goods, 293

Holy Scripture, proves God's presence, 55-56; badly interpolated by heretics, 129;—on greed, 282;—on bequeathing of property, 298

Honorius, 178 n.44

Hunneric, King of the Vandals, 199 n.21

Hunnic-Roman alliance, 197-198

Huns, 115, 120, 141

Hypatius, father-in-law of Salvian, 241;—a pagan at the time of Salvian's marriage, 243

Illness, bodily, mother of strength, 30-31

Imperial messengers entertained, 139

Increase in wealth brings lack of restraint, 270

Indignity to an honored person, 168

Individual watched over by God, 57

Inhumanity of individuals toward selves, 317

Injustice, 150

Inquilini, 144

Interest for others above interest for self, 323

Israel, interpreted as 'seeing God', 58

Israelites, depart from Egypt, 45;—pursued by Pharaoh, 45; malcontents among, 48;—and Christians equally cared for by God, 48; punished for worship of golden calf, 49

Italy and its calamities, 172

Jerome, St., 13, 317 n.32

Jerusalem, holy places of, 231

Jesters, 156

Job, 88, 254

Jonah, 247

Judges and officials, 134

Judgment of God, 296

Judgments of God Differentiated 66

Judgment seat of God and almsgiving, 323

Just, prayers of the, heard by God, 56;—and unjust regarded by God, 56-57

Justice of God, magnitude of, 107-108

Justice and judgment of God evidenced by calamities, 180

Julian, Emperor, 3

Lactantius, *Institutiones Divinae,* 27 n.1

Latifundi, 142 n.16

Latin liberty, 330

Law, and good and bad lives, 113-114; barbarians ignorant of, 116;—not a hindrance,

127;—and morals, 127-128, 371;—the antidote, 128; salvation and life in the, 128; heretics and the, 129; barbarians and the, 130;—read and trampled on by Christians, 131; heretics ignorant of, 131; —and legality, 298

Law of the Twelve Tables, 231-232

Lawsuits, method in, 189

Lazarus, 337

Legacies, to unworthy heirs, 277;—profit nothing to the dead, 321; to unholy—do not avail at Judgment seat, 324; —to the good an act of piety, 325; legitimate, 325;—and justice, 351;—bequeathed as an honor, 359

Leniency of God to man, 83

Lerins, 4, 5, 13, monks of Lerins, 237; teaching at, 239; Salvian's request to monks of, 239-240; 255 n.2

Levies, tributary, 138

Levites and property, 306-307

Limenius, 253

Litigation, 105

Litorius, 198 n.18;—captured by barbarians, 198-199;—an example of God's judgment, 199; long captivity of, 199

Livy, 247

Lord, belief in, with mind and wealth, 312-313

Lot, 44, 211

Love, qualities of, 237;—and paternity, 273-274; parental —for children, 274-275;— beneficial to parents and children, 276-277

Lyconia, 231

Mainz, games not performed at, 164; 175 n.40; continuation of vice in, 175-176; conditions within—while being captured, 176

Malice, 80

Man, perversity of, 94; nature and wickedness of, 94;—trusts in men but not in God, 313

Mankind, multiplication and wickedness of, 40-41; punishment of, 41

Manna, 48

Maro, 28

Mars, 170

Marseilles, 237 n.1

Marriage, uncomsummated, 297

Martin, St., of Tours, 13

Mary, daughter of Moses, 51; punishment of, 51-52

Masters generous to slaves, 330

Master and slave both runaways, 96

Maximus, emperor, 199 n.21
Medianites, 195
Mercury, 170
Mercy of God, 145-146;—and justice, 249; mercy and almsgiving, virtues proper to all Christians, 319
Merit of cup of cold water, 345
Metals, fusion of, in furnace, 205
Minerva, 170
Monasteries of Egypt, 231
Monk and holiness, 297
Monks, reception of, by Carthaginians, 231
Moors, customs of, 120
Moses, a proof of God's governance, 45;—hears God speaking, 45;—receives the Law, 46-47; God speaks to, 47;—judges the blasphemer, 50; 51
Mount Sinai, 47, 49
Multiplication of Christians and weaker faith, 270
Multiple interests and God, 319-320
Murders, 84
Murmurings, 80
Music halls, 156

Nabuchodnosor, King of Babylon, 203
Nabal, 60
Nadab, 50
Nadab and Abiu, God's judgment of, 50-51
Name, no profit in a, 257
Nathaniel, true Israelite, 298
Nativi, 144 n.19
Neptune, 170
New Law, why more demanded under—than under Old Law, 300-301;—and restrictions of, 300; almsgiving commanded in—and Old Law, 310
Nineveh, 247
Nine peoples, 187 n.4
Nobility, and crime, 86-87; homicide and lewdness, capital sins of, 87;—worse than slaves, 98; social status of—when converted to God, 101-102
Nobles, abuse slaves, 98; marriages of—with their slaves, 99;—debase nobility, 100
Noah and the Ark, 41; a proof of God's governance, 41-42
Noe, 88

Obedience, qualities of — in slaves, 78;—to God's commandments, 82
Obscenities, 155-156

Officials, crimes of, 97-98; unjust rule of, 137
Offerings mitigate, not absolve sins, 288
Offspring not to be preferred to one's soul, 324
Og rebels, 52
Old Law, severity of, 71;—on bequeathing of property, 298; —was the Gospel, 299;—and indulgence, 299-300;—why less demanded under than under New Law, 300-301
Opponents of divine word, 370
Oppression of the lower classes, 137-138
Opulence leads to destruction, 314
Orosius, 14, 132 n.6
Ownership and usage of property, 278
Oza, the Levite, 169

Palladia, 4; wife of Salvian, 241; her request to her parents, 244-246; as a child, 245
Pagan, philosophy and belief in God, 28-29;—profanations, 155;—god of theaters and circuses, 158;—law protects monks, 232
Paganism and Christianity in Africa, 227
Pagans and poverty, 32
Pantomimes, 156
Parents, love and greed in, 273; —accumulate riches for offspring, 273; legacies to the good and holy, 321;—seek out blood relatives indiscriminately, 322;—deny legacies to offspring in religion, 325-326;—prefer children in the world to children in religion, 322
Parental possessions and children, 273-274
Parentage, nominal, and adopted sons, 322
Passion of our Lord, 294
Passover, 45
Paternity a cause of evil, 273
Patrick, St., 5
Patrocinia, 142
Patronage, 142; methods and evils of, 142-143; unequal barter, 143
Paul, St., on mortification of the flesh, 33, 34; infirmities of, 34;—follower of Christ, 74; tribulations of, 74-75;—an ideal disciple, 77;—and charity, 77;—on the rich, 86, 279-280, 314, 320;—and the charity of God, 108; his love for God, 109;— and transgression, 118-119;—on the Law,

125, 127;—on penance, 146; —and corruption of the mass, 151;—on the 'acceptable people,' 160-161; titles bestowed on, 241;—on the burden of each, 295;—on what is owed to God, 301-302;—on widowhood, 302

Paulinus of Nola, 189 n.6

Penance at the hour of death, 287

Penitentials, 15

Perfection, seeming harshness of call to, 272

Perjury, 79;—and fraud of businessmen, 85

Persecutions of Christians, 121

Peter, St., on lukewarm Christians, 124-125;—punishes Ananias and Saphira, 152

Pharaoh, destroyed in Red Sea, 45, 49

Philistines, 42

Philosophy of religion, 309

Plato, 220 n.53;—and Platonic schools, 27

Pliny, 150 n.24

Plunder, 150

Poison of flattery, 352-353

Poll-tax, exemptions from, 9

Poor, suffer from envy and want, 138; position of, 140; reason why not all—flee to barbarians, 140-141;—and patronage, 142; penury of, caused by rich, 142; and needy are bankers, 320;

Portrait of a dying man, 350-351

Possessions, an impediment to perfection, 272-273;—ordered by God for children, 276;—revert to owner at end of usufructory tenantry, 278-279

Poverty, temporary and eternal punishment, 316;—in present life more bearable than eternal poverty, 324

Prayer, and its answer, 36-37; —and crime, 85

Precarium, 278

Prince of Tyre, 205

Profits derived from paternal observance of God's commands, 340

Promised Land, Moses and Aaron enter, 54

Property, a divine gift, 277-278; —bestowed by God for His own honor, 278;—indiscriminately transferred, 281;—offered with compunction and tears, 288;—pleases not as a purchase price, 288;—must be offered to God in humility,

288;—should be offered to God, 289;—and disinheritance of self, 300;—and early Christians, 334-335

Proprietors, and *latifundi*, 10;—and the poor, 11;—and the State, 11

Public processions, 156

Pythagoras, 27

Quieta, mother-in-law of Salvian, 236

Raca, 72
Rapacity, 150
Rapsaces, insult of God by, 151
Ravenna, theater at, 167
Reasons, for denial of legacies to offspring in religion, 326-327; —for generosity to God, 360-361
Recompense to God, 109-110
Recreation and impurities, 161
Redemption, meaning of, 290
Relatives, indiscriminate choosing of, 341
Religion is knowledge of God, 308
Religious zeal, 124
Religious, and penance, 147; debtors to God, 293; benefits enjoyed by, 293-294; unbecoming for—to think themselves better than laymen, 296;—not to be presumptuous of salvation, 297; bequeathing of property of, 297-298;—indebted for their possessions and selves, 302;—owe more to God than laymen, 308; their profession a pledge of devotion, 308;—and irreligious, difference between the debt of, 308;—should bequeath wealth, 316;—have use of but not rights to property, 329;—likened to Latin freedmen, 331; reasons for their being disinherited, 332; who forsake the world in dress rather than in heart, 354;— and belief in almsgiving, 362-363;—guilty of crime of forgery, 363-364

Repentance, necessity of quick, 285; late, consequences of, 287; first step to salvation, 293

Rich, theft and highway robberies of, 97; human race a prey to the tyranny of, 97; lust of the, 99; quarrels of, 139-140; —sell *patrocinia*, 142, selfishness of, 142;—Christian, first duty of in this world, 320;— —Christian and legacies to his children, 320-321

Riches, purpose of, 280; evil abuse of, 280;—a hindrance to piety, 315; their profit after death, 347

Rome, captured, 172;—pays tribute to barbarians, 183; in bondage to the barbarians, 183-184

Roman, people suffer what they deserve, 110;—society not all corrupt, 113;—vices, 114;— heretics, 132; — indignities, 135; — citizenship debased, 136; Romans delight in games, 157-158; — cities, games in, 164-165;—recompense to God for His gifts, 181-183; — presumption of strength, 196;—weakness generally known, 196; freedom, meaning of, 330

Roman army, defeated by barbarians, 198;—and prayer, 200;—defeated in Spain, 200; —overconfident in Spain, 200

Roman Empire, calamities prove evil of, 93; crime in, 100;— to barbarians, a judgment of God, 195;—overthrow ascribed to sins, not to God, 203

Roman Forum, 248

Roman treasury, penury of, 165; expenditures and waste of, 165; squandering of resources of, 167-168

Roman politics in fifth century, 7

Roman world, a desolation and a curse, 166; morals of affluent, 167; poverty of, 168;— uncorrected by punishment, 180

Romans, attitude of — toward State, 32; crimes of—and God's judgment, 111; self-righteousness of, 111;—think themselves better than barbarians, 111; lack of charity among, 133;—flee to barbarians, 135;—prefer not to be Romans, 136; they suffer no injustice among the Goths, 141;—eager to live under barbarians, 141; calamities fail to correct, 145; pride of, 145; hard-heartedness of, 146, perversity of, 166;—still desire games, 166;—prefer to die than to live without vice, 177; —not corrected by gifts of God, 181; God's gifts to, 181; —of present compared with those of past, 183; weakness and misery of, 185;—not amended after punishment, 185;—miserable and pleasure loving, 186;—and barbarian nations compared 187;—un-

INDEX

chaste among barbarians, 193; — continue impurities among Goths and Vandals, 222; — suffering by God's judgment, 225;—kindle flame which burns them, 226

Sabbath day a day of rest, 49
Sabine-Roman War, 247-248
Sacrilege among officials in Africa, 228
Safeguards against insults to the person, 168
Saints, and sinners, difference between, 296-297;—almsgiving, 367;—disinherit themselves, 368
Salonius, bishop, 255 n.2; letter to, 256-263
Salvation, and performance of God's commandments, 79; three steps for acquiring, 293
Salvian, works of, 5-6; 15-16; style of, 6; his attitude toward the Germans, 14 n.20; estimation of his own style, 25-26;—proposes to refute adversaries, 66;—is writing for a Christian audience, 69; born in Gaul, 174 n.37; arguments of, 185;—does not present arguments, 185 n.1;—on forthrightness, 224; Letters of, 237-263; his reception by monks of Lerins, 238; his status in society, 238; his willingness to help those in need, 239; his wariness in asking favors, 239; his request to his parents-in-law, 242-243;—separated from parents-in-law, 243;—and Palladia's objectives, 244;—contrasts own pleas with pleas in Roman Forum, 249-250;—on position, honors, and ambitions, 253-254;—compares first Christians with Christians of his own day, 269-270;—bases arguments against avarice on Scripture, 283-284

Saphira, 152
Sardinia and Sicily, 173
Saul, 201
Saxons, 115, 118, 207
Scandal of the eyes, 81-82
Scriptures Holy, and belief, 68; —and the mind of God, 69; Christians have complete—129; Christians do not observe, 129; heretical teachers corrupt,—Quotations from or references to Biblical writers or Biblical books, 130
Acts, 59 n.10; 106 n.33; 152 n.5; 270 n.1; 334 nn.13, 14, 15 and 16; 371 n.22
Apocalypse, 123 n.60; 369 n.17

INDEX

Daniel, 287 n.24
Deuteronomy, 194 n.9; 271 n.3
Ecclesiastes, 58 n.6; 97 n.16; 176 n.41; 279 n.16; 280 n.18; 283 n.22; 308 n.21; 350 nn.32 and 33
Exodus, 45 n.22; 47 nn. 23, 24, 25, 26; 49 n.28; 116 n.47; 169 n.26; 214 n.50; 282 n.21
Ezechiel, 88 n.33; 194 n.8 and 10; 204 n.34; 205 n.35, 36 and 37; 206 n.38, 39 and 40; 321 n.6; 335 n.17; 352 n. 38; 357 n.6; 354 n.12
Genesis, 38 n.10 and 11; 39 n.12; 40 n.13; 41 nn.14, 15, 16, 17; 42 n.18; 43 n.19; 44 n.20; 104 n.28; 177 n.43
Hebrews, 357 n.7; 369 n.19
Isaisas, 91 n.4; 103 n.26; 149 n.23; 151 n.3; 203 n.32; 224 n.1; 226 n.2; 303 n.15, 352 n.37
James, 79 n.23; 86 n.32; 92 n.8, 9 and 10; 281 n.20; 281 n.20
Jeremias, 58 n.8 and 9; 91 n.6 and 7; 99 n.22; 166 n.23; 191 n.7; 200 n.23 and 24; 201 n.25 and 26; 202 n.30; 203 n.33; 232 n.17
Job, 255 n.1; 333 n.11
John, 72 n.6; 73 n.11; 102 n.24; 107 n.36; 133 n.7; 229 n.10; 230 n.14; 321 n.7; 356 n.5
Jonas, 247 n.6 and 7

Josue, 151 n.1; 213 n.44
Judges, 195 n.11; and 12; 196 n.14 and 15
Kings, 60 n.12; 61 n.13; 62 n.14; 63 n.15 and 16; 64 n.18; 65 n.19; 122 n.57; 151 n.2; 169 n.27; 177 n.42; 195 n.13; 201 n.27; 213 nn.45 and 46
Leviticus, 50 nn.30 and 31; 51 n.32
Luke, 73 n.9; 77 n.20; 131 n.5; 150 n.25; 161 n.18 and 19; 173 n.36; 187 n.3; 198 n.17; 229 n.8; 262 n.6; 308 n.20; 311 n.26; 320 n.3; 336 n.19; 337 n20; 351 n.35
Mark, 81 n.29, 276 n.11 and 12
Matthew, 59 n.11; 67 n.1; 71 nn. 3 and 4; 72 n.7; 73 n.10; 76 nn.17, 18 and 19; 81 n.28; 104 n.27 and 29; 119 n.54; 167 n.24; 188 n.6; 213 n.47; 258 n.3; 260 n.5; 271 n.2; 272 n.4 and 5; 276 n.13; 281 n.19; 304 n.16; 307 n.18 and 19; 310 n.24 and 25; 311 n.27; 315 n.30; 318 n.33; 319 n.1; 320 n.2 and 5; 345 n.27; 346 nn.28, 29 and 30; 349 n.31; 351 n.36; 355 n.2; 358 n.8; 360 n.9; 361 n.10; 364 n.13; 368 n.15; 370 n.20
Numbers, 49 n.29; 52 n.33; 53 nn.36, 37 and 38; 54 nn.39,

40 and 41; 169 n.28 and 29
Osee, 91 n.5
Paul, 30 n.3 and 4; 33 n.5; 34 n.6 and 7; 37 n.9; 69 n.2; 72 n.5; 72 n.12-16; 77 nn.21 and 22; 79 n.24; 80 nn.27-27; 94 n.11; 97 n.14; 107 nn.34, 35 and 37; 108 nn.38 and 39; 109 n.41; 110 n.42; 112 n.43; 114 n.45; 118 nn.45-51; 119 nn.52 and 53; 122 n.55; 123 nn.58 and 59; 124 n.61; 125 nn.64-68; 127 nn.1 and 2; 146 n.21; 151 n.4 152 n.6; 153 nn7-9; 157 n.12; 160 nn.13-15; 171 n.31; 211 n.43; 213 nn.48 and 49; 219 n.51; 226 n.4; 227 n.7; 232 n.16; 251 nn.1 and 2; 273 nn.6 and 7; 275 n.9; 280 n.17; 290 n.25; 291 nn.26 and 27; 295 n.1; 296 nn.2 and 3; 298 nn.6 and 7; 299 nn.9; 300 n.10; 301 nn.11 and 12; 302 n.13; 305 n.17; 314 nn.28 and 29; 320 n.4; 335 n.4; 335 n.18; 343 n.25; 344 n.26; 354 n.1; 369 n.18; 270 n.21
Peter, 44 n.21; 122 n.56; 124 n.62 and 63; 160 n.17; 364 n.11
Proverbs, 55 n.1; 83 n.30; 90 n.2; 95 n.13; 114 n.44; 170 n30; 198 n.19; 226 n.5; 279 n.15; 296 n.4; 355 n.3
Psalms, 52 n.34; 53 n.35; 56 nn.2 and 3; 57 n.4; 58 n.5; 65 nn.20 and 21; 66 nn. 22 and 23; 85 n.31; 91 n.3; 105 nn.30, 31 and 32; 108 n.40; 135 nn.11 and 12; 145 n.20; 146 n.22; 198 n.20; 201 n.28; 202 n.29; 226 n.3; 229 nn.11 and 12; 232 n.15; 260 n.4; 275 n.8; 297 n.5; 303 n.14; 308 n.22; 310 n.23; 339 n.21; 340 n.23; 351 n.34; 356 n.4; 369 n.16
Tobias, 257 n.2; 287 n.23
Wisdom, 58 n.7; 316 n.31
Zacharias, 229 n.9
Scylla, 149
Scythians, rites of, 120
Seius, 208
Self-righteousness and guilt, 72
Serfdom, 144
Servius Galba, 248
Sestertii, 295
Siba, 65
Silvanus, 241, 242
Simei, 65
Sin, an offense against God's divinity, 103;—and mental guilt, 167;—and madness, 179
Sins, of intention, 72; acknowledgement of—wished by God, 146

Sinner, dead, excluded from confession of his sin, 339
Sisara, 195
Slander, 80;—and plunder, 105
Slaves, obedience to masters, 78;—and masters, 83;—accused by rich, 94-95; conditions of, 95; customary allowances of, 95;— become nobles, 98; murder among, 98;—better than their masters, 99;—less blameworthy than nobles and freeborn, 100;—and Roman freedom, 329-330
Socrates, 220
Sodom, destroyed, 44; angel messengers sent to, 44; 104; 211
Sodom and Gomorrha, 43, 44;—compel their own destruction, 44
Sodomites, destruction of—proof of future judgment, 44
Soldiers and pillage, 85
Soul, eyes, the windows of the, 81;—disinherited of its wealth, 318;—is the most precious possession of man, 349
Spain, cities of, 98;—delivered to Vandals because of impurities, 194;—given over to Vandals by God, 194; reason for its being given to barbarians, 194-195

Spaniard, 136
Stewardship of God, 57
Stoics and God, 27-28
Storehouses, imperial, 173
Subjection of the flesh, 252
Swearing, 79
Syrian merchants, habitual perjury of, 115

Tanit, 226 n.6
Taxation, in the hands of brigands, 100; its effect on the poor, 101; 138; remedies, misappropriation of, 101; inequality of levies, 138
Tax levies, public, 138
Taxes, misappropriation of, 133-134;—and imperial messengers, 139;—a burden on poor, 139; mitigation not for poor, 140;—and reliefs, inequality of, 140; poor continue to pay, 143
Tertullian, 154 n.11
Testament of God sufficient proof of performing and ordaining all things, 68
Testators, precautions taken by, 343-344;—do not think of judgment of God, 348; intentions of, 358-359
Thamar, 63, 64

Theaters, abhorred by God, 158
Theft, 111
Thedoric I supplicates God, 199
Timothy, 256, 257, 241, 242; infirmities of, 34; his works not apocryphal, 256-257
Tobias, served the needy, 299
Toulouse, captured by Visigoths, 7 n.16; 198 n.18
Towns and municipalities, 134
Transference of property at moment of death, 343
Transgressions, consequences of man's, 38
Transitory nature of wealth, 323
Treasures ordered by God for children, 275
Trial in worldly courts, preparations for, 342
Tribes, wanderings of, 201-202
Trier, probable birthplace of Salvian, 3; games not now at, 164; destruction of, 164, 174-176; effect of sacking on, 174; its description of during capture, 174-175; — wealthiest city of Gaul, 175 n.39;—stormed four times, 175; continuation of vice in, 175; its description of after capture, 177-178; 179-180;—and public spectacles, 179;—destroyed three times, 180;—uncorrected by destruction, 180
Trinity, heretical beliefs on the, 130
Tumblers, 156
Twelve Tables, Law of, 231-232

Ulfilas, bishop, 129 n.4
Urias, the Hethite, 61
Ursicinus, 240
Use, not ownership of property bequeathed to religious, 328
Usufructory tenants, 278

Vandals, 132, 141, 172 n.33, 194, 197; in Spain, 172-173; —cross into Africa, 173;—call prosperity a gift of God, 197;—demand help from God, 197;—trained by evil teachers, 197;—and prayer, 200;—heretics more reverent than Roman Christians, 200; their success proof of God's judgment, 201; reasons why they not remain in Gaul, 202-203;—realize Roman weakness, 203;—driven by divine command to Africa, 203;—sent to Africa to cure it of sin, 204;—compared with Africans, 214;—untainted by Africans, 215; their law in Africa, 215; their conduct in

Africa, 216-217;—cleanse Africa, 218; their law just, 218-219; their measures to correct vice, 218-219;—and marriage, 219;—and Socratic laws compared, 220-221
Venus, 170
Veranus, 255 n.2
Verus, 253
Vice, and impurity native characteristics of Romans, 164;—and opulent security, 186;—second nature to Africans, 204;—cause of Rome's downfall, 223;—of Salvian's day, 270;—of heirs, 365
Vienne, 255 n.2
Violence against clergy, 135
Virginity and holiness, 297
Virgins, and the law of love, 304; ten, parable of, 304-305; ten—and almsgiving, 304-305
Virtues of pagans, 31-32
Visigoths, 172 n.33

Wealth, of former times lacking, 183;—and the purchase of beatitude, 311; abundant—is eternal poverty, 335; interest in bequeathing—to the holy, 365-366
Wicked, unhappiness of, 29-30
Widowhood, and property, 297; name of—insufficient for salvation, 302; criterion of, 302-303
Will, the compensation of good, 26
Winebibbing and over-indulgence, 105
Wisdom, and goodness, 153;—at the hour of death, 355-356
Wordly, pomp, pleasure and ties, 73;—care and professed religious, 315
Word of God, superior to the reasoning of men, 68;—is uncorrupted truth, 69
Words do not replace deeds, 349
Wrestling schools, 170

www.ingramcontent.com/pod-product-compliance
Lightning Source LLC
Chambersburg PA
CBHW032024290426
44110CB00012B/656